Europe
Violence - Rac

C000116025

European Studies in Education

Europäische Studien zur Erziehung und Bildung
Études Européennes en Sciences de l'Éducation

Christoph Wulf (Ed.)

Volume 5

Violence - Racism, Nationalism, Xenophobia

Ed. by Bernhard Dieckmann,
Christoph Wulf and Michael Wimmer

Waxmann Münster/New York

Die Deutsche Bibliothek - CIP-Einheitsaufnahme
Violence - Nationalism, Racism, Xenophobia / ed. Bernhard Dieckmann,
Christoph Wulf, Michael Wimmer
Münster, New York: Waxmann 1997

European Studies in Education; Vol. 5); ISBN 3-89325-487-0
NE: Dieckmann, Bernhard; Wulf, Christoph; Wimmer, Michael [Eds.]; European Studies

ISBN 3-89325-487-0

© Waxmann Verlag GmbH 1996, Postfach 8603, D-48046 Münster, F.R.G.
Waxmann Publishing Co., P.O. Box 1318, New York, NY 10028, U.S.A.

Umschlaggestaltung: Bärbel Lieske

European Studies in Education

The political, economic, and social developments in the European Union pose new challenges to education in Europe, where each country has its own system. Under these circumstances, the relation between national, regional, and local traditions on the one hand and supraregional, transnational aspirations on the other must be conceived. The field of education is seeing the rise of new issues, responsibilities, and research requiring scholars from different European cultures to work together.

European Studies in Education constitutes an international forum for the publication of educational research in English, German, and French. The multilingual nature of this series mirrors that of Europe and makes it possible to portray and express cultural diversity.

The present volume was written in the framework of the Network Educational Science Amsterdam (NESA), in which more than 30 European and a few non-European faculties and research institutes cooperate in the area of education.

We sincerely thank the Faculty of Education at the Freie Universität Berlin, which facilitates the collaboration of the network's educational institutions, for its support in funding the publication of these research results.

Christoph Wulf

Content

Preface

III. Descriptive-Empirical Studies

Preface

Violence.
Racism, Nationalism, Xenophobia

Terrorist acts of violence, ethnic and nationalistic conflicts, violent attacks on resident as well as nonresident foreigners, drug-related crime, and familial violence have become constant occurrences in the countries of Europe. The claim is repeatedly made that we in Europe today live in societies which are more non-violent than any previous ones. At the same time, however, we are plagued by the problem of violence.

The problems of violence, with which the current European states have to deal, have made a renewed reflection about violence necessary. Within the framework of this international discussion extending beyond the bounds of individual academic disciplines, we must engage in a fundamental consideration of the phenomenon of violence and its manifold manifestations. Scholars from a wide variety of disciplines and from different countries in Europe and North America have made an attempt to do this in this publication.

We are faced not only with the problem of finding adequate political, juridical and pedagogical reactions, but, even more, with the question about the political and moral basis of democracy and any type of civil society. Because apparently not directly politically motivated aggressiveness and willingness to employ violence against others or foreigners arising from religious or sexual differences are often treated as normal and because violence occurs not only in the dealings of people with each other but can emerge from national or state systems, it must not be met with the setting up of analytical taboos or with the quick answers of a moral majority. Although the public may with good reason react with moral indignation, it remains the task of scholars to inquire into the structure, the possible causes of and motives for xenophobic, racist and nationalistic violence in an interdisciplinary manner and with their various respective instruments.

The differences in the national scope of experience serve as the background for this volume, in which not merely integrative attempts at explanation with their various perspectives on the societal, political, cultural sociopsychological and anthropological situation are presented. On the contrary we have tried here to free the phenomenon of violence, especially the acts of violence of extreme right-wing youths - but also those committed singly and which cannot be attributed to these youths - from possible theoretical prejudices and to examine the phenomenon of violence anew in a conceptual-theoretical, hermeneutic-historical and descriptive-empirical manner:

- It may not be possible to explain the explosions of violent behavior without understanding the crisis of the basis of reproduction of the capitalist system in the states of Europe.
- Acts of violence and brutality - whether they be viewed as predetermined, as tendencies or as unavoidable risks in the various intellectual disciplines - could be rationalized or minimized by social scientific or anthropological inquiries, if they should, in denial of reality, conjure up and revive only the autonomous subject in spite of its evident barbaric deformation.
- Perhaps the cultures of Europe themselves provoke the emergence of violence, so that evil cannot be made to disappear along with the delinquents.
- »Human nature« must not be overlooked if evil is to be explained.
- Perhaps the founding of the history of humanism was itself an act of violence.
- Violent behavior on the part of individuals or groups happens to victims who are seldom taken into consideration by a theory of behavior in society.
- »Europe« is an historical dimension just as identity and self are biographical dimensions, which arise by means of multitudinous forms of delineation against others, as long as otherness is not assumed to be dissimilarity and automatically transformed into enmity.

Whoever speaks of violence must take the trouble to conceptualize differences. Discussions about violence must bring to light not only the possible violent quality of language but also the difference between force and violence in order to establish criteria that distinguish between the legitimacy of force and the arbitrary violence of xenophobic attitudes or racist behavior and their possible goals. If a discourse about violence ignores the differences that characterize the concrete forms of violence - the physical, the symbolic, the structural or the official - then it can no longer distinguish between the lawful from the unlawful, the legitimate from the illegitimate, justice from caprice.

How would a method of discourse look, if it took into account this reflection itself as a social phenomenon? What possible other versions of the concept of violence would it force us to consider? In any case, the growing discrepancy between the »new« situation of increasing violence and xenophobia in Europe and the old ideas will not be resolved without an intensification of speculation about concepts and without efforts to revise the language of this discourse.

Where, corresponding to the rationality of society, the irrationality and heteronomy of the subjects grow, their destructive blows to the »civilized order« as an expression of the natural history of the human race could paradoxically demonstrate their subjectivity. This, in any case, was the basic idea of the »Dialectic of the Enlightenment«, the concept that namely the form of social control of human nature strikes back against the society and its individuals, who no longer master their own circumstances. Then all moralizing as a social means of debarbarization fails once and for all. Understanding acts of violence against foreigners and others means also understanding the logic of the functioning of social and communicative systems, which, nevertheless, do not make ethical maxims about behavior outdated.

The various contributions in this volume approach the questions and the area of the phenomenon of racist, xenophobic and nationalistic violence by means different methods and from varying national perspectives. The essays and studies place an emphasis on considering the concepts and metaphors of violence and attempt to differentiate between force and violence in terms of their relationship to power and to justice in order to make visible the continuities and discontinuities that express themselves in the thought of European societies and that have molded their historical identity.

The hermeneutic-historical emphasis is centered around the relationship of agreeable self-images and disparaging images of others and their function as a fixed devices for interpretation, which can overarch all internal social differences. Analyses provided by the media as well as ethnological and historical explanations and interpretations can no longer explain xenophobia and racism in exclusively political or moral categories. The previously widely accepted assumption was that every society itself gives rise to violence, which is, however, expressed, channeled and, to a great degree, neutralized in various social and cultural institutions. It now seems that the open explosion of xenophobic violence has demonstrated the impossibility proving this putative institutional containment. Do these theories and models, meanwhile so familiar to us, still suffice to illustrate or explain our current experience of violence and the expression of ethnocentrism, which culminates in the intention to exclude others and, finally, in an ideology that shapes language and governs perceptions? Is a relationship to an other conceivable, in which sameness is not confused with identity, which does not lead to nationalism as a movement as the source of integration and identy, and which, upon recognizing differences, does not tragically proceed to set up a corresponding hierarchy of values?

The willingness to engage in violence and the economic and sociopolitical reasons for the growth of nationalism constitute a further focus of these studies.

Whereas the establishment of Europe as a political entity was conceived of as an effort to overcome a number of manifestations of nationalism, these very sentiments are now experiencing a renaissance at the national level and, expressed as a strong tendency toward autonomy and decentralization, at the regional and local levels as well. Bearing in mind that racism and xenophobia are not purely national or European problems and that in different countries varied forms of disorder can be observed, it is necessary to name the conditions and factors which would make it possible to decide whether in each country the same causes of the definitely diverse manifestations of violence are to be found or whether qualitatively different structures and sets of conditions underlie the multitude of expressions of violence and the willingness to engage in it. To what extent are common factors such as global social developments or particular lo-cal reasons responsible for these developments in all countries? Are we, as a result of type of »economic ethnocentrism« on the way to a »fortress Europe«, which translates the dichotomy of rich versus poor as European versus foreigner? How are inclusion and exclusion marked respectively and then made into the very highest barriers? How far are political myths, programs and the use of symbols in-creasingly replacing necessary and complex conceptions of the world?

Since racist and xenophobic acts of violence are largely commit-ted by young people, the socioeconomic conditions of youth: under-qualification, unemployment, the collapse of traditional social envi-ronment; the forms of and possible shortcomings in their educational and familial socialization and upbringing; and, above all, the influ-ence and effects of the mass media on attitudes and behavior must be examined. The studies on this subject in this volume decisively reject the idea of an »aggressive core of human beings as an anthropologi-cal constant« as well as the corresponding necessity for coercive measures and emphasize, above all, the importance of young people's uncertainty about their future, their fear of social decline, their expe-rience of powerlessness, their role as victims of complex tendencies toward modernization and social disintegration, and especially the role of the mass media.

On the conceptual plane as well as in actual practice pedagogy is confronted by the acts of violence of young people with new prob-lems, not least of which is the problem of whether it can itself be conceived of as noncoercive at all, even if it is meant to be a »pedagogy of debarbarization«. It also is faced with the question of whether it should or can satisfy the unreasonable demand repeatedly made on it as an »all-purpose cure« to find the missing answer to unsolved social problems.

The Spanish novelist Jorge Semprun regarded evil as well as good as accounted for in freedom. Acts of violence were neither the result of a abortive »taming of the human being« nor a remainder of his or her supposed animality - evil is immanent to the very humanity of humans. The propensity to evil of human beings can no more be eradicated than the concrete expression of their will to do good can be forbidden, which, given the in the end irrevocable freedom of human beings and depending upon the circumstances, is called courage, solidarity, dissent, sympathy, self-sacrifice. In the examination of the structure, the forms and the expressions of violence it must not be forgotten that humans are free to resist evil, even when evil disguises itself in the tinseled finery of the good and the »best for everyone«.

Bernhard Dieckmann
Christoph Wulf
Michael Wimmer

I.

Conceptual-Theoretical Perspectives

Floya Anthias

New Racism and Nationalism - Social, Cultural and Scientific Approaches and Solutions: Rethinking Racist Exclusions and Antiracisms

Introduction

Recent writing on »race« and racism (Miles 1993; Goldberg 1993; Anthias and Davis 1993) indicates the continuing demise of old deterministic and unitary conceptions of race phenomena and their related axes of exclusion and subordination. There is a greater interest in ethnicity and nationalism now, and the idea of a new racism (Barker 1981) embodies a shift in the central organising elements of racist discourse away from explicit biological notions to culturalist or nationalist ones. The interest in ethnicity and nationalism has characterised theoretically much of the recent discussion on issues of racism as opposed to older frameworks that focused on racism and colonialism, race and class or race and prejudice and discrimination. The argument is that much racist discourse is now couched in terms of cultural identity and national boundaries rather than using the idea of the biological inferiority of groups (Barker 1981; Gilroy 1987; Miles 1989). The »new racism« as it has come to be called has been the subject of much debate (Miles 1989). The notion of the plurality of racisms as opposed to some unitary system of representations and practices has now become common place (Cohen and Bains 1988) although a core of racism must lie in any definition of racisms in order for the term to be meaningful (see Anthias 1990 and 1992).

The issue of a specific European racism, at times posed as an essence of European culture and at other times posed as a unity of

21

concrete forms, has also become current in debates on new forms of racism. Whether this form is new or not has been variously asserted or contested (see Miles 1992). There has also been a shift away, somewhat unfortunately perhaps, from a concern with racial disadvantage to a concern with group identification and culture, with a postmodernist tendency to talk about the proliferation of identities and the growth of new ethnicities (Hall 1988). An equally significant development, is the increasing use of notions of diasporic populations (R. Cohen 1993; Gilroy 1993; Hall 1991) identifying new social processes and new conceptual tools for understanding movements of population and settlement across and between nation state borders. The focus here is on the development of new transnational identities but the issues of racial exclusion do not become of less significance even within this problematic.

There is much confusion on issues of »race« and racism in academic and policy debates concerning the bounds of the object to be tackled and how that object should be tackled. The legal framework has not been up to the task of tackling racist violence and the institutional structures of the race relations industry have been largely paralysed by lack of resources, cooptation and confused interventionism. The multiculturalist and anti racist practices in schools have been seen as less than effective, working with fairly simplistic notions of prejudice formation and a belief that racist responses, which are seen as irrational, should be tackled by rational means (Rattansi 1992).

Conceptualising Racisms and their Objects

The way we think about race and racism is central to formulating anti racist strategies and for building a truly participatory and multicultural democracy. One of the most important problems in anti racist strategy is to think out *what* indeed is to be tackled and *how* it is to be tackled. Before being able to focus on the question of *how*, that is of strategy and struggle, there needs to be a fairly clear conception of *what* it is that is being fought against and what is being fought for. There are dangers otherwise of ineffective and indeed possibly reactionary outcomes that may reproduce the categories and inequalities.

At one level it is crystal clear that prejudice, discrimination, disadvantage and violence, all forms of racism (Wieviorka 1991), are to be countered. This is not at issue. What is at issue however, is the modes by which these operate and the targets to which they apply. Much literature in Britain has challenged the race relations tradition which has tended to concentrate on the relations between so-called race groups, and instead prioritize the exploration of racism(s). Miles (1993) believes that »race« concepts and race relations concerns should be abandoned and racism and its trajectory become the central concern for understanding this series of phenomena in modern Europe. He stresses the importance of a historical perspective on the central role of migration in the development of capitalist social formations and on the expression of racism within these and he explores the interrelation between immigration and the economic, political and ideological integration of the EC.

The main thrust of the critique of the category race is that it neglects interpersonal relations, it homogenises practices that should be separated and that it reifies the phenomenon to which it refers. Historical analysis can reveal different and specific racisms towards outsiders ie there have been ideological and political reactions to migration and towards insider minorities such as the Gypsies and Jews, the enemy within. However, according to Goldberg (1993), racial definitions and the attendant racist articulations emerged with modernity and change with modernity. He tells us: »The concept of ›race‹ enters European social consciousness more or less explicitly in the 15th century ... It is only from this point on that social differentiation begins increasingly to take on a specifically racial sense ... There is considerable evidence of ethnocentric and xenophobic discrimination in Greek texts, of claims to cultural superiority, yet little evidence that these claimed inequalities were generally considered to be biologically determined« (p. 21).

We find a subtle historicised account of the extremely fluid referents of race terms. He looks at the shifting definitions and usages of the term stating that it is »a fluid, transforming, historically specific concept parasitic on theoretic and social discourses for the meaning it assumes at any historical moment.« (p. 74)

We can reject the view that racism is a product of the irrational prejudices of individuals (as or that it involves »irrational appeals to irrelevant categories« (Goldberg 1993, 7). Racism is rational (p. 11). It is not a question therefore of being a set of false ideas or a specific form of ideology that can be countered by knowledge or rational argument.

In rejecting this view writers like Goldberg posit a totalising version of racialised discourse it with the whole of culture in the modern period. Racism therefore is omnipresent and ubiquitous; at the very heart of the social order. The race category serves to naturalise the groupings it identifies and treats then as unchangeable. This notion of the fixity of race is not new (see Rex 1973; Hall 1988). If »race« is a naturalising discourse how are we to distinguish between notions of generic class or sexual difference as natural and »race«? What is missing is the object to which this is applied. What is missing is the common social ontology specified by racial expressions. I would suggest that we can see them as one form of ethnic articulation concerned with constructing boundaries around populations identified by the notion of differences of origin and destiny. It is misleading to treat »race« to be about physical difference and ethnicity about cultural difference since cultural difference can become treated as generic and unchanging.

As Miles (1993) states »the boundary and meaning of the concept of racism is the site of theoretical struggle« (p. 7).

His own position is that the origins of racism lie in precapitalist societies, thus explicitly rejecting the equation between racism and capitalism found in Cox (1970) and Sivanandan (1982) or that its origins are in colonialism. The reproduction of racism is determined by both nation state and colonialism (see also Miles 1989, 38-40, 99-100, 111-121). Wallerstein's (1988) view attempts to produce a dual theory of origins seeing the ideology of universalism with its requisite of exclusion of certain categories from the universalist umbrella, to coincide with capitalism. In this formulation, racism was invented to explain the subordination generated by capitalism. For him, it is a subordinated form of inclusion, therefore, rather than the exclusion or expulsion produced by xenophobia. For Wieviorka (1991, 1992), the growth of racism in France since the 1970s has been the result of the decline of industrial society and the disappearance of the proletariat as a social movement. The object of analysis for such an approach must be racism and its modalities.

It is interesting to contrast Miles and Goldberg who are very much apart on the issue of the conceptualisation of the limits of the object of racism. Miles wishes to confine the concept of racism to a system of false ideas about groups treated in a deterministic way. and tied to the development of capitalism and the nation state form: to nation building projects in a period of capitalist expansion. It is a specific system of ideas tied to the categorisation of sections of the populations as essentially inferior on the grounds of stock attributions. Not all social categories are racialised. For Miles there are exclusions of class (and presumably of gender although he has really nothing to say on these) which co-exist with racialised exclusions. Miles is opposed to including institutional effects or other exclusions in defining racism. He does not therefore have a totalising version of culture and action as racist in modern society.

Goldberg inflates the concept to include all discourse, acts and consequences (therefore including institutions, structures, practices and outcomes which he sees as discursive). Racism is omnipresent and it is difficult to see how it might not become coterminous with Western Culture. He sees the whole of modern culture as endemically racialised at its very centre. His empirical examples come mainly from the US, South Africa and to a lesser extent Europe. Miles draws mainly from the British and the European experience.

There have been attempts to provide typologies of racism, such as those that are based on inegalitarianism and those on difference; the distinction between subordination as a form of inclusion and separation and exclusion or exploitation and extermination. The recent work of Wieviorka (1991) distinguishes between prejudice, discrimination, disadvantage and violence. The problems with these typologies is that they tend to be a bit like shopping lists and it is not clear how they begin and where they can end. It may be preferable to distinguish between the discourse of racisms and their systemic implications for action (Anthias 1990). We can designate ideological/discursive, practices/intersubjectivities, and outcomes as three different modes for identifying racisms.

Racisms come in different guises. All are, however, underpinned by a notion of a natural relation between an essence attributed to a human population, whether biological or cultural, and social outcomes that do, will, or should flow from this. It is not possible to seek an exhaustive list of racisms and their empirical identification as though we can discover their essential truths. However, what are referred to as racist practices and outcomes cannot be understood exclusively as outcomes of race categorisation. There are invisible Others not addressed by the issue of »race«. These include insider minorities, outsider minorities and new migrants.

It is necessary to specify the distinguishing feature of the general case of racism in order to clarify what the particular racisms are. This is given by the naturalisation of difference and the internalisation of this difference to produce boundaries of identity that then give rise to racial exclusion. Racisms promote exclusions on the basis of membership of supposed race groups (however they are taken to be constituted). This includes *racist institutions* and *racist outcomes*. Power is central in this formulation since subordinate groups may use an ideology of naturalised inferiority which might lead to social exclusions but they do not have the facility to put this into practise (see also Anthias 1992).

In some literature racism is regarded as an ideology specifying biology, evaluated negatively and self reproducing (e.g. Miles 1993). What is missing from this definition are exclusions as outcomes and their institutional framework. Exclusionary practice is distinguished from racism rather than being part of it since racism is conceived as only ideological. This is a very limited and virtually useless definition for identifying racism in contemporary societies, particularly given the growth of culturalist forms of racism that do not specify biological inferiority but rely on cultural difference and notions of undesirability.

The delineation of racisms does not arise from the project of being able to label inequalities. The discussion is motivated more by being able to identify constellations of social meanings and practices that are regressive from the point of view of participatory social democracies. The identification is for elimination rather than for labelling with regard to any concrete effect for any one individual or group. We must refocus on the question of democratisation and increasingly breaking down ethnic enclavisation and the border constructions that lie at the heart of both racisms and multiculturalisms. We must also interrogate the cultural imperialism that lies deep in multiculturalist policy.

Race categories, identities and meanings are complex and multidimensional. This is more and more acknowledged (eg the title of Cohen and Bains: Multiracist Britain 1988). This acknowledgement is part of a postmodernist tendency to recognise fragmentation and difference. However, despite this recognition in some quarters, there is a sense in which certain types of race categories and racism creep into much academic discourse and policy discussions.

For example, within arguments around »neo racism« in Britain, the assumption has been that there has been a shift of focus from biological notions of race difference to cultural or nationalist notions as they present themselves to *Black people*. So although the new racism allows for a different type of racism which uses culturalist arguments rather than biological ones, the victims and perpetrators have been defined in racial terms as Black and White. However, the notion of cultural racism cannot be used when the object of racism is not so clearly *culturally* visibly distinct. If Black cannot be seen in cultural terms in as much it doesn't denote cultural difference it then becomes an issue of the extent to which the symbol of colour stands for national belongingness and the impossibility of being authentically a member of a European »nation« and also Black. It is blindness to this which problematises the view of »neo racism« as focused on culture rather than colour. The latter can become a sign of culture and national belonging despite the lack of contents which might justify this. Young people who do not appear as culturally different may still be subjected to racism eg young Asians and Blacks who see themselves as British and whose culture cannot be depicted therefore as undesirable. The growth of syncretic cultures (Gilroy 1993), of hybridity (Bhabha 1990), needs to be incorporated as well as the existence of transethnic solidarity amongst young adolescents.

27

Racisms are forms of ideology and practice that serve to inferiorise and exclude (or include in subordinate positions) all groups whose boundary is defined in terms of an ethnic or collective origin (Anthias 1992). The boundary does not have to be a racialised one in order for racist exclusions to operate therefore. We can no longer treat anti racist struggle as organisable around the question of blackness nor can we see racism as a system of beliefs about groups (only as an ideology) as in Miles (1982, 1989, 1993). A restrictive use of racism is unhelpful but we need to be able to specify what is common to racisms also. We should note the danger of inflating the category too much (found in Goldberg) so that it subsumes the totality of inequality faced by groups conceived as »races« in society. Such an approach treats racism as a totalising discourse deeply entrenched in European culture and it is difficult to see the forms which would allow effective contestation.

The object of racialisation is not exclusively constructed in terms of colour racism but can use culture and religion as symbolic markers of difference, inferiority and undesirability as the debates on nco racism have pointed to (Barker 1981). Black may nonetheless be situationally understood and politically important. However, as an analytical category or explanatory category it is largely wanting. The contextual nature of identifications with such a political category that denotes a common experience of racism needs to be acknowledged. For example Asian women in a study of S.E. London (Anthias and Yuval Davis 1992) said they shared this depiction with Afro Caribbeans because of their colour but do not see themselves as Black when they are asked to define their identity. They say they are Sikhs or Asians. But pan-Asian itself may be a reactive category and also one that is used about the groups rather than by the groups - in the ethnic Census question Asians wanted the country of origin distinction included for this very reason whereas African Caribbeans did not wish the Caribbean islands to be included. To a large extent the value of the term Black as a political category needs to be judged with reference to its potential for forging solidarity with regard to fighting racism and in terms of its political effects.

The term Black cannot articulate processes of racialisation in general or in their specificity. It is both too limited because it excludes those who do not experience what Brah (1992) calls colour racism. It is not necessarily wrong to see the targets of racism in Britain as primarily Black (although the notion of Blackness has some problems (see Anthias and Yuval Davis 1992). However it is clear that such a depiction cannot recognise the forms of racism faced by Cypriots, Jews, the Irish, the Turks, the Kurds and Gypsies in Britain as well as Third World migrants nor by Muslims who may be defined (or define themselves) more by their non Europeanness or Otherness than their colour. It is too broad because it cannot tackle specific forms of racism such as those against Asian women or Afro Caribbean youth, in the first case linked to gender and sexuality (eg the practice of virginity tests at immigration control) and in the second case linked to gender, generation and unemployment (criminalisation). It reduces racism to a homogenous set of experiences and practices organised around the centrality of skin colour as the visible marker of racist intentionality. Racism is therefore defined in intersubjective terms, being seen as exercised in and against subjects with particular ascriptive characteristics rather than being a set of outcomes of a large range of legal, policy, institutional and discursive practices (Anthias 1990).

There is the argument that colour visibility makes assimilation into the hegemonic culture and structure of a society impossible. Racism is here usually confined to the product of colonialist discourse of »the Other«, which is seen to have ongoing effects in the present, often derived from class interests (as in the work of Rex 1973; Sivanandan 1982). In some arguments this prototype is seen to predate the colonial experience and to be a product of the historical signifier of blackness (Jordan 1974).

Gilroy (1987) stresses the existence of a Black culture and organisation that is not merely structured in, and through, the experience of racism. However, he assumes a homogenous cultural and political entity. Miles (1989) extends racism beyond colour, and indeed points out that racism is not the privileged domain of whites, and that blacks can be racist. This needs to be modified, however. Racism is not just about beliefs or statements (discourse in this narrow sense). Racism also involves the ability to impose those beliefs or world views as hegemonic, and as a basis for a denial of rights or equality. Racism is thus embedded in power relations of different types. From this point of view, although racialised groups may be racist in terms of believing that some groups are endemically inferior, they do not usually possess the power to effect change.

There are good reasons, therefore, for rejecting a unitary subject as victim and culprit around the binary opposition of Black and White. In both the British and the broader European context a multitude of ethnic exclusions and otherness exist that bear no resemblance to Black categorisation. Different ethnic groups experience racism differently - it has different *outcomes* depending on class location, political position, forms of regulation and control exercised by the state, forms of citizenship and so on.

Where is the Missing Term: Ethnicity?

Racism can be regarded as the most extreme form of the exclusionary face of ethnic phenomena (which can also involve practices of extermination, repatriation, exploitation, slavery as well as racial harassment and unequal social rights and denial of access to resources of different types). Other forms of the exclusionary face of ethnic phenomena are to be found in ethnocentrism (the belief in the naturalness or taken for granted superiority of the ways of being of the ethnic group) and xenophobia or the dislike of outsiders which becomes racist when the group has power to exclude as already noted in a diverse number of ways (Anthias 1992).

There is a view that »ethnicity tends to emphasise a rhetoric of cultural content whereas race tends to resort to a rhetoric of descent« (Goldberg 1993, 76). Here we can pause to delineate the distinctiveness of ethnicity and racism. There are more and less benevolent forms of the articulation of ethnic processes. Ethnicity is dedicated to boundary formation and assertion in the face of difference and threat to the group; whether the group is more or less powerful will determine the form it takes. Racism is dedicated to maintaining existing borders and resisting usurpation by minority or subordinate groups or to attempt to dominate over these groups. Racism is both defensive and expansionist, defensive of the border but expansionist in terms of areas of domination over other groups and resources. Ethnicity is a resource that can be marshalled in the exercise of both usurpation and exclusion and can be used by both racists and antiracists in order to provide effective political mobilisation through the assertion of common interests that override those of class and gender.

Racisms do not rely only on race categorisation, but use the ethnic category more generally as their essential building block. The historical manifestations of racism, however, are linked to a diversity of economic and political projects and do not, therefore, emanate exclusively from ethnic processes (Anthias 1990, 1992). A useful question to ask is what the ontological referents of racisms are. It is not possible to see these as being »races« only since this would delimit the recognition of inferiorising and excluding populations to only those who discursively have been regarded as a race. A more inclusive and sensitive application of racisms would seek the specificity of racism (as opposed to sexism or class inequality) to lie in its working on the notion of ethnic groupings. It is a discourse and practice whereby ethnic groups are inferiorised. Racism need not rely on a process of racialisation in the sense of constructing its object in »race« terms. As Balibar has suggested it is possible to think of a »racism without race« (Balibar 1991). Racism can also use the notion of the undesirability of groups, as well as the notion of biological inferiority. Undesirable groups need not be conceptualised in explicit racial terms but as Others more generally. This may lead to attempts to assimilate, exterminate or exclude groups. These attempts may be justified by the negative attribution given to culture, ethnic identity and personality as well as racial stock. For example, anti Muslim racism in Britain relies on notions of the »non civilised«, and supposedly inferior and undesirable, character of Islamic religion and way of life, rather than an explicit notion of biological inferiority. However what allows us to refer to all these discourses and practices as racist, is to be found in the attribution of collective features to a given population. This population is endowed with fixed unchanging and negative characteristics, and subjected to relations of inferiorisation and exclusion.

Indeed the question of power and racist effects is central to racism. For example, subordinated and powerless groups may hold beliefs that other groups are inferior. Such beliefs and attitudes may be characterised as racist (or women may be sexist towards men) but this is not coterminous with the racism propagated by dominant powerful groups. This is because the beliefs of powerless groups cannot produce social effects of subordination or inferiorisation. Racism is not just about beliefs or statements (discourse in this narrow sense), therefore. Racism also involves the ability to impose those beliefs or world views as hegemonic, and as a basis for a denial of rights or equality. Racism is thus embedded in power relations of different types. From this point of view, although blacks may be racist in terms of believing that some groups are endemically inferior, they do not usually possess the power to effect change (Anthias 1992).

Another Missing Term: Where is Gender?

Racist exclusions operate differently also on the basis of the sexist relations within ethnic and racialised groups to produce different outcomes. For example men from such groups may use sexist rules and power in order to counteract ethnic and racialised exclusions as in the super exploitation of women within »ethnic economies« eg the Clothing industry (Anthias 1983). Phoenix (1990) has argued that gender relations relating to motherhood amongst young Afro Caribbean women are not derived from a static cultural attribute but are produced in interplay with the sexist and racist nature of British society. Bhachu (1988) has argued that Sikh women in Britain are taking an important role in the development of business enterprise as a response to racist exclusions that the whole of the Sikh community faces. In other words gender relations are also not static but are produced in interplay with class and racialisation processes.

I have argued before (Anthias 1991) that gender divisions are central to understanding the social placement of minority ethnic and racialised groups. This does not merely mean that men and women from ethnic minorities are positioned differently in relation to each other. It also means that the social and economic position of men and women from ethnic minorities is partially determined by the ways in which gender relations, both within the ethnically specific cultures of different groups and within the wider society interact with one another. This interaction has implications for both the positioning of men and women from these groups on the one hand and for the whole of the minority or racialised group on the other. There are therefore two sets of gender relations that are involved, those of the minority and those of the dominant majority. These gender relations then produce a particular class structuration for different groups in conjunction with labour market processes and racialisation.

Racialisation processes, which relate differently to men and women and the class disadvantages already attendant on migrant and ethnic minority status, will affect the way in which gender relations within the groups may be dynamically constituted in the setting of a racist exclusionary society also. Therefore gender relations should not regarded as static or as pregiven as in much feminist analysis of the labour market (see Beechey 1977).

The sexist bases of ethnic culture (which includes racist articulations) both of the minority and the dominant majority, limit the place to which women can be positioned but in different ways for different groups. For subordinate ethnic groups two different modes of sexist ideology and practice, internal and external to the group, may operate in different directions and thus intersect to produce distinct effects. For example where the notion of women as economic dependents is primary in white working class gender relations this may not be the case for African Caribbean gender relations (Phoenix 1990). Yet the ideology of economic dependency is implicated in producing outcomes for such women in their day to day lives through the postulate of economic dependency as »normal« and such women as pathological and abnormal. Minority ethnic and racialised women are not only subjected to racist exclusions unlike dominant majority women. They are also subjected to two sets of sexist relations.

The centrality of gender for the understanding of racist articulations and outcomes has hardly been touched upon in the available literature. Where the fact of family labour, for example, has been noted (Ward and Jenkins 1984; Wilson and Stanworth 1988), the implications of this in terms of the centrality of analysing gender relations have been totally missed. Phizacklea (1990) on the other hand is aware of the importance of gender but misses the double set of sexist relations that are implicated for minority ethnic and racialised women, ie those internal to the group and those of the dominant group and the state. For example, a quick perusal of labour market processes in Britain as they relate to »ethnic minorities« acts to nullify notions of a unitary category of the racialised which is positioned only through racism or the internal choices of groups (two alternative explanations adopted by writers and policy makers (Anthias 1991)).

Countering Racisms

There is an urgent need to refocus the terms of reference of discussions on antiracism and multiculturalism. The first takes as an object a race (a given group who is the victim) and racism. This fails to note what the positive goal is and instead concentrates on the enemy. The kind of society (anti racist) that is implied cannot be assumed merely in these negative terms. Similarly in multiculturalism (and they are not the same animal every where), the problematic is that of recognising and facilitating cultural diversity and preserving difference. The assertion of group rights contained in race conscious policies versus individual rights for the rest of society (liberalism classically focuses on the latter) is problematic not least because it means that some individuals only emerge as members of collectivities (the race and ethnic groups identified) whereas others (dominant race and ethnic groups) emerge in terms of their rights as individuals (the rest of society).

The tendency to treat categories of the population as unitary and static is found in debates on antiracism whose target is seen as a group defined as race who experiences racism. In multiculturalism the target is a group defined by a difference in culture whose preservation and reproduction is to be encouraged. Both these positions fail to note the dynamic character of culture and ethnic and race identities are defined as possessive properties rather than fluid and processual social relations. They may have the effect of ethnicising and producing modes of struggle that focus on culture and identity, repeating for themselves the static and ahistorical nature of racialised definitions. They serve furthermore to promote forms of politics that can be divisive.

Greater *inclusion* in the polity has resonances both in terms of the representation of diverse cultures and groupings on an equal level, as constituencies of advocacy and on an individual level in terms of social and political rights; what may be broadly termed those of citizenship. There is also recognition that anti racisms need to work on a number of fronts in terms of socio-material conditions, the discursive apparatus and mechanisms of subjective identification.

Formulating anti racist practices pragmatically, however, is laden with problems. For example one of the weakest parts of Goldberg's argument (1993) is when suggests »unannounced testing and auditing« (p. 226) for seeking out discriminatory practices in industry. He also suggests that »where a verbal racist expression - an epithet, a joke, a story, for example - can be shown to be not just offensive but harmful«, all those witness to it should register their objections through letters to the local press. It is clear that penalties need to be imposed through legislating against racist practices. It is not so clear, however, that a »big brother« approach in industry will have a positive effect in terms of countering racism in the workplace. It is also not clear that responding to racist verbal expressions through vocal dissent, or writing to a usually racist press and for a usually racist audience, will be very effective. At one point he also states that »charges of racism and sexism can be mistaken« (p. 228) such as when »A student charges racism of an instructor for using the work ›niggardly‹ in class, while another demands that a reproduction of a Klimt nude hanging in her instructor's office be removed because it is sexist« (p. 228). He suggests the first student should be asked to look the word up in a dictionary and the second be given a good reader on censorship and pornography. What is missing is the attempt to deal with the real disquiet of the subjects in this case and the failure to consider what is going on in the interaction process. Goldberg is assuming some objective yardstick here for measuring what is racist or sexist and a prescriptive approach is given.

Nor is it possible to coherently argue the rights of cultural practice, found in some forms of multiculturalism. The rights of culture - of a way of life - can only be sustained as part of the goal of struggling against exclusion and is not an end in itself. It is because denial of validity to cultural practices symbolises the denial of rights that it is an arena for struggle not because any culture has its own rights. The problem of racism is both one of being included in the polity and society on subordinate terms or outcomes, and of being excluded completely,

A distinction can be drawn between multiculturality (which involves diversity, cultural penetration and hybridity) and multiculturalism (difference, cultural reproduction and enclavisation). Multiculturalism uses the notion of separate communities espousing the rights to autonomy on a cultural level but not a polity level, and therefore depends on a separation of state and society,or what Rex (1991) has called »the two domains thesis«. The object of multiculturalism is the community and the aim is to allow and celebrate cultural diversity as a mode of pursuing egalitarianism.

Culture, however, can never be lost. The fear of loss and the need to preserve confounds the meaning of culture as the existence of a patterned way of doing and knowing with the contents of the things we know and do. The existence of patterns to knowing and doing does not entail that the contents are fixed either in terms of the symbols and rituals themselves or their meanings over time and space. Multiculturalism in the sense of cultural diversity is, in any case, a reality; we need to pose the question as one of democracy.

Multiculturalism is the interventionism that seeks to reproduce and preserve. Multiculturality is the removal of barriers to the legitimacy of different ways of being and is not dedicated to reproduction. Multiculturality goes along with both hybridity and assimilation. Neither is to be feared as a loss or a demise of a group although assimilationism is an ideology and practice of forced acculturation and therefore deeply delegitimising. Multiculturalism focuses on the reproductive processes of culture rather than the transformative ones.

Conclusion

There is a general recognition both in academic and policy discourse, that there is a crisis in racism and anti racism. This appears to be informed by a number of advances and a growth of a more sophisticated critical awareness and therefore has a positive aspect. There is a recognition for example that race categories and meanings are complex. A critical re-examination of race categories and the political uses to which they are put as well as the unpacking of what constitutes racism are important elements of this advance. Concepts after all contain sets of assumptions about the object of intervention and how this intervention should take place. Ideas about the social forces and networks that dynamically constitute and reproduce racisms are important elements.

That the tackling of racisms needs to be done on many fronts is now more generally accepted than in the past. But one important issue is whether it is correct to talk about tackling racism as such and what this means or whether to tackle naturalising discourses more generally as well as sites and practices of exclusion which reproduce inequalities. If culture is a sphere of knowing and doing, historically emergent, then to build a culture that is non racist requires the manipulation of social conditions and a rational challenge to its forms of classification and ordering. This requires sustained and radical theoretical work in the social sciences and scientific discourse.

It is clear that policy makers and activists, dedicated to fighting racism in the 1990s, must be aware of the dynamic and shifting nature of the terrain of racism and how ethnicity may be used in both the pursuit of racism and its attack. The static and reified notions of difference embodied in much multiculturalist policy, from education to support and funding of the voluntary sector, need to be abandoned. Attention must be paid to the complexities involved. The European framework highlights these complexities further by providing different instances of ethnic and racist practices. For example, there has been the growth of racism and hostility in Spain and Greece towards migrants from Poland and Albania. In Germany and the Netherlands the Turks have been targets of racist hostility but more recently

Rumanians and Poles in Germany have been the subject of neo Nazi attacks. But more than anything it is the growing malignancy of racist violence and the increasing ramifications of what has been termed »ethnic cleansing« (or the extermination of populations by ethnic (racial?) violence) that has alerted us to the urgency of rethinking »race«, ethnicity and racisms. There is still much work to be done in order to enable a more multidimensional, historically and situationally sensitive, theoretical and political intervention in this sphere of overwhelming human tragedy and loss.

References

Amos V., P. Gilroy and E. Lawrence (1982), »White Sociology, Black Struggle«, in: Robbins, D. et al. (eds.), *Rethinking Social Inequality*, Gower.

Anthias F. (1983), »Sexual Divisions and Ethnic Adaptation«, in: Pizcklea, A. (ed), *One Way Ticket*, London.

Anthias F. (1990), »Race and Class Revisited - Conceptualising Race and Racisms«, in: *Sociological Review*, Feb. 1990.

Anthias F. (1991), »Parameters of Difference and Identity and the Problem of Connections«, in: *International Review of Sociology*, April.

Anthias F (1992), »Connecting ›race‹ and ethnic phenomena«, in: *Sociology*, August.

Anthias F. (1994), »On ›race‹ and ethnic phenomena and the disconnection of ›race‹ and racism«, in: *Sociology*, November.

Anthias F.and N. Yuval Davis (1992), *Racialised Boundaries - race, nation, gender, class and the anti-racist struggle*, London.

Balibar, E. (1991), »Racism and nationalism«, in: Balibar, E. and L. Wallerstein (eds.), *Race, Class, Nation: ambiguous identities*, Verso.

Barker, M. (1981), *The New Racism*, Junction Books.

Beechey, V. (1977), »Some Notes on Female Wage Labour«, in: *Capital and Class*, no. 3.

Bhabha, H. (1990), *Nation and Narration*, London.

Bhachu, P. (1988), »Apni Marzi Kardhi. Home and Work: Sikh women in Britain«, in: Westwood S. and P. Bhachu (eds.), *Enterprising Women*, London.

Brah, A. (1992), »Difference, diversity, differentiation«, in: Donald, J. and A. Rattansi (eds.), *Race, Culture, Difference*, Sage.

Castles, S. and G. Kosack (1973), *Immigrant Workers in the Class Structure in Western Europe*, Oxford.

Cohen, P. (1988), »The Perversions of Inheritance«, in: Cohen, P. and Bains (eds.), *Multi Racist Britain*, Macmillan.

Cohen, R. (1993), »Notions of Diaspora: Classical, Modern and Global«, paper presented to International Seminar organised by UNESCO-CRER, *Emerging Trends and Major Issues in Migration and Ethnic Relations in Western and Eastern Europe*, University of Warwick, 5-8 November.

Cox, 0. (1970), *Caste, Class and Race: A study in social dynamics*, Modern Reader Paperbacks.

Gilroy, P. (1987), *There Ain't no Black in the Union Jack*, Hutchinson.

Gilroy, P. (1993), *The Black Atlantic*, Verso.

Goldberg, D. T. (1993), *Racist Culture: Philosophy and the Politics of meaning*, Oxford.

Hall, S. (1978), »Racism and reaction«, in: *Five Views of Multi Racial Education*, Commission of Racial Equality.

Hall, S. (1988), »New Ethnicities«, in: Mercer, K. (ed.), *Black film/British cinema*, ICA, Document 7, London.

Hall, S. (1990), »Cultural Identity and Diaspora«, in: Rutherford, J. (ed), *Identity: Community,Culture, Difference*, Lawrence and Wishart.

Jordan, W. (1974), *White over Black*, Oxford.

Mason, D. (1994), »On the dangers of disconnecting race and racism«, in: *Sociology*, November 1994.

Miles, R. (1982), *Racism and Migrant Labour*, RKP.

Miles, R. (1989), *Racism*, London.

Miles, R. (1992), »Le racisme européen dans son context historique«, in: *Genesis*, 8.

Miles, R. (1993), *Racism after »race relations«*, London.

Omi, M. and H. Winant (1987), *Racial Formation in the United States*, London.

Phizacklea, A. (1990), *Unpacking the Fashion Industry*, London.

Phizacklea, A. and R.Miles (1980), *Labour and Racism*, RKP.

Phoenix, A. (1990), »Theories of Gender and Black Families«, in: *British Feminist Thought*, (ed) T. Lovell.

Rattansi, A. (1992), »Changing the Subject? Racism, Culture and Education«, in: Donald, J. and A. Rattansi (eds.), *Race, Culture, Difference*, Sage.

Rex, J. (1973), *Race, Colonialism and the City*, Weidenfeld and Nicolson.

Rex, J. (1991), »The Political Sociology of a Multicultural Society«, in: *Gandhian Perspectives*, vol IV, no 1.

Rhodes, P.J. (1994), »Race of Interviewer Effects in Qualitative Research. A brief comment«, in: *Sociology*, vol 28, no 2. May.

Sivanandan, A. (1982), *A Different Hunger*, Pluto.

Ward, R. and R. Jenkins (eds.) (1984), *Ethnic Communities in Britain*, Cambridge.

Wilson, P. and J. Stanworth (1988), »Growth strategies in small Asian and Caribbean businesses«, in: *Employment*, Gazette, April.

Wieviorka, M. (1991), *L'Espace du racisme*, Paris.

Winant, 0. (1993), »Difference and Inequality: Postmodern racial politics in the United States«, in: Cross, M. and M. Keith (eds.), *Racism, the City and the State*, London.

Christoph Wulf

Violence, Religion and Civilization

I. Mimesis and Violence

1. One theory of violence places the origin of violence in human beings' ability to imitate - the mimesis (René Girard). The starting point of this theory is the insight that mimesis, on the one hand, makes possible the development of the human race in as much as attitudes, skills and behaviors once acquired can be passed on from one generation to the next and can be creatively modified. On the other hand, there lies in mimesis, a necessity inextricably connected with being human, a reason for the emergence of violence among humans. Mimetic appropriation of attitudes and behaviors creates competition and rivalry, which then become the starting point of acts of violence. Violent behavior especially is imitated. In earlier cultures every act of violence was followed by a retaliatory act of violence, an occurrence which threatened the cohesion of the society.

2. Two strategies present themselves as methods of mastering the potential for violence emerging from mimesis: prohibition and ritual. By means of prohibitions everything which threatens the sense of community is supposed to be excluded. These include conflicts of competition, rivalry and violence, to all of which mimesis gives rise. Mimetic behavior which aims at eliminating differences which are essential to the structural maintenance of the internal order of a society, such as those behaviors necessitated by hierarchies and the division of functions, is forbidden. These essential types of behavior must be preserved because they fulfill an integrative function and the society would be threatened if unlimited mimesis were allowed. It is necessary to restrain mimesis with prohibitions in order to strike a balance between its powers of social cohesion and social dissolution.

For this reason mimetic behavior in the form of rivalry and competition for the most desired objects is above all forbidden.

3. While prohibitions strive to suppress violence that threatens the cohesion of a society by excluding the mimetic rivalry which contains the potential for such violence, rituals represent the attempt to channel manifest mimetic crises in such a manner that integration within the society is not endangered. When prohibitions are violated, a mimetic crises that jeopardizes the social consensus as a result of a vicious circle of reciprocal violence arises. It is the task of rituals to master the danger to the cohesion of a society in mimetic conflict by involving its members in a cooperative act. By mimetically creating an awareness of the dangerous dissolution of the society and thereby strengthening the powers of and the desire for integration, rituals serve to avert menacing crises. While prohibitions aim to prevent mimetic crises from arising in the first place, rituals pursue the goal of overcoming such crises by the repetition of certain acts intended to foster integration and the maintenance of the society. The purpose of the repetition of these rituals is to make the integrative forces relevant and to overcome the corrosive violence found in rivalry. If they both are carried out, the community can, through the mimetic process, benefit from their reconciliatory power. Rituals and prohibitions are thus various means to the same end. They serve to avoid or overcome crises of inherent violence.

4. Many rituals are brought to an close with a sacrifice that confirms the end of the mimetic crisis staged by the rituals themselves. Sometimes these sacrifices are executed by one person; at other times, by many so that it resembles a lynching The decisive factor is that the sacrifice should take place in the name of everyone. While the community presents itself within the framework of a ritual as if it were in a crisis with its basic consensus threatened by self-destructive acts of violence, the sacrifice changes the situation immediately. The entire community is now against the victim, which cannot defend itself and the death of which, because of the victim's powerlessness, will give rise to no further acts of violence. The sacrifice itself is in fact an act of violence, but it is one which is expected to close the circle of

violence, to be the very last and to effect a reconciliation within the society.

5. Given the differences in rituals of this type the unanimous solidarity of the collective against the victim, which is often chosen by chance, is surprising. The reason for this can be found in the mimesis of the antagonist, a development which brings about an alliance against a common enemy and, thereby, the end of the crisis. Two processes come into effect here. Firstly, the victim is made responsible for all acts of violence and ascribed a power it does not possess. Secondly, the capacity for effecting the reconciliation the society experiences after the death of the victim is attributed to it. In both cases it concerns attributions and transference which guarantee that the sacrifice brings about the expected results. The return of peace seems to prove that the victim was responsible for the mimetic crisis. In reality, however, the situation is different. It is not the society which suffers from the aggression of the victim, but rather the latter which suffers from the violence of the society. In order for this reversal to function it is necessary that both transferences not be seen for what they are. Should they be understood, then the victim loses its reconciliatory, liberating power.

6. A scapegoat is sacrificed. It represents the sacrifice that society makes in order to master its own inherent violence. According to Girard's studies the concept of the scapegoat can be traced back to the caper emissarius of the Vulgate, a translation of the Greek apompaios meaning »he who removes plagues«. In this manner the Septuagint carries over the Hebrew term, the translation of which means »destined for Asasel«, an ancient demon. Also where the term scapegoat is used figuratively such as in many rituals, which can be called »scapegoat rituals«, the same structure can be found. The victim becomes the bearer of the misdeeds of the society for which it makes reconciliation possible by dying. A generally accepted belief in the guilt of the victim is decisive for the success of the sacrifice. The belief also determines who plays the role of the victim. The victims are often marked by frailties such as a limp or a humpback. They are thus bearers of a sign that makes them scapegoats. Or they are chosen by an

apparent random method that, nevertheless, guarantees that the sacrifice will not lead to revenge being taken on society. Mimetic rivalry is often the reason for the sacrifice of »doubles«. They jeopardize difference and are especially suited to reconciling the violence in mimetic rivalry by their death. Romulus and Remus, Cain and Abel are proof of the fact that a double must die. Whereas in the case of Rome the death of Remus because of his provocation of Romulus appears justified, the killing of Abel by Cain was regarded from the very outset as a crime. A characteristic of the Judeo-Christian narrative, which distinguishes it from the myths and rituals of other cultures, emerges here: the account is told from the point of view of the victim, not, as in other cultures, from that of the victor.

7. According to Durkheim the sacred demands the renunciation of self-referential, gain-oriented acts and the development of devotion and self-denial. In its aura terror and horror mix with attraction and enchantment. This is the reason for its ambivalent character. A definition that confines rituals and their victims to the sphere of the sacred alone misses the mark. It is ritual sacrifices themselves which produce the sacred with its mixture of horror and attraction. Many forms of violence exercise this ambivalent fascination. So that society does not destroy itself by self-destructive violence, the act of violence is centered on the victim, whose death brings reconciliation. »The sacred is violence itself.« The religious is the enormous effort to establish or maintain peace. In Girard's words, »If the religious honors violence, then it only does so because it assumes that violence brings peace. The religious is oriented entirely towards peace, but the ways to peace are not entirely free of great sacrifices.« The effectiveness of sacrificial mechanism in producing the sacred depends upon these mechanisms being misjudged. In societies in which they are eventually seen through, they lose their power to focus the existing potential for violence on the victim. The fascination of the sacred declines.Freedom and non-violence do not, however, necessarily follow. On the contrary, the danger arises that an attempt will be made to overcome the crisis of the system of sacrifice by increasing the number of victims. Acts of violence carried out in the context of the vanishing of the sacred no longer bring the peace mentioned in connection

with the religious. In other words, the sacred is full of violence; the religious is its confirmation and the vain hope for overcoming it.

8. There may be the risk today of secularized societies having to make continually greater sacrifices of money, material and life precisely because of their rejection of sacrificial offerings. For some time now the sacred has been mixed with the profane and a game with simulacra and simulations of the holy has been played. A situation now exists in which the holy and the profane can hardly be distinguished from each other. Overlapping and transposition take place. Commodities are invested with an aura of holiness and that which was once sacred becomes profane. The standpoint, on the basis of which clear distinctions can be made, is missing. Under these circumstances violence has become the great problem facing humanity. Should this problem not be mastered, then the end of the human race and many other forms of life will be the result.

II. Universalism, Difference and Violence

9. Religions are systems which provide a universal interpretation of the world. They present answers to unanswered questions and demand acceptance of these answers. They insist on the validity of the answers and demand subjection to their interpretation of humanity, the world and the universe.

10. Since religions offer all-encompassing interpretations and endeavor to gain acceptance of their validity, there is in religion no room for deviation. Religions resort to violence in order to prevent deviations, since they qualify the claim to universal validity and threaten its effect.

11. In this manner religions exclude of necessity everything which does not belong to them. With spiritual, intellectual, social and physical violence they prevent contradictions. They advocate homogeneity not heterogeneity. The exclusion of disagreement and heterogeneity leads to violence.

12. In politics, the sciences, culture and religion the maintenance of dissent, the safeguarding of the rights of others and radical pluralism are imperative. The claim to universal validity, especially that of religion, is often accompanied by violence in its effort to gain acceptance from the particular individual or collectivity. The European civilization process offers many examples of this. The annihilation of the Indians in Latin America is a striking case, in which the extermination of others was called for.

13. European civilization has, in its obsession with understanding human beings, destroyed many expressions of humanity in other cultures with symbolic, structural and physical violence. This is especially true of the modern era. In other words, in order to constitute man/woman (according to the European model with the help of capitalism, science and technology) many cultures were wiped out. They were sacrificed to the delusion of a European civilization process.

14. In this perspective human rights can be interpreted as an expression of the bad conscience of European peoples with regard to the peoples they have oppressed. It is time to reexamine the suitability of human rights for the present situation of these peoples and, if need be, to modify it to accentuate the particular rights of an individual collectivity, the right to disagree and the right to be different.

15 Violence can be avoided, if disagreement is conceived of as a condition of the possibility of intercultural communication. Consensus must consist in mutual recognition of the right to contradict. Variability, pluralism, otherness and renunciation of the demand to understand whatever is foreign is necessary. The starting point of a less violent behavior of peoples and individuals toward each other has to be the insight that it is impossible to understand the other, the different one. On this basis it is then possible to communicate and cooperate.

III. Complexity, Insecurity and Violence

16. Universal claims lead to a reduction of complexity. They lessen fear, and the abatement of fear through the reduction of the foreign to the familiar serves as a justification for violence. It is necessary to restore particularism to its rightful place in relation to universalism. In this way the complexity of social relations will rise. The prevention of this rise in complexity by violent means must be avoided.

17. It is essential to develop heterological thinking and a corresponding behavior that tolerates otherness, foreignness and the complexity involved in the confrontation with it, so that the increase in complexity need not be answered with reduction or violence.

18. A hitherto unknown degree of complexity of relations in the European civilization process is on the rise. This development affects the relations of the European people to each other and to the political, social and cultural relations within a people as well are subject to it. This applies also to the development in the humanities. This degree of complexity, which has been rapidly increasing since the death of God and man, is creating insecurity to an extent previously unknown.

19. As far as the future development of Europe is concerned, uncertainty is the most certain condition of development.

This uncertainty arises form the process of transformation of nation-states into a supranational Europe. In Central Europe we are experiencing a crisis of nation-states, which is being intensified by the recent emergence of antitotalitarian politics, which had for some time been longed for. The security guaranteed by authoritarian Socialist politics and the nation-states has been shattered. Disassociation, antagonism and fear of the future are the results.

In this crisis it can come to the decline of the political, to the loss of any sense of responsibility, indeed to the collapse of civilization in Central Europe. At the moment we are experiencing the endangerment of the present by the past: the revival of ethnic entities and the decline of the forces of order which had until recently functioned.

In the end the uncertainty about the future of Europe is connected to the crisis of the world society, a crisis caused in large part by Western culture and civilization.

20. How the development in Europe will continue is an open question. Will the principle of association or of disassociation triumph? Will there be one united Europe and a collective responsibility in Europe? These developments will take time. Not an acceleration, but rather a deceleration of these processes is called for. Whether a multiple catastrophe in the areas of atomic energy, ecology and politics in Europe can be avoided is more than doubtful. Europe constructed the modern world and is surprised at its contradictions, its paradoxes and the violence in it.

Yves Michaud

Violence, Identities and the State

The revolts and the popular wars of the 1960s and 1970s, with the insurrections, dictatorships, terrorisms and counter terrorisms which accompanied them, as well as the apparantly unshakeable stability, dissent notwithstanding, of the totalitarian socialist regimes and the oriental despotisms, produced a profound disorientation of European political philosophy. Anglo Saxon thought, for its part, remained as always immunized against history.

On the one hand, numerous intellectuals persisted in defending on principle the cause of the liberation movements and the right to revolt against the violence of the state and that of the dominant right. In so doing they merely took up the marxist denunciation of the violence dissimulated behind every dominant order. For exactly the same authoritarian and libertarian reasons however, it was more and more difficult for them to defend the legitimacy of the political consequences of revolt: it was difficult for them to recognize the legitimacy of the authoritarian states which, in each case, took over from the liberation movements, and they could even less accept with closed eyes the means of the revolt itself. In France, those who were known in the 1970s as the »nouveaux philosophes«, intellectuals like André Glucksman or Bernard Henri Lévy, were examples of this contradiction. Their point of departure was a Marxism-Leninism nuanced, so to speak, by Maoist variants. With the support of an aging Sartre, they started by justifying the right to revolt[1] but shrank back before the perspective of terrorism on the model of the Baader gang in Germany or the Red Brigades in Italy[2]. They had to reconcile themselves rather quickly to recognizing the evidence of state totalitarianism which prevailed in the countries which they had for a long time held up as their models: The Soviet Union, Maoist China, Albania, Cuba, etc. There, under the idyllic traits of realized utopia, reigned barbarism with a human face. Sartre and Glucksman, with the surprising collaboration of an elderly Raymond Aron, were to be seen working together to sollicit the intervention of the president of the Republic Giscard d'Estaing to furnish humanitary aid to the Vietnamese who, as heroes in the struggle against American imperialism, had received not so long before the resonant support of the Vietnam base committes, without thinking that many of them would rapidly become boat people seeking to flee by sea the paradise on earth.

On the other hand, the partisans of liberal democracy had also been shaken by the dominating analyses and were no longer able to thing the conditions of liberty and eqality in a world governed by profit, technical rationality, competition of social groups and the means of mass communication. The divided and ambiguous positions of a writer like Hans Magnus Enzensberger are typical of this bad conscience of a post-marxist democrat with a disabused but still militant view of the contemporary world.

The concept of violence has served for twenty years to apprehend this disorder, one could say this chaos of political phenomena.

Its indiscriminate use reflected at the same time the disorder of the thoughts and conceptualizations in the face of this disorder.

There was indeed a time not so long ago when everything was categorized and denounced as violence, from rampant colonialism to elementary education, from brain washing through propaganda to publicity for soap, from terrorism, whatever its origin, to bourgeois law, from war to the auto-repression of the desires.

In a book entitled *Violence et politique* (Michaud 1978), I undertook to establish that this recent and probably temporary use of the concept of violence in political theory was at heart characteristic of a way of thinking henceforth incapable of conceiving of the political world in terms of social contract, incapable also of tracing the line between the legitimate and the illegitimate - or simply incapable of believing in the validity of the distinctions and legitimation criteria still in effect.

As in all similar intellectual situations, the diagnostic of this incapacity reflected less a direct weakness in thinking than a crisis of the traditional models of the political community and the novelty of the situations to which they were persistently applied. The history of science presents numerous similar cases of the crisis of paradigms and vogues of hazy substitutive concepts (phlogiston, ether, catastrophes, chaos, etc.).

As to the actual use of violence within societies and between states, it seemed to me to flow from two series of closely linked factors: on the one hand the disapearance of landmarks and normative points of reference in a social and historic context where everything was apprehended as permitted, and on the other hand the irrepressible rise of technical instrumentalization.

The weakening of norms, the disenchantment of everything that could pass for legitimate, the suspicion directed from all sides against the surreptitious function of domination or oppression in norms, made possible a national and international porno-politics, where everything could happen because everything was permitted. The state terrorism and the terrorism against the state of the 1970s and 80s were a perfect illustration of this porno-politics where any end at all could justify the worst means. The murders committed by the death squads in Latin America echoed the attacks of the Red Brigades or the terrorism of ETA on the same level of murderous banalization of behaviour.

As to the instrumentalization of violence under the sign of technology, it did not introduce any radical novelty but gave instead an unprecedented scope to known phenomena.

Violence has always been a normal and fairly efficient means of action in the human animal, whose aggressiveness serves him to dominate his habitat and chase off rivals. War, prime means of procuring riches, has been the proof throughout history. In the same way crime, gangsterism, domestic and familial violence have shown that violence is a paying means of arriving at one's ends.

As to the process of rationalization and instrumentalization of violence, it is also no newcomer on the scene: it has since the earliest times accompanied the development of technology and one looks in vain for a technical invention whose initial motivation or application did not originate in violence.

What has considerably changed since the 19th century is the scale, the efficiency and the rationalization of the management of violence. With the First World War, the first war of the industrial era, humanity came into the epoch of the industrial production and management of violence - and has not ceased to make baffling progress ever since.

In the 1990s history seems to offer new challenges. The ethnic wars that oppose fragmented communities reduced to savagery, the return of xenophobia and racism, the rise of anathema bringing fundamentalisms strike us as just as many new manifestations of violence. At the same time we are seized by a doubt in the face of what appears also as a return to stages of archaic inhumanity.

At the moment when Francis Fukuyama diagnosed in a typically postmodern fashion the end of eschatological history, history itself, with its noise, its fury and its absurdity, returns like a sort of pre-lived nightmare. There is a mixture of old and new here which deserves to be closely studied, but more than ever we must be wary of the temptation to localize the evil in the past or in the future.

Four series of facts, it seems to me, call for reflection.

1. The totalitarianisms and the authoritian regimes have collapsed. This can hardly be just a fact to be stated. Everywhere or almost everywhere the authoritarian regimes have collapsed. And they collapsed almost of their own accord, more through their incapacity to continue to come to terms with the economic and political situation than through the blows of identifiable adversaries. This was the case in Latin America during the 1980s, when the military regimes often gave up power on their own which the guerrillas had failed to wrest from them. This was the case more recently in the countries of the defunct Eastern Bloc following the fall of the Berlin wall in 1989. Even in Africa the authoritarian powers are disappearing or are being shaken. This certainly does not mean that everything is for the best in the best of all possible worlds. As can be seen in the countries of Eastern Europe or in Africa, the disappearance of the state leviathan, whether it be a large, small, or miniscule leviathan, leaves the individuals and groups to their former confrontations, most often without the help of the intermediary bodies or the traditions which would permit them to deal with these confrontations. The analyses of Hobbes regain on this view all of their depressing pertinance.

Incontestably the individual and the social group attain here the liberty that the revolutionaries, the dissidents and the democrats had tirelessly but unavailingly laid claim to. At the same time they find themselves caught up in transactions that range from competetive cooperation to open conflict without the aid of norms of behaviour. While the tryingly scholastic books of Charles Bettelheim and his disciples tried in the late 1960s to theorize the passage of the liberal economies to socialism and the mechanisms of a transition economy, it is the opposite which has been on the agenda for the last years. Whole countries have to learn new ways to act and interact, to fit themselves out with property codes and commercial law, democratic habits that the young generations know nothing of and that the elder generations cannot recollect. This applies to the countries of the ex-Soviet Union as well as to South Africa and Togo. It brings to mind the revolutionary and Napoleonic epoch in Europe when under the shock of the changes in France numerous countries had to reconstruct entirely their legal system in appealing to personalities and jurisconsults like Bentham.

The negative consequences of this disintegration of the authoritarian regimes were a collapse of norms and a freeing up of the violence of individuals suddenly deprived of their social adherences, their local orientations and their traditional obligations. There followed situations of generalized civil war, from before the social pact or after its collapse, between national groups or within states. The theses of Hans Magnus Enzensburger on the molecular civil war (cf Enzensberger 1994) take on here their full significance. The return to freedom is also the return to the war of all against all. The worst is that a rapid issue to these crises is not in sight. From Thucydides to Hobsbawm (cf Thucydides; Hobsbawm 1971) all the analysts of civil conflicts, confronted with dizzying progressions of vengeances and counter vengeances, with a balance-sheet of massacres and responses to massacres, have underlined the slowness and the difficulty with which shared norms of conduct and stable conventions of interaction can be reconstituted in a torn society, conventions which permit new and confident expectations by which the state of peace can be defined. Hobbes already, as is too infrequently remarked, does not define on principle man as a wolf for man, but sees him rather as fundamentally social and benevolent. But he remarks that what hinders the natural laws of sociability from operating is precisely the absence of guarantees of reciprocity in the state of nature. There is violence when no one knows what to expect, when nothing can any longer be counted on, when anything can happen, - when the rules are lacking that render behaviour forseeable and ground the expectations of reciprocity in interactions.

2. Second observation: in the democratic countries on the other hand we feel a new need to distinguish between the legitimate and the illegitimate in social and political action. The Italian-style »clean hands« operations, the increased power of judges, the denunciation of corruption are the first steps in this direction. From the theoretical point of view, the renewal of interest in thinkers like Hannah Arendt, the slow penetration of ideas such as those of John Rawls and Michael Walzer, a certain return to Raymond Aron and Paul Ricoeur are symptomatic of this change of attitude. It is difficult to continue saying that everything is ultimately violence when we have the feeling that there is nevertheless a difference between aggressors and those aggressed, between assassins and victims. It becomes once more indispensable to set out distictions with legitimating functions. Even if the punks and skins are often not better off than the immigrants they attack, and are themselves rejects and victims of the social order, it is hard to see how not to condemn their violence. Where previously there was only oppression, overt or hidden, we must once more be able to draw limits and operate condemnations.

The theoretical difficulty is that this work is just starting, and it must be carried out against the background of a conscience disenchanted through years of the thinking of suspicion.

Practically, the difficulty is further that these preoccupations have not yet had any effect on the doctrines of the political parties. These remain frightfully lacking with respect to reflexion on social cohesion, the city, education - and the elementary deontology of behaviour. The collective ideologies are in an even worse state: the rising awareness of the malaise seems only to translate by an antipolitical hankering which for the moment serves to further the fortunes of none other than the demagogues. There is nonetheless one encouraging exception, seen in the ludicrous forms of a runaway humanitarian conscience transformed into a televised commercial product.

3. Third observation, the double evolution in the instrumentalization of violence.

On the one hand, the rationalization of the means of violence and their use by the police and the military ushered us long ago, well before the advent of 1984, into a science-fiction world whose reality and irreality alike were demonstrated at the time of the Gulf War.

The Gulf War was a transparent and literally telegenic war, where the »technological damage« was apparantly staggering without our being able to know exactly the scale of the human damage, and without our being able to know the real effect of the »technological damage«. Saddam Hussein is still well in place and no one knows exactly what percentage of scuds the patriot missles are able to shoot down.

At the same time, violence as a pre-technological and even archaic means of political competition is making a massive come-back in all localized conflicts, from the Balkans and the Caucasus to Africa or Mexico. It is true that there are enough arms for sale, or even up for grabs, to keep the combattants well supplied.

As Raymond Aron laid out in *Peace and War* (Aron 1966), the duopoly of the American and Soviet imperialisms had frozen the risk of localized wars. With the end of this duopoly, war and violence have become again, even at the heart of the so called developed countries, the continuation of politics by other means. Whoever knows a little about the history of the Balkans over the last six centuries can not be surprised at what is happening there, nor can they be horrified at the violence that is taking hold there in its worst forms.

What does scandalize us however in the events in Bosnia is that they are taking place within a world that we believed to be unified and pacified. Not only are we horrified, we are also rationally shocked by this return to archaic modes of territorial conquest, as vain and as murderous as those of the 1914-1918 war or, closer to us, of the war between Irak and Iran - which lasted, let us recall, 8 years.

4. Last observation: in comparison with the set of these developments where the last cry of technology and the vestiges of barbarism are continually set off against each other, the grand novelty, so to speak, is the reappearance of even more primitive forms of violence, linked to the search for identity on the part of groups without identity or,

what amounts to the same thing, of perfectly disoriented individuals. Such is the violence of the skinheads, of the neo-fascist groups in Germany and in the Eastern Bloc countries, the *Cabezas Rapadas* in Spain, the Hooligans in England or Holland, the »casseurs« of the suburbs in France. This is the violence of groups against outsiders, against immigrants,- against others in general, against the »them«, that is to say those who are not like »us«.

This violence has the surprising characteristic of being pure violence - I employ volontarily this provocative adjective - that is to say non-instrumental, gratuitous. A vagrant or a passing immigrant is killed, a home for refugees is attacked, or the supporters of the opposing club, an underground passenger whose face does not please the aggressors.

Psychologists have long recognized that ultraviolent pathological behaviour arises in general in people who have been victims of violence in their childhood (murderers were often beaten as children). We know also that violence is the weapon of those incapable of managing (for example verbally) a too-complex situation. Moreover, despite all the social mechanisms of control and ritualization of violence (sports, automobile accidents, autodestruction through drug abuse), and probably because of them as well, there remains a form of violence which seeks means of exteriorization above all in moments of extreme social change that disrupt the traditional mechanisms of control.

The conjunction of these factors is today at the root of the gratuitous violence, without instrumental aims, whose sole significance is the impossible affirmation of the self in the refusal and the negation of the other.

It is extremely significant that the neo-nazis, the skins, the hooligans, the »casseurs«, have never had the slightest program or concerted action. They act erratically, randomly. In fact they seek to exist only in exteriorizing their violence against others. What shocks us is here again a major contradiction: that this brutal and gratuitous search for identity should express itself within democratic - or recently »democratized« - societies whose principles, juridical as well as political, fundamentally exclude violence. The gap between principle and reality is here at a maximum. We experience it with even greater disbelief and outrage that we no longer have the means to condemn the principles of this democratic organisation in the name of an ideal society of the future, or in the name of a nostalgically reconstructed traditional communal society.

In these conditions we need the intellectual courage to face up to the paradox that it is the very principles of democratic society that engender this search for identity.

All of the principles of modern democratic society that enhance the rights of the abstract autonomous individual in creating duties of real individuals and of the state, tend in fact to detach the individual's links to a localized community and to an easily assignable identity, and affirm the principle of equality and liberty not only within the state but also outside it in all other democratic states. This is the idea behind the different declarations of human rights (Universal Declaration of the United Nations, European Convention of Human Rights, African Charter, etc.) which release the individual from his subjection to the state and generate a fundamental cosmopolitanism. This cosmopolitanism is already that of the »jet set« of the wealthy individuals who are everywhere at home. It is also that of the hordes of tourists whose comings and goings homogenize the continents. But it is in the same way the cosmopolitism of the migrants and immigrants who come in search of the benefits of the right of the individual elsewhere than »at home«. This cosmopolitainism is also the principle behind the legitimations of what is called humanitarian interference, or the right to humanitarian invervention.

At the same time as the principles of this cosmopolitanism as a stoic world citizenship is spreading, there remain entire groups who escape completely this cosmopolitanism even while they are submitted to the effects of its dedifferenciating power. For these orphans of the state, dispossessed of all belongings and adherences, violence is all they have left to exist. In many respects they bring to mind the vagabonds whom the enclosures movement threw onto the English streets under the reign of Henry VIII, or, further back, the ragged crusaders who left to liberate the tomb of Christ.

Alone a reflexion on the contemporary identity and its possible roots will bring us out, practically as well as theoretically, of our present situation. We will have to take up once more the dialectic of the particular and the universal, of the local and the planetary. We will also have to come back to the question of education. But my purpose here was merely to establish a diagnostic.

Notes

1 *On a toujours le droit de révolter* is the title of a work by Pierre Victor (1974).
2 The terrorist episode of Action Directe was precisely an episode, and did not receive the support of the intellectuals.

References

Aron, R. (1966), *Peace and War: A Theory of International Relations*, New York.
Enzensberger, H.M. (1994), *Cicivl War*, London.
Hobsbawm, E.J. (1971), *Primitive Rebels*, Manchester.
Michaud, Y. (1978), *Violence et politique*, Paris.
Thucydides, *History of the Peleponnesian War*, Book III.
Victor, P. (1974), *On a raison de se révolter*, preface by J.P.Sartre, Paris.

Ulrich Albrecht

The Challenge posed to Theory in the Social Sciences by Ethnosocial Wars in Europe

Changing the Research Paradigm

Peace and conflict studies are now facing a new challenge; anyone planning to investigate war in Europe nowadays, whether their intention is to develop procedures to end or merely restrict the violence will be confronted with this new development. Politics, in practice, is in a similar situation. Neither of the two conventional dominant war scenarios, that of internal or civil war and war between two separate countries, covers what is happening at present in a disintegrated Yugoslavia or in the Caucuses. Consequentially, previous ways of dealing with the conflict no longer work. These concepts of dealing with conflict remain fixated on the nation-state as *the* basic element within an international structure (compare Ropers 1992, 1); either war is internal within the nation-state (primarily to force a change-over in power or to prevent one) or else the nation-state, possibly as part of an alliance, wages war against other states. Neither of these are more than marginally applicable to the ethnosocial war in modern Europe.

The new type of problem stems from large unions of states, as for example, the former Soviet Union or ex-Yugoslavia, disintegrating in the course of the transformation which has become apparent since the end of the cold war with single ethnic groups trying to violently force secession, claiming the right of a people to self-determination, while other ethnic groups violently try to stop them. In the area previously under socialist control ethnic wars have arisen not because these were previously successfully repressed (which, in addition, they were) but because minorities wrongly imagine their previously marginal position has changed during the political and economic crises. A further reason is the general crisis in the state opening up the chance for an ethnic group to participate in the re-shaping of their own political and social situation.

International law or United Nations' resolutions are powerless in the face of this phenomenon. Many of the bloody incidents committed in the new ethno-war are therefore better covered by the Russian term »pogrom« or similar terms than the Geneva Conventions. We are not dealing solely with massacres or pointless bloodbaths, but with directed acts whose driving forces have to be revealed.

The general problem cannot simply be defined as a transitional difficulty caused by the change-over in the political system in previously communist-ruled states to a parliamentary democracy, or as the change-over from a command economy to the free-market. It's certainly hard to imagine a more dramatic change in social structure than the one taking place in the political and economic system of central and eastern Europe; and, indeed, this transformation entails many various conflicts, offering to some opportunities for outbreaks of violence. However - and this is the first thesis - the genuine roots of the ethnosocial conflict we want to analyze are not to be found here.

There is certainly an element reflecting the reaction to the thorough repression of ethno-culture and ethnosocial desires and the completely undifferentiated former East Bloc policy towards the various nationalities within their (see Balekjian 1991; Grotzky 1991; Nowikow 1991; Auch 1992; Halbach 1992; Bundesinstitut für Ostwissenschaftliche und Internationale Studien (German Federal Institute for Eastern Europe and International Studies) 1993; Umbach 1993). The underlying force which turns the crisis into war, however, comes from another source.

After the end of the East-West conflict Europeans were confronted by a new type of war which had been considered extinct in civilized societies, especially those within occidental cultures. Research until recently, wars of secession and anti-regime wars or racist pogroms were primarily located in Third World countries (Krell 1990, 233).

However, the recent wars in central and southern Europe are directly comparable in form to well-known ethnosocial conflicts already involving military action in western and southern Europe, like the Northern Ireland conflict, the Basque struggle in Spain or even the secessionist desires of the Corsicans.

The alternate pogroms of the Hutsi and Tutsi in Ruanda or Burundi are exactly the same as the »ethnic cleansing« of in the former Yugoslavia. This would support our first theses, which is that the transformation in systems may be the trigger but is not the cause of the new wars in the eastern part of the continent; this naturally implies the conflicts will not be limited to the transformation period itself but will carry on beyond it.

There are estimated to be 5,000 ethnic groups worldwide which would have a potential right to their own sovereign state were they to decide to claim their right to self-determination. There are at present roughly 260 ethnic groups who do militantly claim this right. The total number of ethnic groups determines the upper limit of potential conflicts and, in addition, the total membership of a future United Nations. Our second thesis says the phenomenon of ethnosocial war has a vast potential for expansion. In an older statistic relating to our topic, there were around 50 ethnic conflicts counted in the western part of the continent in handbooks of western European regional movements; this is equivalent to one per cent of the total number of ethnic groups worldwide (Blaschke 1980; Miroglio/Miroglio 1978). In Europe, 200 national minorities were counted in total if one included ethnic distinctions not leading to militant action (Focus 11/1994, 254).

As is usually the case with fresh starts in the social sciences, there has been an abundance of new terminology which is moving away from the orientation towards a national state.

Terms arise like »pluri-ethnic conflicts« (Krippendorf); »ethnonational conflicts« (Ropers); »identity conflicts« (König); »ethnoterritorial conflicts« (Halbach); »ethclass« wars (Gordon). These have developed alongside older terms such as »secessions conflict« (Horowitz); »anti-regime war« (Gantzel); »regional movement«; »minority conflict«; »irredentism« etc. There are yet other writers on the topic who see socio-cultural factors (especially religious ones) and social contradictions as key variables.

This multitude of terms reflects a lack of analytical assurance. Many of the various terms are not convincing. It's simplest to see this in the explanation of the religious dimension (cf especially Scheffler 1985; Dehdashti-Zadeh 1993).

European mosques and churches are not fuller than they used to be. Labelling conflicts as »ethno-religious« doesn't mean they are wars of religion, as we know them from the period after the Reformation in Europe. Religion bestows identity, at least in terms of one's own historical experience. However, we cannot draw the conclusion out of the diversity of material that the combatants stem from some fanatical religious sect.

After all, the epithet »religious« proves itself to be (along with the reference to the genesis of the conflict) far more a simple method of ordering the material in order to divide up the opposing conflicting groups. Thus, in Northern Ireland, there are the Catholics versus Protestants, in the former Yugoslavia Catholics against orthodox Christians or Muslims, and in Lebanon there are Sunni Muslims vs. Shiites vs. Druse vs. Maronite Christians. Dehdashti-Zadeh (1993, 124) sees a particularly close »connection between the fragmentation of religious denominations in a society and the political conflict.« However, the result is that as analytical categories religious labels have nothing more to reveal in a secular world than a notion of origins. They are neither able to bring out the underlying object of the conflict, nor are they able to make the pattern of the behaviour of those involved - let alone, how the war could develop - clear to an outsider.

The epithet »ethno« does not fare much better. The term is highly problematic in itself. The basic textbooks in ethnology and political science largely indulge in lists of qualities in an attempt to explain the term, along the lines of a »historically developed unity« which »through particular characteristics like language, shared race, cultural tradition, ethnic characteristics, etc differs from other ›peoples‹. An individual identity is claimed for each of these ethnic groups.« (Blaschke 1980, 15) A number of these characteristics take the political scientists into treacherous waters which they try to avoid, as for

example, terms like »belonging to a racial group« or »ethnic character«. Constant use of such connotations of the term ethnocentricity, like irredentism or nationalism, don't lead us much further.

At present, the discussion is going round in circles, as when Barth
(1969), for example, is in actual fact going back to Weber, who categorized people into ethnic groups: »By reason of the similarity of
their external *habitus* or mores or both or by reason of memories of
settlement and migration leading them to cherish a subjective belief
in a communal origin.«

Furthermore, according to Weber ethnicity is a socially defined
»inclusive category« which goes beyond the »belief in tribal bonds«
(*Stammverwandtschaftsglauben*); this »inclusive category« in the
same way as the class of terms dealt with above is made dependent
on a definition of characteristics like religion, tradition, habits, and
physical appearance.

Simply the fact that an agglomeration of inexact terms can hardly
be expected to lead to analytically differentiating concepts ought to
be enough to make one discontinue in this direction of war analysis,
but there are other reasons too.

Firstly, the ethnic identity of warring groups or factions is problematic especially in modern states; this is also true historically, if
one follows in detail the authoritarian population policies of different
countries. Secondly, for an explanation of why there is war, or why
human rights are systematically and brutally violated, or why there is
such a readiness to use violence in places where wars break out, the
term »ethno«, as little as the category »religion«, has no explanatory
force at the end of the twentieth century.

Unlike religion, the idea of »ethno« appears to be not only back-
ward-orientated but also subjectively to feed the flames of the conflict. Thus, in contrast to religion, in what follows we ought to examine the escalation parameters to openness to violence for the purposes of a more exact definition.

War cannot be explained either by the argument that we are dealing with an identity conflict of larger ethnic groups. Certainly, the
prohibition of mother tongue usage, or hindering the structures wanted for self-organization, no doubt leads to a situation more emotio-
nally-loaded and an increased readiness to use violence. The repres-

sion of natural processes which construct identity or endow identification in the previously communist governed areas is still a manifest
reason why conflicts of this type break out in a particularly virulent
form in that part of Europe. Helmut König (1992, 3) defined identity
conflicts as follows: »Identity conflicts... have a fundamentalist character. In no time at all there is a lot at stake. It is difficult to introduce compromise in such conflicts and they are not usually open to a
calculated weighing up of advantages and disadvantages. They result
from deep-seated existential uncertainty. And are related to the fear
of being overrun, assimilated and alienated.«

However, war as the mere act of killing, as the pernicious destruction of identity symbols like the cultural monument of Dubro-
vnik is not explicable in this way either. The idea that worries about
identity lead directly to aggression will soon be found to be lacking.
In a similar way to the term »ethno«, the problematic nature of
»identity« has to be brought into play to understand the escalation of
violence.

Last but not least, the use of the term »ethnosocial« will also be
found inadequate. Various essential dimensions fall under the use of
this term and become apparent: social differentiation in the war areas
show discrepancies, suggest social envy, insinuate an aggressive potential. One line of argument for the causes of the new wars in Europe is, without doubt, to be looked for in the »dynamic modernization
process which is incomplete and asymmetric« (Ropers 1992, 8).
However, nowadays, social discrepancies are usually dealt with in
another way than simply by fighting wars. Connecting the gap between rich and poor with aggression would too simple; it would be
far from being a viable thesis to explain the cruelty in how some wars
are carried out. Nonetheless, a look at social differences as a variable
of cruelty in the new wars within Europe would be worthwhile.

It must be emphasized, in addition, that the societies of central
and eastern Europe are not simply returning to a market economy and
a democratic party system after decades of state socialism and a brief
period of German occupation in the Second World War. The period
between the World Wars was consistently marked by authoritarian,
militaristic, nationalistically involved policies, partly leaning towards
fascism - with a few exceptions, as in Czechoslowakia. The range of

research into these changes should go further back than the end of the Second World War in 1945. And the momentum for ethno-nationalism starts with historical conditions which took place long before this crucial date.

Thus, we can conclude that a new topic has arisen through the discussion of social science and war in Europe, making it clearly necessary to develop further previous analytical concepts. The result of our brief survey has been to show that religious labelling is solely putting a badge, as it were, on the opponents but has no further analytical significance. The terms »ethno« and »identity« were considered as being a step closer to the process of analytical breakthrough, because they imply possible escalation, which can be expressed succinctly by saying we are dealing with an »ethno-war«. The ethno-dimension or related hypotheses will admittedly be unable to completely explain war and pogroms. The acceptance of the use of violence and the negation of all civilized limits in the course of the conflicts make it vitally important to strengthen present efforts to provide an analytical understanding of this bloody phenomenon.

The objection doesn't hold that certain acts of war explicitly appeal to such categories, as, for example, »ethnic cleansing« by those involved in the war in the former Yugoslavia, the brutal expulsion of minorities, or ordering mass rape of defenceless woman. As Duerr (1993) in particular has pointed out in his outstanding study in two volumes, when such measures are viewed as part of a detailed study of a war they appear as a means of psychological deprivation of the men involved in the war on the other side; in other words, as a means of war. Thus, we return once again to the question of the roots of the wars in present-day Europe. The second part of this paper is an attempt to answer this question.

Extending the Paradigm

The multiplicity of ethno-conflicts in Europe alone brings home the need systematically to introduce concepts from peace studies and to narrow down the focus for theoretical considerations. A part of these European conflicts will remain latent; at least, we can say with relative certainty they will not escalate into violence, as, for example, with the Channel Islanders, Belgians of German origin, or the Inuit in Greenland. The topic we specifically wish to discuss is ethno-war, not simply ethno-conflict; after all, there will always be conflicts and disputes about problems and tensions between ethnically and socially differentiated groups in a population.

To want to try to remove all of this would be a utopian undertaking. In fact, competition between groups has even been recognized in democratic theory as having a positive potential.

Helmut König (1992, 1) points out that our problem area contains within it particular potential for escalation when he writes: »In general, ethno-national movements are determined by claims about identity or at least include a momentum which easily leads to the domination of aspects of identity over rational and negotiable interests. Where questions of ethno-nationality are central, negotiations are difficult, compromises rare, and violent conflicts common.«

A little further on (ibid., 2), König emphasizes the »enhanced danger of escalation and increased readiness to use violence. Apparently, there are no suitable methods within these societies nor in the larger international framework for solving the conflict peaceably.« We can only agree with him; the specific connection between ethnosocial struggle and the general transformation in areas previously under state socialism is to be found within the societies themselves; above all, it is to be found in the almost total absence of intermediary institutions such as political parties and associations which could have been effective in informally directing disputes and conflicts of interest. As Friedhelm Neidhardt (1994) put it, in general intermediary organizations have »to deal with the discrepancy in expectations in differing reference groups.« Within the political landscapes of western societies, the symbolic political forms indicate a comparatively wide-spread potential to bring out ethnosocial contrasts in a non-violent way.

The main question, according to Neidhardt, is what leads to an escalation of conflict into violence, public pogrom, or war. And here we are not dealing with war as it understood by the Hague Convention, where in an ideal case the civilian population does not even notice that two sovereign powers are fighting each other. Civil war is almost the complete opposite: the civilian population bears the brunt of the war, and the uniformed combatants suffer almost no casualties. Here we are talking about strategic violation of human rights for a majority of the victims, about mass rape of women as a means of waging a war, or about ethnic cleansing, which is at the very least the forced expulsion of large groups (cf most importantly the edition 2/1993 of *Sicherheit und Frieden*; Duerr 1993; Seifert 1993; Stiglmayer 1993). To cite just one fact as an example: according to UNICEF, by the end of 1992 approximately a million children in the former Yugoslavia had suffered war trauma sufficient to warrant therapy (Neue Züricher Zeitung, 10.1.93). This is a picture of war more or less contrary to the attempts in the European tradition to limit the theatre of war and the suffering of the innocent.

The basic question is which analytical tools are suitable to deal with this recurring wasteland of violence. Pogroms and massacres are not simply consequences of the way a war develops, nor are they even strategic steps in a war. My personal suggestion is to combine research into ethno-wars with research into extremism. The word »combine« is meant literally: what the social sciences have worked on in ethno-wars ought to be brought together with work from extremist studies to explain the escalation in cruelty during a conflict.

One particular connection to extremism, for example, is to be seen when considering the moments which induce escalation towards the use of violence: in both cases, they are not only formally similar.

This suggestion to extend the paradigm of peace studies into extremist studies introduces a completely new dimension. To meet these demands it is necessary to define new goals in studying and dealing with conflicts in a number of European and neighboring Asian states going through a forced process of societal transformation, in which there are radicalized ethnic groups engaged in violent conflicts or pogroms. Such conflicts may also be of a cross-border nature.

Admittedly, it would simplistic to see the cause of extremism solely in a revival of attitudes long thought to be overcome, as for example, nationalism or religious fanaticism, or else to attempt to establish a social psychological »narcissistic indignation« in those individuals involved, and to bring these divergent elements together in a suitable combination in the process of research. For the increase in extremism, one can assume there are also genuine political factors which could explain the central component in the various manifestations in this country and abroad. Extremist activists and their supporters consider new societal structures unable to satisfy their demands on the state and society. At least in a transitional process there are attempts, which also include violence, to shift the new lines marking the internal division of power for each group's particular gain. This process culminates in the rejection of the new state: it becomes an adversary because it has not succeeded in finding workable forms for the coexistence of antagonistic ethnic groups.

A suggested approach

Practical application: The latest work (Burton and Galtung) specifically emphasizes the need for »therapeutic« intervention to solve conflicts, in addition to the necessary analysis of the conflict itself. Galtung has even gone as far as to develop a training curriculum. The task of preventing the outbreak of violence is further stressed by Burton and others. Generally one can say the dimension of prevention is being more widely dealt with in peace and conflict studies.

Psychosocial application: »Ethnonational movements« (as König referred to them) prove to be determined to a large extent by claims of identity. Present conflict-resolution models prove to be too full of presuppositions to be effective here. A necessary requirement would be the initial investigation of the de-escalation of such conflicts. After all, there is an analytical connection between causes and development and they don't just develop arbitrarily. Only after this, could we establish what conflict mediation as taught by the social sciences would be able to do.

In conclusion, one can say the above mentioned ways of application refer to two basic streams in the political science discourse: the question of the subjectivity of the actor, as well as the research approach adopted.

Specifications: Scientific work required for this area is:

1. to construct a more exact typology of diverse conflicts (in addition to the conflicts of interests and identity established by Senghaas, locating conflicts between ethnic groups, cultures, languages, and religiously opposed groups;
2. to determine with greater empirical certainty the configurative interlocking or overlapping of these categories;
3. to establish whether there are movements within the conflict configuration, especially with regard to extremist escalation and the extent of violence;
4. to research into intervention points for conflict mediation;
5. to attempt to alter the way of dealing with conflicts and especially the prevention (or, as Burton refers to it, the »provention«) of extremist violence.

Conflict studies is often accused of merely trying to turn manifest conflict back into latent conflict, that is, to stop open violence, without, however, really resolving the conflict. Conversely, conflict studies is also accused of wanting to completely neutralize conflict as a fundamental social phenomenon and is so unrealistic as to want to remove it entirely. The view put forward here of therapeutic conflict intervention (to paraphrase Burton) ought to refute such criticisms.

In concrete research into the development of extremism in Germany, it's particularly important to bear in mind that we are dealing with city violence and that experience of violence within familiar areas (family, school, youth gangs, or similar; cf. Ropers 1992, 8) appears to play a major role. On the other hand, it would also be necessary to look into the role played by supra-national processes, in particular the dynamic effect of incomplete and asymmetrical on-going modernization processes. They lead to a dissolution of tribal identity and bonds and enlarge the individual's sphere for personal choice.

Furthermore, social groups which have an extreme reaction are especially those which do not benefit from the promised material improvements. As Ropers put it: »Without the satisfaction of such needs, the offers of identification with the modern consumer and media society have a provocative effect.«

Peace and conflict studies which are concretely dealing with extremism can profitably adapt Lance Clark's approach. He distinguishes between three levels within relevant factors:

1. Push factors: divisible into root causes and proximate events, thus linking long-term causes to those developments leading to escalation;
2. Variables of intervention, which modify the development of extremism; and
3. Triggering events, which bring about particularly violent acts of extremism.

Peace and extremist studies are not only examining an undoubtably important partial area of social development, but have proved to be variously connected with other current problems and their investigation within the social sciences, for example, as when extremism occasionally collides with adherence to human rights. There are different orientations to, expressions of, and values attached to human rights dependent on the various cultures and ideologies.

Nonetheless there is a wide gulf between the protection of the individual's rights in various cultures and the development of extremism.

The tension involved in developing the internationalization of human rights and the insistence on the individual states' sovereignty under international law, even when there is an apparent extremist development within a single state, currently leads to the question of justifying »humanitarian« intervention - or more exactly, intervention for humanitarian reasons. In the eighties, root causes became part of the international debate about mass movements of refugees, with extremism being accorded an important role in all its various manifestations.

In the final analysis, international extremist studies is to be understood as a contribution to an »early warning system« especially with regard to the mass exodus of refugees caused by political extremism. Thus we can see that in concentrating on ethnosocial conflicts as a central theme of social science we are trying to concern ourselves with a broad-range of social needs.

References

Auch, E.-M. (1992), *»Ewiges Feuer« in Aserbaidschan*, Berichte des Bundesinstituts für ostwissenschaftliche und internationale Studien Nr.8, Köln.

Balekjian, W. (1991), »Konflikt im Transkaukasus«, in: *Politische Studien*.

Barth, F. (1969), *Ethnic Groups and Boundaries. The Social Organisation of Culture Difference*, Berlin/Oslo/London.

Blaschke, J. (1980), *Handbuch der westeuropäischen Regionalbewegungen*, Berlin.

Bundesinstitut für ostwissenschaftliche und internationale Studien (Hg.) (1993), *Aufbruch im Osten Europas*, Köln.

Burton, J. (1990), *Conflict: Resolution and Provention*, London.

Dehdashti-Zadeh, R. (1993), »Ethnizität. Eine analytische Kategorie zur Untersuchung von Konflikten«, in: Clauss, B. et al. (Hg.), *Kriegsansichten - Friedensansichten. Vom Umgang mit Konflikten in Theorie und Realität*, Münster/Hamburg.

Duerr, H.P. (1993), *Obszönität und Gewalt. Der Mythos vom Zivilisationsprozeß*, Frankfurt.

Elwert, G. (1989), *Nationalismus und Ethnizität. Über die Bildung von Wir-Gruppen*, Berlin.

Focus (1994), *Minderheiten in Europa*, Nr. 11.

Gantzel, K.-J./Siegelberg, J. (1990), »Krieg und Entwicklung. Überlegungen zur Theoritisierung von Kriegsursachen unter besonderer Berücksichtigung der Zeit seit 194555«, in: Rittberger, V. (Hg.), *Theorien der internationalen Beziehungen*, Opladen.

Grotzky, J. (1991), *Konflikt im Vielvölkerstaat*, München.

Halbach, U. (1992), *Ethno-territoriale Konflikte in der GUS*, Berichte des Bundesinstituts für ostwissenschaftliche und internationale Studien.

Horowitz, D.L. (1985), *Ethnic Groups in Conflict*, London.

Krell, G. (1990), »Staaten- und Bürgerkriege in der Dritten Welt«, in: Knapp, M./Krell, G. (Hg.), *Einführung in die internationale Politik*, München/Wien.

Miroglio, A./Miroglio, Y.-D. (1978), *Dictionnaire Encyclopédique des Populations de l'Europe*, Paris.

Neidhardt, F. (1994), *Theorie intermediärer Institutionen*, Berlin.

Neue Züricher Zeitung (1993), *Psychologische Betreuung von Kindern im Jugoslawienkrieg*, Ausgabe vom 10.01.1993.

Nowikow, N. (1991), »Nationalitätenkonflikte im Transkaukasus und Mittelasien, in: *Aus Politik und Zeitgeschichte*, Dezember.

Ropers, N. (1992), *Transnationales Konfliktmanagement als Beitrag zu einer weltweiten Zivilkultur*, verv. Man., Duisburg.

Scheffler, Th. (1985), *Ethnisch-religiöse Konfliktte und gesellschaftliche Integration im Vorderen und Mittleren Orient*, Berlin.

Seifert, R. (1993), »Krieg und Vergewaltigung«, in: *Das Argument*, Nr.1.

Senghass, D. (1992), »Vom Nutzen und Elend des Nationalismus im Leben der Völker«, in: *Aus Politik und Zeitgeschichte*, Band 31-32.

Sicherheit und Frieden (1993), Heft 2.

Stiglmayer, A. (Hg.) (1993)), *Massenvergewaltigungen. Krieg gegen die Frauen*, Freiburg.

Umbach, F. (1993), *The »Yugoslavisation« of the former Soviet Union and Western Crisis Management*, Köln.

Weber, M. (1972), *Wirtschaft und Gesellschaft*, 5.A., Tübingen.

Edgar Morin

Discourse in Sarajevo.
The European Intelligentsia between
Mission and Demission.

The war in Bosnia-Herzegovina evokes in me not only a feeling of repugnance for war in general, but also appears to me to be appalling in view of the destruction of a peaceful polyethnic and polyreligious construct, which had distinguished itself not only by tolerance and coexistence but also by exchange, communication, genuine communal life and marriage. This Bosnia-Herzegovina was the concrete anticipation of the Europe that we want. What remains are only some besieged, bombarded, oppressed cities, Sarajevo among them. With every bomb, with every piece of destruction, with every death this Europe in the making is being shattered and is withering away.

What a development since 1989/90! What we thought was a wonderful sunrise was actually the deadly explosion of a gigantic red star. The spring of the peoples of Europe was destroyed by a frost once again and even more terribly than in the past.

When reflecting on this tragedy we must go beyond the direct responsibility of the aggressors. It is always the task of the intelligentsia to put the single case in a context, to view it in terms of the global situation. This global situation is the result of a process in which worldwide unification and separation are inseparable and contradictory. The planetary age in which we live has made all societies dependent upon each other. All human beings, wherever they live, share the same life and death problems and are faced with the same mortal threats. All major problems are beyond the competence of nation-states, even though we are living in an epoch in which nation-states are multiplying and becoming ever smaller.

Why?

It is necessary to understand the modern and at the same time archaic essence of the idea of the nation. The term Heimat, native country, is a concept with maternal and paternal aspects. It encompasses the love and security of the mother symbolized by the earth and simultaneously the protective authority of the father, embodied by the state, to which we have to pay respect and obey unconditionally. Where, however, tribal ties, the extended family and even the nuclear family itself disintegrate, the Heimat revives a mythological family complex which makes the »children of the Heimat« the brothers of those to whom they are in no manner related by blood.

The idea of the nation-state, which arose in Western Europe, was disseminated worldwide in the 19th and 20th centuries and used by peoples subjugated by the Great Powers for their emancipation. They were able in this way to root themselves in their identity and culture, i.e. in their past, by conquering a state that had at its disposal modern technical and, above all, military means of defense. To this extent the nation-state enhances the re-establishment of a relationship with one's own past, the affirmation of the present and the ability to cope with the future.

In addition a crisis of the future that arose in the 70s is spreading throughout the world. Western Europe had disseminated the idea of the certainty of progress guaranteed by the »laws of history«, the inexorable advance of evolution, and the uncreasingly beneficial developments in science, technology and industry. Overall shone on our planet either the Communist promise of a »radiant future«, the assurance that the Third World would develop, or the reliance on the progress of industrial democracies. The future has become uncertain and disquieting. Wherever the future collapses and, above all, the present is plagued by fear and morbidity, there is a return to the past, i.e. to ethnic, religious and national roots.

This is precisely what is happening at present in the crisis of post-communist Europe. Ethnic groups or nationalities are attempting to detach themselves from large polyethnic structures (ex-USSR, ex-Yugoslavia, ex-Czechoslovakia) and are striving to create states of their own. Yet the main difference to the European nation-states in the West like France, England and Spain is that these entities were created by pre-existing states and that these nations have integrated completely dissimilar and even more heterogeneous ethnic groups than those in ex-Yugoslavia. France has integrated the Bretons, the Flemish and the people of Alsace, but only in the course of a long historical process of six hundred years. In the East, however, the state is not creating a nation encompassing the ethnic group, but rather the ethnic group is creating a state by means of which it is becoming a nation.

Not only has Yugoslavia not had sufficient historical time to evolve into a polyethnic nation, but it has had to cope with the violent breaks in its development caused by the Nazi invasion. Nevertheless Yugoslavia contained in its heart a creation both multiethnic and multicultural - Bosnia-Herzegovina, which through its integration of religious and ethnic diversity had come very close to being a model nation.

The war in Yugoslavia has shown that the formation of ethnonations in Eastern Europe has been perverted by the legacy of the three great polyethnic empires - the Ottoman, the Austrian and the Soviet Russian - in which completely heterogeneous populations overlay and interpenetrated each other in the course of centuries. For this reason when an ethnic entity becomes a nation and its open administrative borders become impenetrable national borders, one or more now foreign minorities find themselves in its midst, while parts of the entity are, as minorities themselves, enclosed in other nations. In this manner the problem of mixed ethnic groups is transformed into the problem of endangered and oppressed minorities. A fierce nationalism then manifests itself in a threefold crisis: the national crisis, of which I speak; the economic crisis, in which the society loses the security of a bureaucratic economy without having gained the advantages of a market economy and a political crisis, in which fragile democracies are threatened simultaneously by the crisis and by a nationalism that is interested in silencing every dissenting voice and, in the case of a war, every call for peace. Fierce nationalism gives rise to dictatorships, which, in turn, spur on this fierce nationalism. Apparatchiks, having converted to nationalism in order to save their power, add to this their brutality and cynicism. In this way the justified hopes for a sovereignty of the spring of the peoples of Europe have transformed themselves into a surge of hysterical nationalism with numerous wars, of which the most hideous is taking place here in Sarajevo. Adam Michnik once said that nationalism was the highest state of communism. We can say that ethnic cleansing is the highest stage of ethnonationalism and total nationalism.

Yugoslavia has fallen apart and Bosnia-Herzegovina is about to fall apart. If both of them had never existed, as some claim, why do they then have to be shattered by blows of the ax, by cannons and by deportations?

It is precisely here that the tragedy of Sarajevo, the tragedy of Bosnia-Herzegovina, the tragedy of ex-Yugoslavia and the tragedy of Europe are taking place.

Following the suicide of World War II Europe embarked on a course of unification. France and Germany, former enemies, have joined together to create a European community. Because of the Iron Curtain this process was, to be sure, limited to the West and met with a great many political obstacles arising from the refusal of nation-states to surrender even a small part of their sovereignty. The process pursued an economic path in order to get around the enormous political resistance to it and, with the help of the boom of the years from 1955 to 1975, resulted ultimately in the establishment of the Common Market. Maastricht was supposed to stimulate a new attempt to create a politically interconnected Europe. However, the lack of a confederate political organization prevented the opening of the West to the countries of the East that had turned to it. The West's common market could not be opened to closed economies. The economic crisis it was experiencing also lead to a retreat of the West into itself and the establishment of a small iron curtain against the products and immigrants from the East. Finally Europe demonstrated an alarming incompetence, a deadly blindness, in relation to the war in Yugoslavia without being aware of the fact that precisely this war and especially the dismemberment of Bosnia-Herzegovina was thwarting the entire European project. Like in all of Europe in 1992/93 we now see enormous forces of disintegration spreading in the West.

The decisive splits have not yet occurred. The battle has not yet been decided. Europe's destiny will be decided in the struggle between the forces of disintegration, discontinuity and deepening national, ethnic and religious hate, on the one hand, and the forces of integration, solidarity and confederation, on the other. Instead of having become invalid, the principle of interconnection has gained in relevance as a result of this war. The failure to hold on to or to reestablish unification will lead to new horrors.

It is the duty of the European intelligentsia to reaffirm sovereignty as well as unification. The rights of a people, the rights of minorities, the rights of the individual, and the right of Europe itself to engage in unification must not be separated.

It is the responsibility of the European intelligentsia to resist war hysteria, by means of which a people is hated rather than a system or regime being condemned. This task forces us to put the problem of Sarajevo in a context, that of the insane irruption of ethnonationalism and total nationalism in the crisis of the future, in the crisis of communism and in the crisis of Europe.

It has to be understood that the dismemberment of Bosnia-Herzegovina is a deadly attack on the future of Europe. But the final hour has yet not passed. We must do all we can to save the multicultural cities, the cities of the citizens, the cities of the democrats cities, which are still putting up resistance, especially Sarajevo, and which have to resist the powers of internal disintegration driven by endless and merciless sieges. We must constantly think about peace, for peace is the only way which enables the democratic forces being strangled in Serbia and Croatia to rise again and challenge ethnonationalism and total nationalism. Under the guarantee of the Great Powers this peace will, however, have to guarantee open borders, like those of the European Community, and make preparations for new unions.

I speak here at the University of Sarajevo.

I am formulating a discourse, not as a politician, but as a citizen of Europe.

I am addressing the discourse of an intellectual to other intellectuals.

I am creating a discourse within an organization which is obliged to transcend politics - the university.

The university has a transsecular and transnational purpose:

- because it receives, passes on, teaches and produces a cultural and intellectual heritage.

- because it renews and revitalizes this heritage by reexamining it and passing it on.
- because it produces knowledge and culture.

The purpose of the university is not fulfilled by education alone, by the teaching of professions and technology. It must offer metaprofessional and metatechnological instruction. It must inoculate the society with a culture not created to correspond with the transitory and provisional aspects of the zeitgeist. It must not only modernize the culture, but rather »culturize« the modern. It must defend intrinsic values - first and foremost, the independence of knowledge and the precedence of truth over utility.

The European cultural legacy which must constantly be renewed is questioning. It is here that we find the contribution of this rebirth - the questioning of the world, Nature, God and mankind. This is actually a dialogue, i.e. a fruitful opposition of great ideas: belief/doubt, reason/religion, speculation/proof.

And it is also a question of tolerance, not only the tolerance of the first degree which recognizes the right to express those ideas we regard as erroneous and disputable. It is further the tolerance of the second degree, the one which encompasses the recognition that the opposite of our fundamental truths are also fundamental truths. This is a tolerance which is aware of the truth in opposing ideas.

It is rationality - not only the critical, but the self-critical as well - which openly and actively sets itself in opposition to cold, arrogant and inaccessible reason.

It is resistance to prohibitions of thought, to intimidation, to judgments of those in authority.

The challenge with which the twentieth century opposes these values is not only the result of the monstrous invention of totalitarianism. It is not simply an outcome of a ethnonationalistic or total nationalistic hysteria. It emerges from the pressure of a process promoting specialization and the technical approach. This process demands an orientation towards the latest methods and technology (which soon become outdated) in instruction and increasingly reduces general education to a remnant of its former self. It fosters a mental structure that is no longer able to contextualize and generalize. Thinking can make progress only if it is able to put partial and specific pieces of knowledge in a larger context and to generalize. Intelligence is in the words of Herbert Simon a »GPS«, a »General Problem Solving«, a machine with the general ability to solve problems. In future a double impoverishment will have to be fought against - that of a humanistic culture with no access to scientific knowledge and that of a scientific culture no longer able to reflect on itself and on the blind course of science in the current world. The university should devote itself to a renaissance of a general education which is the fruit of the exchange between the two separate cultures.

We are standing then in a transsecular place devoted simultaneously to the past and the future.

We find ourselves in the middle of an age and are standing in one of the most tragic places of the tragedy of the century. This inevitably forces us to reflect on this century, to understand it and, even more, to resist all barbarities, which threaten the intellect. This includes those which threaten the members of the University of Sarajevo in their state of exhaustion and helplessness, namely the barbarities of isolation, closure and rejection.

Ulrich Herrmann

Discipline and Education.
Pedagogic Aspects of the Transformation
of External Constraint into Self-Constraint

Prefatory Remarks to the Frame of Argument

The concept »violence« has been avoided in the formulation of the theme. As a historian and education researcher, I would like to point out - about something which, perhaps, agreement already exists -, that the violence-*formation* of human behavior and the powerful violence-*activity* of persons and groups is always *also* a result of individual and collective *learning processes* and as such should be observed and from this viewpoint experienced *other* than the ordinary ways.

Therefore, some aspects must be considered which have been mostly overlooked when we are concerned with violence, racism, and hostility to foreigners. As a rule these are discussed as an expression of convictions and (political) options. Thereby it is subordinate - without it being made expressly clear; it is a question of *rationally arguably* comprehensive options which, so to speak, have a solid »cognitive« kernal. However, in regard to young people whose political orientation and options either are still unstable or are first forming, it is not plausible and not explanatory for their behavior, because these orientations and options begin to form first under the impression of prevailing *relevant* - and *changeable* - life experiences. From the *pedagogical* aspect it is not the »cognitive« kernal of behavior that is of interest, but the emotional-affective dimension, dependent on a *life history*, in the course of which the stability of a cognitive attitude first appears as *learning history*.

The *origin-history* of individual and collective life histories and life forms is defined here as the *learning history*: as *socialization* in the sense of *imprinting*, as a *behavioral history* in the context of the learning of *social rleationships*, as a *history of consciousness* in the self-reflexive conduct of life. The event is for some the individual *character* of a person - from the viewpoint of complying with norms, moral convictions and maxims etc. -, for others the superindividual *determination* of behavior in terms of *form* - from the viewpoint of taking over behavior *structures* from the collective. These origin - as well as developmental histories - always occur through socialization and educational influences coming from outside, i.e., active influences whose aim is above all to affect modifications of behavior and consciousness, be it as changing consciousness through behavior or of changing behavior through consciousness.

These changes are *first of all* to be observed in the light of different pedagogic *objectives*: behavior security, demand for creativity, readiness for cooperation, strengthening from a will to achieve, among others (contrary objectives are pedagogically-ethically not allowed). In the center is almost always the tense relationship of »individualization« and »socialization«; that is, the *self-determined* construction of the »Ego« of a person in his relation the the »You«, that is, to a »We« on the one hand and on the other the unavoidable *outside determined* adaptation to social-cultural norms. These changes are *secondly* to be observed - and this is for the following considerations of the more important aspect - in the light of different *forms*, which can indeed not be independent from the respective aims, which as forms represent, however, certain superindividual collective *forms of communication*, that is, *life forms*, within which (or also alternatively to which) we live out our individual behavioral norms: competition, solidarity, dominance, justice, etc.

The tense relationship of »individualization« and »socialization« - as well als »passing« from forms of communication and behavioral norms: individual behavioral norms are adapted (accomodated) to collective forms of communication, social forms of communication are internalized (assimilated) as individual behavioral norms - must be regulated and *learned* in an organized way, because the *self-determination* of a human being as a moral subject can occur first on the basis of an *insight* into these processes and the necessity of their active and successful control, that is, on the basis of a learning history as a formative- and educational history of consciousness, as a history of an intellectual-cognitive gain from *self-reflexivity* and *rationality*. Without this regulation, chaos will resign in the relationship of a human being to other human beings and above all in the relationship *to one's self*. Therefore, the learning histories as origin histories of individual and collective life histories are planned and staged, in order to normalize consciousness and behavior. This begins in a child already with the first nursing and feeding, as well as with language acquisition, finally with the formation of this primary elementary emotional and social contacts. This *must* be so, because otherwise - psychoanalysis and developmental psychology teaches us about this - under the circumstances, lasting undesirable development, if not terrible harm to the personality can occur.

This normalization is necessary as well as unavoidable. It occurs in the transformation (*assimilation*) from outside constraints into self-constraints, as Norbert Elias has designated it in his genetic cultural anthropology and theory. Constraints are applied - causes, forms, methods, duration, intensity, etc., are most controversial and, therefore, variable -, in order that the intended consciousness -, i.e., behavioral imprinting or -modification go into effect and to establish an *attitude* (therefore, one uses this expression in the literal sense) - i.e., *mentality* in the long term. One can imagine the inner psychic process as a modell - the formation of behavior and the formation of consciousness: the impulse to changing, the necessity for assimilation, the control of the modified status and whose final fixation (*accomodation*) forms a circle of rules, which - as far it is a question of *I-active learning* and not only external behavioral conditioning - is open to new impulses and, thereby, to the acquisition of new forms of consciousness and behavior and behavioral content. Thus, learning is carried out in active relationship with oneself and at the same time in a mutual relationship with culture and society.

It is desirable in two ways: 1. a person must learn to take this process of transformation from outward constraint into self-constraint under *one's own* control - that is, he must himself become the constructer of his Ego, his biography, his life relations. Thus, a *subject* derives from an *individuum,* and this develops into a self-responsible *person.* 2. The ever new events in the transformation of consciousness and behavior inwardly must be conveyed to the surrounding everyday world in a social and emotionally controlled way, because this is registered otherwise as »eccentric actions« and »deviations« and, if necessary, sanctioned.

»Discipline« and »Education«

We will now observe a special case of these processes, which at the same time from a *genetic* point of view is one of the most decisive - namely the *life-historical beginnings* of such practive in behavioral forms and forms of consciousness in childhood, under the additional circumstances of guidance of a child's life and learning through elders (children or grown-ups) -, then we note immediately the *violence formation* which, what we call »educational environment«: because behavior coding, behavioral correction, - normalization and behavioral stabilization are modelled through processes of reinforcement of failure - therefore, through *induced learning*: through »reward and punishment« - all »modern« pedagogy begins as a psycho-technique since the Halle Pietism and relational behavior conditioning of the late Enlightenment. This behavior can be alleviated through psychologically instrumentalized manipulation techniques, which in their elementary form we also call »education« - deviation from the undesired awakening of interest of desired attention, etc. - does not, however, entirely lose the character of violence formation, on account of the effective threats of sanction latent in the background. In this way through the circumstance that for the purpose of socialization the child *inevitably* is exposed to a normalizing *discipline,* the experience of violence, in the worst case in the form of bodily aggression or psychic terrorization (e.g., through deprivation of love). All our beginnings in our life- and learning histories are imprinted by normalizing concepts. They open for us, whether we like it or not, the access to the *real experience* of violence formation of life relationships. In this respect a *requisite* setting for social survival takes place outside of the family sphere as well as the private one. The institutions which were created with this aim of socialization - all before school - serve above all for the buffering of social structural violence, so that this cannot (under any circumstances) deform or demolish the young people, who cannot resist it yet with their own forces.

»Education« proceeds out of »discipline«, insofar and in as much as the normalizing influence pursues the goal through other people, that the child learns *to normalize himself*. This can obviously not occur through imprinting or training, but requires communication and understanding with the one to be educated about the content and structure of his *self*-consciousness. In these terms, education in the real sense intends *freedom* (self-determination), and it can reach this *goal* only through the fact that the goal is established as a *means*: one can become self-determined and emancipated only through the possibility of practice in free communication, in self-determined behavior, in self-responsible argumentation. The primary environment of the child, considered as life-historical as well als learning-historical - protection, care, »discipline«, »waiting« -, is transformed into a secondary environment with the adolescent - communication as argumentation, in which the parental violence must be transformed into an authority requiring explanation. »Discipline« is transformed into »upbringing«, »upbringing« into (self-)»education«, *dependence* is transformed into *self-determination* on one hand and *partnership* on the other hand.

Violence as Attitude

It is necessary to become acquainted very briefly with the »small catechism of pedagogic argumentation«, because proceeding from this, it turns out that the violence-*capability* as well als (potential) violence-*propensity* and as well als (manifest) violence activity always have their source *also* in experiences in upbringing and relationships associated with upbringing, and, indeed, to the extent that the above-mentioned transformations in the educational and consciousness forming relationships and processes in the direction of self-determination and partnership had not taken place or had not taken place completely. Violence as behavior is grounded not simply in aggressivity as a so-called »anthropological constant« in the human-biological, i.e., in the behavioral-ethological perspective. It also is not plausible as a consequence of »early childhood harm«, because here the developmental- as well as life-historical *causality attribution* are more asserted than imposed. The experience of violence is *organized* in terms of life-history and biography much more in a *culturally specific* manner - in Europe, for example, differently from in Asia, with children in Italy differently from in Germany, the relationship of the sexes in the Orient differently from in the U.S., etc. Thereby violence as the *adjustment* in behavioral- and consciousness structures, i.e., behavioral and consciousness disposition are *structural*. Violence becomes *everyone's* potential and occurs in *everyone's* behavioral repertoire.

If this is so - irrespective of the other approaches to explanations of violence-propensity and violence-activity - then the phenomen »violence« is obviously mobilizable and actualizable through self- and external cultivation, therefore, on the basis of life- and learning histories. But it is *this* which also opens the perspectives, that violence consequently is also controllable (at least should be), since the genesis and form of violence-propensity as well as the causes and manifestation of violent activity are explicable: the latter through intended *impulses* (partly of the mass media), through creation of situational »more favorable« circumstances (for example, through unemployment, through closing of youth centers, etc.), through the »right« reinforcement (for example, in influential and norm-setting peer-groups scenes) and life-historical perspectives (»What do I achieve through my provocation?«), above all, however, the violation of public taboos.

In this way it is possible conclusively to explain how violence-*prononess* can be produced with educational-manipulative means, not only in totalitarian regimes but mainly in all forms of socialization through the combination of
- the experience of violence in primary relationships related to upbringing,
- the brutalization of conditions of existence in adolescence,
- (mass)media reinforcement of modes of behavior, whose violence-formation can appear as normality.

The phenomen »violence« in the form of public violent activity must always be seen in its *social* origin- and circumstantial connections, in its »social place«, that is, in that perspective, under which this behavior appears as plausible, i.e. »rational« (without which violent activity would be excusable, understandably). What »we«, for example, call »society« in its state and in its non-private organizability, is always also characterized through the institutionalized, rationalized, organized and legitimized violence-formation of social forms of communication: for example, in the subjection of citizens

- as »sovereign« under the commandment of loyalty in contrast to enforced constitutional order;
- as legal subjects under the violence-monopoly of enforced legal order;
- as economic citizens under the achievement- and competition principle of the market within the prevailing economic order;
- as learning and educating under the achievement- and selection principle of the existing instructional- and educational system.

This subjection does not prevent, but on the contrary guarantees the effective perception of basic rights; it also requires, however, irrefutably the principal violence-formation of its guarantee. The other side of the medal lies at hand: if this political, economic, legal basis order appears questionable to any individuals or groups because it does not profit from it, but is put at a disadvantage, then the violence-*formability* of the guarantee of this order must necessarily evoke the violence-*activity* of each, which see no other *real* chance for execution for its requests. It requires only a small trigger in order to transfer latent violence-prononess into violence-activity: annoyance grows out of protest, protest is articulated as provocation; its unhealthy containment inflames counterviolence: the educated supports, only weak wherever possible, of the »learned self-constraint« break away.

Conclusions: The Limits of Upbringing

Violence-propensity in Germany (and naturally not only there) - one must turn to the history of education - was always on a massive scale: in the authoritarian structures of the families and schools, at place of work and in public; in the form of nationalism an racism; in political instrumentalization of war enthusiasm and hatred of foreigners. The examples from the time of the Wilhelm empire, the NS-regime, the DDR can be quickly enumerated: they show the arrest of consciousness in the subject-mentality as a consequence of standarization of behavior through *subjection*; they demonstrate the deformation of consciousness as a consequence of the *defamation of civil courage*: they verify - under the prerequisite of corresponding arrangements of life- as well as learning- and consciousness processes - the dominating effect of imperative collective communication forms over the individual-moral behavior norms.

If this is correct, then the conclusions must be that with instruction and explanation (»education for insight«) violence-prononess and violence-activity are not to be developed, because *first of all* the violence formability of early education experience cannot be corrected later nor can its consequences be set aside for adjustment and behavior potential, and because *secondly* the life experience of daily manifest social structural violence is not *pedagogically* to be denied.

The teaching of history - for society as a whole as well as for the individual life history - unfortunately is: violence-*propensity* under the dominating principles of our social- and economic order means the normality of the to be acknowledged communication forms of the competition- and achievement society, the conquerer and the conquered, the successful and the subject, privileged and the discriminated *must* produce; violence-*activity* is from this point of view functional-*rational*, because it is goal-achieving and practical: violence-activity by juveniles produces offers of help. And its legacy is reactivated through renewed violence-activity. *This* is directed against persons, i.e., institutions.

As long as these relationships as general conditions of life models are organized in terms of the market, i.e., are perceived as such - that is, under the condition of providing only temporarily limited scarce material resources of the needy, i.e., it is not affected by (social)pedagogic means. Moreover: education - as I had to point out - communicates the process of violence-formation of experience and behavior: education structurally cannot avoid this process and, thereby, this experience and, therefore, it cannot cure it even in the period of childhood, where the everyday life of this young person now and in the future must follow other stipulations: the threat of social declassification.

Hinderk M. Emrich

Selfpsychological Explanatory Models of Aggression

When human beings turn towards the world around them they receive conflicting signals. There are those which we experience as familiar and taken for granted, raising neither problems nor suspicions; then, on the other hand, there are those which are suspicious, mysterious, unsuspected and possibly dangerous. This constant inner sorting, weighing up, and comparison between the pleasant and familiar and the mysterious and dangerous always contains in itself the alternative options of retreat and aggression, of consideration and approach. In the following, selfpsychological models and processes dealing with the construction of identity with respect to aggression are connected with these fundamental decision-making possibilities of more developed species.

The development and formation of an aggression neither controllable nor comprehensible must be considered as *the* central problem of civilisation today. This is especially so since, due to technical progress, both actual and potential aggressive energy are far greater today than they ever have been. There is no unified theory to explain the occurrence of the intra-psychological, inner and inter-societal formation of aggression which can help us come to grips with the problem. And this at a time when there is an ever-closer similarity between Auschwitz, camps in ex-Yugoslavia, and the hatred of foreigners in the former GDR culminating in the arson attack on a Turkish family in Solingen.

In depth psychology and psychoanalysis, though, aggression is seen as having a certain positive value. Thus Stavros Mentzos writes in his book *Neurotische Konfliktverarbeitung* (Overcoming neurotic conflicts), »In my view, what is important is the fact that aggression is activated by every obstacle to satisfying the libidinous and narcissistic (self) needs (Bedürfnisse). In this way, aggression ›ensures‹ the implementation of such needs and contributes decisively to the survival of both the individual and the species.«

Cultural and social anthropologists will not be able to accept such an analysis without protest since they are aware of the destructive force in mass phenomena. However, for the psychoanalyst aggression is primarily positive as without it there could be no contact, no struggle and no conflict.

In this connection, what is interesting is the emergence of the aspect whereby aggressive conflict is always re-formulated into terms of spatial location. Conflicts are forever being described as »territorial conflicts« even when these are meant to be understood metaphorically. The issue is »home« territory, social status, job-status, the specific identity of races, of origins and culture - all of which are to be defended. This is reflected in the origin of the word: *agreddi* comes from Latin, and signified »attack«, thus to go against someone or something.

The basic aggressive territorial conflicts are seen as resting on the solid foundation of intra-psychological conflicts, partly conscious, partly unconscious, but which need to be brought to expression. We are dealing with a struggle between alternatives, and alternative options for ways of living. And we are dealing with the conflict between the desire for security and individual autonomy as explicated by the social biologist Norbert Bischof.

Questions about the origins of aggression are frequently answered with reference to a human being's natural drive, the »so-called evil« of Konrad Lorenz. A naturalistic, biological model is conjured up of the nature of the human being, or the dichotomy of a human being's nature respectively, consisting of natural drives and reason with Friedrich Schiller's aesthetic education as reason's motor. It is not the intention here to argue about the basic possibility of such models being right. However, in what follows the thesis is to be put forward that a major part of aggression formation originates in something far less animal and much more human than is often considered the case.

The thesis which concerns us is that rather than aggression formation in humans being primarily attributable to a slipping back into »natural drives«, it stems far more from the process of identity formation and stabilization underlying personal identity being able to be endangered or destroyed, and this ensuing destabilization is then accompanied by aggression formation. If we start from Max Scheler's concept of personal identity, we can see it not as a single »identifiable« structure but more as a special way of »becoming«, of developing; that is, as a constitution of the self. In Robert Spaemann's interpretation of Scheler, personhood is not the result of the process of becoming, but rather the process itself. This implies, of course, the task facing philosophical/psychological theory in this area is to delineate and describe the *dynamic* of this process of becoming.

Selfpsychology and Representation

System theory models of selfpsychological processes, as they are presented in the cognitive sciences at the moment, assume that the intentional connection between the subject and his/her »reality« can be portrayed as neuronal representations, with the connections between intention systems and intentional content as a continuum. (Let it be said here in advance that it is exactly this presupposition which runs into difficulties when it comes down to a satisfactory description of interpersonal relationships.)

One major problem faced by shaping cognitive performance in artificial systems is to show the process of learning in the sense of acquisition of something new; that is, the acquisition of semantic content not yet contained within the parameters of the system. How does such a system cope with the unexpected, strangers, new events, things which have not occurred before, the pre-rational, the acategorial? In what way can one describe the process of the »break« in the intentional process through the non-understood or the acategorial? Here there seems to be a dialectical relationship between intentionality and familiarity; whereas intentionality points to that object which is »intended« at the moment, or is »meaningful«, then »familiarity« relativizes this pointing out. It delimits an area as already known and thus opens the horizon of the unfamiliar, the still strange, and so contains within it the classical philosophical theme of the infinite horizon.

This is a question which Emmanuel Lévinas dealt with in his book *Totalität und Unendlichkeit* (Totality and Infinity). His central argument is that the »grasping« (*Begreifen*) of the Other, the totalisation, is in the final analysis an act of violation for which he develops the term »ontological war« (*Kriegsontologie*), whereas dialogue with the Other allows the infinite horizon to open. He writes: »Metaphysical desire strives after the Other as completely different.« Apparently there is a kind of oscillating process in self-enhancement (*Selbstaufschaukelungsprozeß*) between intentionality and the appropriation of the previously unfamiliar. Starting from the germ of the familiar we successively appropriate unfamiliar parts of the world. In doing so, though, there is always a horizon which remains unbroken. This process, which can be explained within the framework of the intentional-introjectional cycle model, describes the struggle of subjective spheres for their »selfhood« in the shadow of »otherness«. It is a struggle between selfhood and otherness in the sense Lévinas uses to describe the approach to the exterior world. Personal identity experiences this as a painful assimilation and limitation as part of the process of becoming, the process of becoming different in the sense already used above by Spaemann to define personal identity.

How can one imagine this complex organization, this differentiation of selfhood and otherness? For the neo-analytical concepts in selfpsychology the most important point of departure is the theory of the »inner Object«. This theory claims everything is an »inner Object«, both what we are for ourselves and for others, as well as whatever reality, world or object there may be; all of this is based on inner representation. In the final analysis, we are only dealing with this.

The appearance of the »alien«, the »unfamiliar«, is the first impetus towards the destruction of the dynamic balance within internal object-representation between the sphere of the familiar and the area not yet understood, not yet annexed.

This generates a sort of »induced curiosity« which results in an intentionality which incorporates two meanings. Firstly, there is intentionality as directedness towards the external not yet subjugated, and secondly, there is intentionality as the »what is meant« (*etwas Meinens*) of the intentional content which has not yet been subjugated nor yet revealed its meaning. The intentional impetus towards the unfamiliar comprises the first step of the intentional-introjec-tional cycle. Within the framework of this cycle, in the course of an-nexing that which is nearest, categories and concepts are driven through into the acategorial exteriority. This process leads to an ex-tension of the sphere of subjective identity and out of the prerational internal structures generates a model of reality, with accessible logi-cal operations, consistency checks and criteria for usefulness and reasonableness. Such differentiated introjection involves selective appropriation and exclusion, equivalent to categorizing, acceptance and rejection.

In connection with this, Lévinas talks of our generally declaring war on the external in this context with an ensuing loss of our own identity. »War,« Lévinas writes, »does not show exteriority and the Other to be other but rather destroys the identity of the Self.« And if we have understood Sartre correctly, Flaubert too had clearly seen that this process of appropriation we have described was one of counterfeiting. In his monumental work »L'idiot de la famille«, Sartre describes through the use of his protagonist Flaubert how the catego-rization of the unknown by »words« is a never-ending act of counter-feiting. He tries to show how Flaubert refuses to speak since he sees in words the danger of a violent alteration of reality. Botho Strauß goes a step further in this direction; in his constructivist-critical play »Schlußchor«, he has the female protagonist at the end of the play being torn apart by an eagle in a masochistic act of love-making. One can interpret this scene to the effect that underlying human nature so described, subdued through constructive achievement and concep-tualization, revolts against the deprivation of power inherent in the process. It is the revolt of nature outraged against coldly constuctivist reason.

Selfpsychological Concepts and the Non-linear Dynamic

As we have seen, the criticism of psychological identity brought by artists and philosophers corresponds to the endangering of identity from, we might say, »inner reasons«, something particularly plausible in neo-analytical models. The identity of Self is threatened simply by the sheer being (*Sosein*) of the Other. The question then arises of how this threat is made plausible. The preceding section describes a structural-dynamic model which illustrates the transition between the latent and manifest representation of internal objects. What we here assume is that a manifest *Structure 1* is associated with a latent and to a large extent non-annexed, not yet effective *Structure 2*, whose meaning lies in having a type of resonance function with respect to possibilities in external experience and meaning. Unforeseen experiences in life can now activate the latent structure, in the sense of the intentional-introjetional cycle described above, which leads to a transformation of an outer dynamic into an internal one. The structural-dynamic transformation which results has the character of the unforeseen, within the theory of a non-linear dynamic system, and thus entails a threat to the stability of identity established up to then.

Such systems include the unforeseeable in the critical area of so-called »instabilities«. Those systems which are not described within the non-linear dynamic have as a distinctive feature the capability of »deterministic chaos«; that is to say, they tend towards the unforeseen. After passing through instability into a new state they are capable of moving on to a »new attractor«, depending on whether an event happened or not, as with the famous example of the beat of the butterfly's wing causing a hurricane in the USA. It isn't possible to predict the behaviour of such a system within unstable areas since there are too many parameters unknown to the observer. In this case, only development of single instances can be observed and described. Basic possibilities can be established through the creation of models, but these will not predict the actual future development in individual cases.

Description of Cases within Threatened Identity and Aggression

The German writer Heinrich von Kleist's description of Michael Kohlhaas has become a particularly important example in psychopathology, illustrating how a threat to identity is transformed into aggression. The series of aggressive acts Kohlhaus commits are accompanied by an over-zealous feeling of a sense of justice. They are rooted in a row of injustices which threaten his identity as a law-abiding citizen and family father. Four humiliations following close on one another's heels lead through two phases from resignation to ideas of revenge, and then from delusions of grandeur to megalomania. Thus, Kohlhaas becomes a proponent of aggressive self-justice; as Kleist wrote in the Preface to his book: »A sense of justice, though, turned him into a thief and a murderer.«

Such descriptions are not only of literary value. They allow us to see how a particular form of aggressive sense of mission with patients suffering from so-called »delusions of grandeur« is accompanied by previous and subsequent repeated disturbances in identity structure and the resultant sense of injury. This pattern I have found in my own practice. One of the patients I examined was a customs inspector suffering from aggressive delusions of grandeur. He was at that time 55 years old. It transpired that he had a history of repeated humiliation, sometimes having been driven to the very edge of a total loss of identity. A characteristic example would be his experience as a German Luftwaffe pilot in 1944. He flew 60 missions and was shot down six times and wounded twice. However, he was interrogated by the SS surrounded by trees on which were hanging the bodies of highly-decorated officers and the SS made a game of betting on whether he would be hung too or not. There are many other examples of humiliation from patients examined by court order. Even the psychopathology of Hitler, as the central apocalyptic figure of the 20th century, isn't free from these kinds of typical symptoms. (I have published a pathographic sketch to support this argument: see Emrich 1992.)

However, in the following we would like to deal with current problems. It appears nowadays as though the main aspect of identity and aggression can be found in the transcultural formation of aggression, in connection with mass migration, which brings with it the question of the relationship between »own« and »foreign« and thus relates to basic questions of interpersonal relations.

Looked at in the context of migration problems, radical cultural change and societal re-organization, aggressive behaviour in periods of transition endangering a sense of identity are not based primarily on drives but rather have their roots in the existential threat to the identity forming structures as described in selfpsychology. Such processes can clearly be seen in research into, for example, refugees and displaced persons, or the traumatizing effects on those interned in camp-like conditions. Just one example among many is the report compiled by Zarah Mohammadzadeh on the care of refugees in Bremen. In one case she describes, the wife of an Afghani became pregnant. The married couple were refugees from Afghanistan, living in shared accommodation and in this aggressively-laden atmosphere the husband became violent. The wife went to the women's refuge and there was advised to have an abortion. The uprooting of the family which entails the threat to identity thus led to aggression and, in this case, very nearly to abortion. This is, of course, the side of the victim. It is more difficult to explain the other side where there is no uprooting and yet migrants are attacked, verbally and physically, in a range of acts from humiliation to the arson attack in Solingen.

The »all-pervading power to kill« within an individual's »pathology of conscience« remains, in the final analysis, non-comprehensible, as Joachim Zeiler recently showed in a psychogram of the Auschwitz commandant Rudolf Höß. However, there are indications that in his case, he was in a kind of permanent identity crisis, coupled with a permanent state of »self-destruction«. He wrote: »It frequently happened that when I was at home suddenly matters relating to the extermination of the Jews crossed my mind. At such moments I couldn't bear the intimacy of my family but had to get out ... I had to appear cold and heartless ... had to watch callously as mothers went into the gas chambers with their children, sometimes in tears, sometimes laughing ... I was compelled to watch all the steps of the procedure ... I had to do all of this - because I was the one everyone was looking at.«

The difficulties of finding a philosophical basis for a psychology of aggression in relation to such cases are enormous. One possible hypothesis which could lead to a solution of this problem assumes that such acts of violence represent frequently painful identity forming processes which have been avoided. To act certain extent, what is attacked in others is what endangers the stability of one's own Self:

that is, challenge, attraction, temptation, the »unlived life«, the partially repressed difference between wish and reality, between the picture of the other and that of the self.

This is the area of »projective perception«, as it is called, or identification, in which one's own problems are seen as others' problems. The theory of the »shadow« which C.G.Jung developed is especially important here. The theory comprises the notion that the unappealing dark sides not recognized in one's own self are found and fought against in the Other and in the unknown. One type of »therapy« which could help this is taking seriously the process of maturing in young people and the crises this involves; talking about and being aware of the painfulness of the identity forming process, which in the end means it leads to a de-theorizing about life, freeing one from abstraction and bringing one back the concrete processes of maturing.

When we consider this aspect we can see that rather than the »territory« on which these conflicts take place being limited to a single person or individual, it is far more necessary to assume an »interpersonal self«. Inside this »interpersonal self« it is possible to describe intra-psychological domains which, due to conflicts within them, lead to identity problems, developmental disturbances and destabilization; aggression is necessary to completely overcome a part of these problems.

The aim of therapy from the psychotherapeutic standpoint can be defined in selfpsychological terms as the training of a »coherent self«. If one posits this as the aim of therapy for the interpersonal area, then the task of our present cultural development is to generate a coherent interpersonal self and such a process cannot take place without abrupt transitions and then development of aggression. René Girard's 'scapegoat theory' is a particularly succinct example of a theory taking such socio-cultural processes into account. The theory assume that the scapegoat has the function of being the victim for an »underlying violence«, free-floating and circulating within society. Without being channeled towards the scapegoat, this free-floating violence would lead to a destruction of the community. There are, of course, other alternative constructs.

In any case, cultural achievement aims at preventing abrupt transitions and crisis-like identity conflicts in the changing micro- and

macro-social structure from leading to dehumanization and the destruction of communities. The selfpsychological models here described in order to understand such processes may be categorized as
resonance-conflict models; their main thrust is to point out how resonance phenomena arise between latent elements in (unconscious)
self-experience and expected experience of the »unknown« where
resolution entails solutions involving conflict. This theory is in
agreement with the ideas of Heinz Kohut (1979, 106) in which destructiveness from a selfpschological perspective leads us not to
consider it as a »manifestation of a primary drive, slowly revealed by
an analytical process, but rather (judging it as) a point of disintegration«.

Stavros Mentzos writes something similar when he distinguishes
between »functional« and »destructive aggression«. »Purely destructive and ›a-functional‹ aggression characterizes a product of the disintegration process.« A similarity between the selfpsychological and
cultural-anthropological concept of systems could be found in them
both converging towards the intended avoidance or resolution of the
interpersonal and social disintegration process. The theoretical difficulties this involves most likely stem from the fact that the modern
notion of consciousness is so fixated on the subjective as to make any
concept of an irreducible interpersonal self problematic. However, it
is only as dyads, or triads respectively, that people are what they are.
If we split this they are no longer what they are and they loose their
identity. One has to assume that within this dyad or group identity,
that is in the realm of the »interpersonal self«, territorial conflicts
take place between cohesion and disjointedness, between familiarity
and the unknown, with an intentionality aimed at annexing the new
but fluctuating between a longing for the secure and desire for the
independent; it is this which initially creates the complexity of cultural development, but also makes the danger of ungovernable aggression formation possible.

In conclusion, we can say that contemporary selfpsychological
models of depth psychology assume dysfunctional aggression formation relates to the inner coherence of the parts of the self being under
threat or disturbed. Thus, a reduction in aggression must aim at increasing both social and intrapsychological coherence.

Interpersonality and Identity

The question which arises in considering the topic of the interpersonal nexus is: how are we to describe the real world of relationships between people, that is the »in-between world«, the inner area which binds two people together and yet which neither of them possess outright? Michael Theunissen has dealt with this in his large-scale study of contemporary social ontology (*Der Andere*). He has shown how the interpersonal realm, Martin Buber's »ontology of betweenness« (Ontologie des Zwischen), continually confirms and simultaneously transcends the intentional pattern through the double poles of recognition and acceptance and the ambiguity of talking in »talking to« and »talking about« (»Anreden« and »Bereden«). Thus, selfpsychology confronts the unresolved problem of interpersonality which has not only theoretically implications but also concrete and practical ones.

Dichgans, a neurologist from Tübingen, recently showed in a review of neuro-plasticity and learning processes in humans that the early childhood link forged between mother and child in the interpersonal »betweenness« frequently occurs in such a way that the child is merely perceived as an object of care but not of acceptance (»Anerkennung«). This is clear from a lack of eye-contact between mother and child during breast feeding or bottle feeding. Such lack of contact can be carried to extremes: in Rumanian orphanages, babies were bottle fed from wire frames thus precluding any construction of an interpersonal world.

In highly-developed western countries, that babies are frequently brought up according to a theory which is at least problematic, if not wrong probably has to do with the modern approach to subjectivity since this theory doesn't do justice to the early intersubjective reality of the mother-child relationship. The result is mistaken advice to young mothers and parents to see the babies and toddlers as »events in the world« and not as subjects in their own right or as part of an interpersonal Self. In this way, the core of identity creation is wrongly placed in the baby, namely in the »I« and not in the »we«. The implication is that we have, to an extent, learnt the wrong lessons from Kant and Fichte's transcendental philosophy: it is not the transcendental subject as a solipsism which is crucial for the theory of personhood, it is rather the transcendental subject as »interpersonal«, as »we«.

When asked »Is that your mother's breast?«, the twenty-one month old toddler Lydia, already talking well, and occasionally drinking from her mother's breast, sometimes answers »Yes, it's mummy's breast« and sometimes answers »Lydia's breast«. She indicates that her mother's breast in reality occupies a »between world« between mother and child and cannot be attributed totally to one of them or the other. To a certain extent, it is the reality of an »interpersonal self«. Later on, this realm is only metaphorically accessible although it has more effect on us than we psychologically imagine. After all, clashes and disputes within the family which shape the inner life of people and their neurotic development, are not in fact arguments between single entities, but rather take place in the realm of the 'interpersonal self' as we have described it. It is here that psyche can be hurt, and it is here that the loss of relationships is felt.

Paradox

This article puts forward the thesis that we are unable to describe the decisive transition from threatened identity to aggression using contemporary philosophical or psychological language - including that of selfpsychology. This is because we are unable to render a reconstruction in system theory terms of the factuality of the interpersonal structures in the »ontology of betweenness«. As Michael Theunissen has shown, within the ontology of betweenness, »talking to...« means »the revolt of the I-You-relationship against the web of intentionality«; this itself implies that the ontology of betweenness can be indicated but not explicated. On the other hand, it is precisely this ontology of betweenness which makes people into people. The nature of the structure as not-being-able-to-be-explicated is one of the reasons why the problem of transition from identity crisis to aggression can not be resolved by psychology alone. There is far more need for philosophical psychology as a science experienced in dealing with paradox. From such a perspective, one may develop the outline of a

»system theory of the interpersonal self«. Not only have we not, as yet, come to grips with the subject-object relation and the body-mind problem, neither do we have terms for interpersonal relations in the meaning of »between«. However, we are confronted by a non-comprehended aggression which arises in this unclear realm.

References

Bischof, N. (1985), *Das Rätsel Ödipus*, München.

Buber, M. (1994), *Ich und Du*, Gerlingen.

Dichgans, N. (1994), »Die Plastizität des Nervensystems«, in: *Zeitschrift für Pädagogik*, 2/1994.

Emrich, H.M. (1992), »Der überwertige Charakter: Prozeß, Identität und Wertewelt«, in: Pflüger, P.M. (Hg.), *Gewalt - Warum?*, Olten.

Jung, C.G. (1971), *Das Typenproblem in der Menschenkenntnis*, in: Gesammelte Werke Band 6: Psychologische Typen, Düsseldorf.

Kleist, H.v. (1982), *Michael Kohlhaas*, Paderborn.

Kohut, H. (1979), *Narzißmus*, Frankfurt.

Lévinas, E. (1987), *Totalität und Unendlichkeit. Versuch über die Exteriorität*, München.

Lorenz, K. (1983), *Das sogeannte Böse*, München.

Mentzos, S. (1984), *Neurotische Konfliktverarbeitung*, Frankfurt.

Mohammzadeh, Z. (1993), *Persönliche Mitteilung.*

Sartre, J.-P. (1980), *Der Idiot der Familie*, Reinbek bei Hamburg.

Scheler, M. (1933), »Reue und Wiedergeburt«, in: *Vom Ewigen des Menschen*, Berlin.

Spaemann, R. (1993), *Oberseminar Robert Spaemann »Person und Anerkennung«* vom 2.-4.Juni 1993, Kloster Zangberg, Ampfing.

Strauß, B. (1991), *Schlußchor*, München.

Theunissen, M. (1965), *Der Andere*, Berlin.

Zeiler, J. (1991), »Psychogramm des Kommandanten von Auschwitz: Erkenntnis und Begegnung durch Zerstörung. Zur Autobiographie des Rudolf Höss«, in: *Psyche*, Vol. XLV, Nr.4.

Christiane Buhmann

Hostility and Foreigners in the Light of Lacanian Theory of Aggressiveness

This article is devoted to the examination of the sources of aggressiveness potential in the phases of the subject's developmental history. These phases are not overcome at their conclusion, but can be reactivated at any time in their predominating relations-mode. Lacan speaks about every phase having a tendency toward aggressivity, of a wish to get rid of the other and of the possibility of overcoming this wish, which aims at the destruction of the other or of the removal of his otherness. My theme is the sources of this aggressive relationship to the other, not the realization of the more destructive wish in violent action. The question of the turning of a *tendency* into *violent behavior* remains open and refers perhaps to a limit to clarification, to the discursive assimilability of violence.

In the second part I will go into some aspects of the contemporary adolescent forms of violence in Germany and relate them to the Lacanian concept of rejection of the symbolic, which returns on the level of the real, of the body.

The Mirror Stage

In 1936 Lacan delivered a lecture concerning the looking-glass phase at the Fourteenth Congress of the international psychoanalytic organization. Thirteen years later, in 1949 at the Sixteenth Congress in Zürich, Lacan extended his research on the meaning of this phase for the genesis of the I: »The Mirror Stage as Image of the Ego-Function«.

Through the invention of the mirror stage, Lacan revealed the sources of racism. Actually racism obtains its power from the original fascination of an individual for his fellowmen: the captures vision of the form of the body of the other as mirror. On the contrary, this point of view excludes the alien, the one with whom I cannot identify: it would break my mirror.

The other skin color, the obviois obstacle - the image does not arise in the mirror. This other does not reflect the ideal image of the unscathed, similar body, but another which must be attacked. Being disabled shows that the body is vulnerable; the others skin color or also the other physiognomy relativizes one's own ideal.

According to Lacan, the dual relationship involves the other, the mirror relationship, a tendency for aggression. A feature of the mirror relationship to the other is its transitivity.

Transitivity designates the reversibility, the exchangeability of both positions. An everyday example from the Kindergarten is the expression of a child who has hit another child: »He hit me«, or in unedited form: »He began it«. The tit for tat is also an example of this. A says: »You are crazy«. B answers: »Whoever says this is so himself«. It is a question of the reversibility of subject and object in the utterance. These are harmless examples which can be observed in any encounter between children, and, therefore, the self-comprehension and the personal logic of more difficult violent criminals corresponds to this thinking- and perception mode.

The hostility that subordinates the victim, greed, and unpredictability distinguishes the perpetrator in his behavior to the victim. His thinking schemata in relation to the object of aggression is transposed into the action of the perpetrator. He is dangerous, greedy, and destructive. In the »mirror«, this time of the German liberal weekly (*Der Spiegel*) and also in other mass media, the perpetrators are presented as cold, inconsiderate monsters. The monstrous behavior subjecting the victims by the perpetrators is constantly used in the media. And fascinated, we the readers, the viewers read reports of violence with digust, horror and indigantion. The perpetrator becomes a social monster. I will come back to this aspect later.

A further characteristic of the dual imaginary relationship to the other is the either-or-logic, the »You«-or-»Ego«-logic; a logic of mutual exclusiveness. You and Ego are set in quotation marks, because in this logic there is no You which could be acknowledged in its subjectivity, therefore, also no I which first arises out of the recognition of the subjectivity of the other.

For Lacan aggressiveness results, which characterizes the dual relationship to the other out of its nature toward the alienating mirror experience. The self-constructing Ego in this experience is an other. I am the other. This arrest by the complete, total image of human form has a manifold meaning. It makes possible the production of a unity, an imaginary wholeness of the body image over the abyss of a multitude of chaotic, discordered bodily feelings of a dissociated body image. The achieved form of unity is extremely fragile, a form only incompletely cemented together out of fragments, which threatens to fall apart again in crisis developing under the circumstances. The danger established »within« will be located »outside«. It is the delirium of a beautiful misanthropic soul which reflects the disorder onto the world which extinguishes its being.

An essential concept which is inseparably connected with this concept of the Ego-construction is narcissism. This structural relationship of transitivity, the fusing unity between I and the object, is a narcissistic one. Lacan emphasizes the mortal character of this naricissistic identification, which loses itself in the image of the other, in which I see myself. One may, thereby, visualize the myth calmly - Narcissis bending over the mirror image loses himself in this mirror. Mortal self-love. In concluding this section about the dual relationship to the other, I would like to cite Herbert Lang (Lang 1973, 53; translated by C.B.): »Lacan calls this mode of intersubjectivity dual or imaginary. It is thereby characterized by the fact that here the subjects do not unite in an informal recognition, but each strives to cancel the other-beingness of the You, in order to fuse with it into an illusionary unity of the Ego. Narcissus wants only himself in the You. Fascination and aggression, therefore, form a circle in which this imaginary relation operates. Sympathy, horror and jealousy perform by virtue of their tendency toward seduction and dominance in it«. That the subjects here do not unite in casual recognition - it is a question of the recognition of the other, the recognition of the fact, that it is my mirror image, my imaginary creature, which breaks through the vicious circle of fascination and destruction.

The Complex of the Intruder (*l'intrus*)

In his article »La Famille« Jacques Lacan discusses the identification crises of the subject further from a psychogenetic perspective. This crisis is distinguished by a reinforcement of aggressive tendencies. The »complex of the intruder« occupies a prominant place here. The intruder is, for example, the milk brother from the *Confessions of St. Augustine* who writes, that he has seen and observed very carefully, with his own eyes, a very small child as it developped the feeling of jealousy; it could not yet speak and could only observe his milk brother with his hostile, poisoned glance. Here an object arises, which is a question of jealousy, the object of the other, of the milk brother, the milkgiving mother's breast. Also here is the imaginary passion to occupy the brother's place in order to enjoy it like he does, whereby the enjoyment given to the other is an absolute, an unlimited one, fullness. Exactly to the extent in which this enjoyment for the child watching is impossible, it becomes enormous in his imagination. The rivalry with the brother can find another solution rather than the destructive passion of jealousy. Sigmund Freud also has demonstrated this way out in »Mass psychology and Ego-analysis«. The initial wish to destroy the other in order to take his place is substituted by a reaction formation which is transformed into the requirement for equality and justice. No one should wish to be distinguished, each should wish to be equal and have the same - according to Freud. Social justice means that one denies oneself a lot, thereby others must renounce much. This demand for equality is the root of social conscience. The basic mistrust toward the stranger arises perhaps from this assumption, that he is not subject to the same renunciation; through his otherness he undermines the demand for equality.

Lacan presents the alternative for the subject in terms of the intruder. Therefore, it turns out that through identification the subject entangled in jealousy before a new alternative in which the fate of the rivalry is conclusive: either it finds the maternal object again and clings to the denial of reality and the destruction of the other, or it allows itself to be led to another object, which in human communication takes on characteristic forms: as communicable object, because competition at the same time as rivalry and agreement occurs:

thereby, however, at the same time it recognizes the other and the socialized object. It turns out that for Lacan human jealousy is an »archtype of social feeling«. Let us once again sum up the two possibilities: destruction of the other and return to the direct enjoyment of the mother-object or recognition of the other with general renunciation of pleasure and the substitution of the primary object by a communicable one. In language, renunciation of the direct object occurs, recognition and agreement occur.

Was this not also the way out of the mortal rivalry of the brothers after the mutually committed patricide in the myth of »Totem and Taboo«? Thus as the unlimited possession and enjoyment of all women of this primal father is mythic, so also is the evidently unlimited enjoyment of the brother at the mother's breast. First the passion of jealousy, the imaginary passion rises to the image of a feeling of pleasure, which the subject has not experienced in this way. The contract contains the renunciation of mythical pleasure and the pleasure of the destruction of the other and generates social feeling among brothers - and sisters?

I would like to end this section with a quotation from Lacan (a lecture examining aggressiveness, which he gave 1948 in Brussels), in which he appears as an analyst to be commited to the principle of brotherhood. From this quote, moreover, it appears that he also relates the lack of relationship among people in the modern age to a multitude of social desintegration processes. »In this ›liberated‹ person of the modern world now this being, who has been torn into pieces until now, is at the basis of the existence of its enormous split. It is the neurosis of self-punishment with the hysterical-hypochondriac symptoms of its nonrealization of the other and the world, with its social consequences of breakdown and crime. It is this moving, fleeing victim that otherwise is irresponsible, that has broken with all conventions which damns modern men to the most tremendous social wandering, whom we receive when they come to us. Our everyday task is to reveal to this existence of the nothing-new the way of its meaning in a discrete brotherhood, to which we are always too unequal«.

Just briefly some more observations on the Oedipus complex, the third crisis: here in the best case is the idealizing destructive relationship to the other removed through th insertion of the ego-ideal, which contains the renunciation of the direct, also sexual enjoyment of the infantile love object. The insertion of the ego-ideal implies the rejection of cannibalism and incest. The recognition of the symbolic order also contains the recognition of the lack, the renunciation of the imaginary vision of the totality, the entirety.

In conclusion I would like to go into a few specific aspects of contemporary violence in Germany. My thesis is that for these young people the process of symbolization has not taken place to a sufficient extent, that the decisive point, which adolescence represents in the development of a person, is activated on the level of the body.

In Germany 65% of all holdups are carried out by children, adolescents and young adults between the ages of 10 and 20 (e.g. Stüwe 1993, 346). This type of crime has risen dramatically in the last twenty years. What is it that is robbed? - The universal means of exchange, money, but also, and this in increasing quantity, items of clothing from other children in the schollyard, from other adolescents on the street. As a rule in terms of these items of clothing it is a question of the trademark, therefore, not so much their actual function, but more their symbolic value. The subject could, in order to be recognized, be distinguished by a certain trademark. The greed for this symbolically valuable object of the other is translated immediately into violent action.

This demand for a trademark, which is worn on the body or on the feet (frequently shoes are stolen) - we think of the meaning of shoes in fetishism and feet in the name of Oedipus -, I could point out as a part of the symbolic. There are, perhaps, new, very individualized and violent rites of passage in adolescence in which it is attempted to obtain fragments of the symbolic, but in a violent way? In order to be recognized as »brother« in the clique, I put on the jacket of my »brother« because of its trademark. Thus, new clan signs, markings arise out of trademarks.

There is yet another specific form to mark one's own body in the name of belonging to a clan. It is the swastika, which is the symbol not of an order based on contract, but an arbitrary order. Again a fragment of the symbolic. The swastika on the breast or even on the face and at the same time skinheads make the adolescents an alienated part of our society. At the same time carrying the signs of the perpetrator and the victim of the Shoah on their body, they become the new monsters of our society. It required two generations in order to bring forth a psychotic. The Skotom, rejected in the grandfather generation in the symbolic sense, returned on the level of the real, the body. These adolescents have certainly no psychotic structure. It is a question of a parallelization of two generations.

Forty-nine years after the liberation of Auschwitz, the police chief of a large German city cannot guarantee the security of a state sponsored game because it takes place on April 20th! The behavior of the powers in authority is a scandal, which is no worse than the behavior of the adolescents committing the violence.

And the monstrous behavior of these adolescents conveyed by the media developed perhaps their worst effect: the imaginary overevaluation of the power of adolescence and the retreat of the power of authority. In the schools as well as prisons not-wishing-to-see and silence appear to be the dominating modes of encounter between the authorities and adolescents committing violence: resignation, anxious flight and ostrich-like politics toward violence, instead of discussion, strong prevention tactics and also punishment. This is a very mild, lenient interpretation of the behavior of the authorities, i.e., the administrative power. At least with organized violent behavior against asylum apllicants the non-intervention of the police, the extreme restraint and also surrender of the communal administration in the form of resettling the refugees can be judged as passively admitted consent to the intentions of the right radical perpetrators of violence.

What concerns the newly inflamed racism of the adolescents in the most recent years is, according to my suggestion, that these adolescents are carrying out what was withhold from them in the media. The recognition of guilt was withheld from them, or at least the communication of the concern over the Nazi-crimes committed in the name of the German people by their grandparents. What was symbolically condemned returns again in reality on the level of the body.

In psychoanalysis, mind you not in terms of legal justice, it is a question of a substitution a symptom by a question.

References

Lang, H. (1973), *Die Sprache und das Unbewußte*, Frankfurt.

Stüwe, G. (1993), »Jugendcliquen im Kontext von Gewalt«, in: Merten, O. (ed.), *Rechtsradikale Gewalt im vereinigten Deutschland,* Bonn.

II.

Hermeneutic-Historical
Approaches

Jagdish Gundara

Inclusion and Exclusion in Europe

Social Diversity and the European State

The two European organisations which have had an impact on the educational developments which relate to social diversity in European society, are the Council of Europe and the European Community. Their impact on the national educational policies has however, been limited because the European states have not allowed these organisations to interfere in the educational domain, which is seen as only being part of the national jurisdiction.

The Council of Europe and the European Community have focused issues revolving around social diversity, through their concerns about the education of »migrants«. The migrations which informed these policies started in the late 1950's when de-colonisation process began to gather momentum.

The Council of Europe began to survey the position of »migrant« children's education in 1966. During each subsequent year resolutions were adopted by the Council on different aspects of the education of »migrant« families. This process culminated in the launch of a five year »Project No. 7« in 1980.

The European Community developed a programme in the 1970's, and it also initiated discussions about education of »migrant« workers, and issued a Directive to this effect in 1977.

While, the Council of Europe has increasingly focused on an intercultural approach to education, the underlying assumption appears to be that the European nation states are cohesive and coherent. What has so far developed in relation to educational policies, such as they are, is a response at the wider European level which does not take into account the underlying diverse natures of European societies. It instead focuses in on the immigrant dimension and ignores how for

115

instance, educational policies for immigrants ought to be formulated in the context of general educational policies which include indigenous European minorities and policies towards their education.

This is particularly a problem at the present time because governance of nations, particularly in Europe, has become an extremely problematic issue. The rise of violence and instability is made worse by the ways in which economic decline in many areas of Europe is leading to a rise in tensions and a disintegration of communities. Where these communities are diverse the tensions are greater. The development of narrow nationalisms east of the Elbe have had dangerous consequences in the western European context of providing strength to presumed purer identities which construct an imagined past which excludes diversities.

Social scientists in the so called developed countries have been concerned for a long time with the integration of the new nations in the developing countries. What has been forgotten is that national integration is a permanent issue for all nations whether old or new; »developing« or »developed«. The tendencies towards disintegration may be linked to different factors in different contexts but the need to re-examine the basis on which nations are governed require continual appraisal. Those who govern most of the European polities seem immune to the dangers that the polities confront unless measures to ensure inclusive citizenship rights are implemented. At another level the education and media systems have a major role to play in ensuring that the educational and informational process does take on the substantive issues of the »belongingness« of all groups to the polity. The representation of »the other« and images which construct the immigrant as an alien do not help.

The national project which set out to make »one out of the many« has faltered and there is a lack of solidarity because people have become surplus to the requirement of the state. This solidarity of all groups within Europe has to be an inclusive proposition so that the national minorities, immigrant communities and the under-class are all seen to belong to it.

The notion of a nation state which is caring and nurturing of all the citizens has received a serious setback. Within western Europe the malaise of racism has assisted in disintegrating communities, which may yet aid and abet the process of disintegrating nations, as it has in the case of the now fragmented clear and acquiring Yugoslavian state and parts of eastern Europe (e.g. Denitch 1990). There is a present danger of the rise of the violent notions of »ethnic cleansing« a legitmately in Europe, merely fifty years after they were defeated. The spillover of this abominable notion into other parts of Europe would have catastrophic consequences.

If citizens within the state feel that they are treated fairly, that they belong, and are accorded their full rights, they would then fulfil their obligations. Therefore, the accordance of full citizenship rights would lead to the loyalities which are necessary for nation states to function. In the recent phase of frenzy about the market, social rights of groups have also been negated with a consequent withdrawal by groups from their social responsibilities. Yet, this is far from the case, and if anything the issues are getting worse not better. In the absence of greater equalities seige communities are being established which hark back to narrow nationalism and fundamentalisms (Gundara 1992).

The secular nation state has received set-backs at various levels. The lack of a commitment by politicians to secular ideals and a corruption of the polity has led to an increase of what Galbraith famously described as private wealth and public squalor, and this has lost the state the loyalty of many people. In Britain the reference to monarchy raises issues of whether they are worth keeping for financial reasons. Yet, at the underlying level a narrow minded government has unleashed this argument by undermining the legitimacy of the Crown by denying that there is any notion of society at the underlying level. This market-orientated approach applied to every aspect of British life, propelled by new conservativism has led to destroying the glue that has held the imagined British national community together.

The marginalisation of large groups of people from different localities, regions and nationalities in European countries undermines the fabric of European nation states. If at times of hardship and economic crises, immigrant groups are seen as being the only element of diversity in societies, they can be constructed as being the problem. In many European contexts they are being blamed for causing many of the social problems, thus activating the syndrome of blaming the victim, for being cause of the problem.

These European nation states have indigenous diversities on the basis of religion, language, and social class through regional or national minorities. Now, in the post world war period, many of these countries have acquired new group of settlers. These groups have different patterns of settlement, social class affiliations, legal statuses as well as levels of family reunification.

The earlier distinction between the countries into which people migrated in northern Europe and the southern European countries from which emigration took place has now changed. Even the emigration countries in southern Europe have now become immigration countries. Schools in both northern and southern Europe have extremely diverse student populations.

With the signing of the Maastricht Treaty and the establishment of an open market in the European Union, a newer pattern of intra-European Union migration is also taking place. The position of the earlier postwar immigrants from outside Europe, who had to fight for their and their children's educational and training rights, is markedly different from the European Union immigrants who as a matter of right, demand high levels of social policy and educational provision for their children.

While the rural and smaller towns in many European countries' may have little in common with the diversity in large urban areas, the new reality might mean that the larger European capitals would have similar potentials and problems to devise educational policies for mixed populations. Hence, a rural area in one country may have similarity with a rural area in another, and urban areas in different national contexts, would be able to develop broader intercultural educational strategies.

As the larger processes of integration take place and there is a greater need for specialisation and social differentiation within societies, each nation state would have to ensure that greater economic, political and cultural policies are developed to enable greater cooperation. Such measures would also have to take account of the local and national peculiarities.

From Migrant To Settler

There have been various types of migration since World War II involving the movement of over 30 million people, of whom about 10 million have stayed on in Europe. Immediately after the war, a massive migration of displaced persons involved 20 million people. This movement on a massive scale included 10 million Germans from Poland and Eastern Europe to Germany and lasted until the early 1950s. During the post-colonial phase very different migratory patterns took shape. The first type of migration consisted of European colonialists who returned to Europe. These included the British from India, French ›pied noirs‹ from Algeria, the Dutch from Indonesia and the Portuguese from Angola and Mozambique.

The second type of migration included, many refugees, particularly from Eastern Europe who migrated to Western Europe. In the 1970s small numbers of political refugees from Third World countries also came to settle in Europe. The third and the largest type of migration consisted of migrant labour which initially came from Italy, a number of Irish migrated to Britain. The fourth type were skilled workers and employees within the Nordic labour market and the European Common Marketand were mostly related to the multinational companies (Gundara 1990, 99). Fifthly, France, Britain and the Netherlands received a large number of immigrants from Africa, the Caribbean and Asia, many of whom were citizens of receiving countries. Germany recruited a large number of workers from 1956 onwards in attempting to catch up with other European countries; these included numbers of Turks particularly since many southern Europeans had returned home. Britain, France and Germany are the largest immigration countries and over 40% of such populations are of third world origin (e.g. Castles et.al. 1984).

Britain stopped the migration of workers in 1962 and only allowed skilled people to enter the country after that date (Castles and Kosack 1973).

Across Europe this discrimination was linked to the European Voluntary Worker Scheme in Britain, the Belgian contingent-system, the French *Office National d'Immigration*, and the West German Federal Labour Office recruiting scheme. In Switzerland, Sweden and the Netherlands there were state regulations which controlled workers coming to these countries voluntarily (OECD 1983). Institutionalised controls even applied to those who came to settle from the ex-colonies of France and Britain even though they were nationals of the country of settlement.

The Guest Worker System was different from the settlement of nationals from the former colonies of European countries. However, both these systems of migration, while facing different policies, laws and bureaucratic rules have led to a somewhat similar issue: settlement. France, Britain and the Netherlands have all enacted legislation to stop the migration of their citizens from their former colonies (for instance The British Nationality Act 1981). The discriminatory nationality legislation has caused an enormous amount of hardship to the disenfranchised citizens because it was enacted with the express purpose of controlling immigration. The stricter the rules against immigration and citizenship have become, the faster has been the transition of temporary stay to a process of permanent settlement.

For example, in Sweden, apart from the Finns and the indigenous Samish peoples in Sweden, it had until 1930 one language and one religion. At the present time 1 million out of 8 million have a non-Swedish origin. In Germany it is estimated that in 1990 there were 6 million Turkish people in Germany. Clearly the issue for educational policies in Sweden and in Germany to accommodate the Ausländer and the Aussiedler are important (OECD 1989, 23-25).

The new settlers belong to the working class because of their relationship to the means of production. However, their relationship to the European working classes is marred by racism, which in turn is nurtured by the state. European governments had expected that with the deepening economic crisis many of the new settlers would return to the countries of origin and that the governments would thus be able to export any accruing social costs. This, in fact, has not happened. In addition expenditures on housing, schools, health and social services have been cut. This has led to an increase in tensions in many cities in Europe. The ruling classes have seized upon these tensions and blamed the very workers who have assisted in the creation of the post-war expansion as a threat to public order and safety, and urban decline. The black community in Britain and the new settlers in Europe have on the one hand been used as exploited labour and on the other hand have been blamed for social unrest and urban decline. In most countries very conservative politicians have whipped up racism by stressing foreign swamping. No European governments have provided the newly settled communities with confidence in their place in European societies.

Redefining Nationalities

As the immigrants have become more settled in Europe there has been a concern about defining their legal and political position within European societies. In Germany the situation is compounded by the »ethnic« Germans arriving from Eastern Europe and Russia and acquiring citizenship rights soon after their arrival. This is in sharp contrast to the auslander who have been resident in Germany for a long time, and cannot acquire such rights.

The new settlers to Europe have come from nation states and most of these states have diverse populations. These settlers are therefore either nationals of the country of origin or of the country of settlement. Their position in legal and political terms is continually being undermined through legislation. This legislation is racist in its intent and is not directed against the »ethnicity« of the new settlers. The use of »ethnicity« by social anthropologists has certainly not helped in clarifying this complex issue. It is necessary for those involved with such issues to undertake a more systematic analysis of the basis of European nation states in historical and contemporary terms so that a clear definition may emerge. For instance, what are the differences between the national minorities and »ethnic« minorities? Do the national minorities (in Jura, Scotland, Brittany, Wales) accept the states as defined by the dominant nationalities? There is furthermore, a need to define the nature of European societies and their relationship to the structures of the nation state.

The national minorities in Europe generally have a territorial basis (Scotland, Wales) which are constitutionally recognised by the state. The newly settled communities however, also occupy urban spaces which may not be constitutionally recognised but nevertheless, represent the birth of new communities. The black community in Brixton, Southall and Handsworth, live as part of a largely disempowered group. Similarly, the Turks in Kreuzberg in West Berlin live in a ›sanctuary‹ against racism which nevertheless, they still experience. Schools in these neighbourhoods reflect the communities in which children live.

Euro Centrism and Education

At the basic level the issue which is being is raised is how does Europe construct itself as an entity and how are notions of inclusion and exclusion articulated, at least in the educational and knowledge do remain.

Knowledge systems confront dual challenges as European integration takes shape. On the one hand Europe confronts a Eurocentric tradition in many domains of knowledge. These hegemonic understandings are informed by the imperialism of Europe. As Edward Said writes:

»Without significant exception the universalising discourses of modern Europe and the United States assume the silence, willing or otherwise, of the non-European world. There is incorporation; there is inclusion; there is direct rule; there is coercion. But there is only infrequently an acknowledgement that the colonising people should be heard from, their ideas known.« (Said 1993, 58)

As a result of the imperial enterprise not only is Europe in the world but the world is in Europe. Ostensibly this has profound implications for the transfer of knowledge. Yet, discourses from the colonised peripheries are still treated as being marginal in contemporary Europe.

Martin Bernal indicated how in the 18c and 19c Europeans developed a historiography which denied the earlier understanding that the Greeks in the Classical and Hellenistic periods had learnt as a result of colonisation and interaction between Egyptians, Phoenicians and Greeks (Bernal 1987). Part of the reason for this new historiography, has been with the rise of racism and anti-semitism in Europe, and the European Romantics and racists wanted to distance Greece from the

Egyptians and Phoenicians and construct it as, the pure childhood on Europe. It was unacceptable from their perspective that, the Europeans would have developed any learning and understandings from the Africans or the Semites.

This historiographic shift has major implications for how European history is constructed, and particularly for how knowledge and linguistic systems from civilisations constructed as being inferior are excluded from the European academe. As Bernal states, the paradigm of »progress« was used to put the Greeks to the fore and to cast aside the Egyptians who were governed by priests. With the rise of the slavery of blacks by Europeans blacks were construed by European thinkers to be uncivilised and consequently distanced from »civilised« Europe.

The notion of a European culture separated from the world south of the Mediterranean is a mythical construction. The contributions to knowledge in the ancient period from this immediate region include Mesopotamian astronomy, the Egyptian calendar and Greek mathematics, enriched by the Arabs. As Samir Amin states:

»The opposition Greece = the West/Egypt, Mesopotamia, Persia = the East is itself a later artificial construct of Eurocentrism. For the boundary in the region separates the backward North African and European West from the advanced East; and the geographic unities constituting Europe, Africa and Asia have no importance on the level of the history of civilisation, even if Eurocentrism in its reading of the past is projected onto the past the modern North-South line of demarcation passing through the mediterranean.« (Amin 1989)

Amin argues that the Euro-Islamic Medieval world ceased to exist during the Renaissance when Europe adopted the road towards capitalism: »In Europe, civilisation gradually wins over peoples of the North and East; to the South of the Mediterranean, Islamic culture gains ground in the Maghreb. Christianity and Islam are this both heirs of Hellenism and remain for this reason, twin siblings, even if they have been, at certain moments, relentless adversaries. It is probably only in the modern times - when Europe from Renaissance onward, takes off on the road towards capitalism that the Mediterranean boundary line forms between what will crystallise as the centre and periphery of the new worldwide and all-inclusive system.« (Amin 1989, 26).

The syncretisms of the Hellenistic period thus prepare the ground for Christianity and Islam and their universalistic message. With the emergence of the Renaissance in Europe the dominance of metaphysics is broken and the material foundations of the capitalist world are laid. Scientific progress becomes manifest in the development of the forces of production in the context of a secularised society which becomes increasingly democratic.

The Renaissance is also a point of departure for the conquest of the world by Europe: »If the period of the Renaissance makes a qualitative break with the history of humanity, it is precisely because from that time on, Europeans become conscious of the idea of the conquest of the world by their civilisation is henceforth a possible objective.« (Amin 1989, 73)

This is to a certain extent marked in 1492 by the mapping of the world, as well as, the construction of a typology of different empires. As the relative strengths of different peoples and societies are tabulated peoples, Eurocentrism is crystallised, and it becomes a global project. This Europeanisation of the globe bears within it an inherent deuniversalisation of knowledge and it developed for three hundred years from the Renaissance to the Enlightenment. It expressed itself as European, nationalist and secular with a worldwide scope. This dominant European culture had to arbitrarily and mythically construct its counterpart in »the Other« and »the Oriental« (e.g. Gundara 1990).

Critical to this is the construction of Greece as »the pure childhood of Europe« and to severe its link from its milieu in the Mediterranean and make it a part of Europe. Endemic to this is the racism of the European who is constructed as belonging to a superior and unified culture.

The implications for constructing images, information and knowledge systems from such a foundation not only distorts knowledge and it's history but remains profoundly racist. The issues for intercultural education and information systems in Europe and perhaps the North American continent are not therefore, as simplistic as critics like D'Zouza assert (D'Zouza 1992).

This legacy of distortion is based on the assumption that the Greek heritage predisposed Europe to rationality, and while Greece was the founder of rational philosophy the Orient is still locked into the metaphysical phase. As Amin asserts: »The history of so-called Western thought and philosophy (which presupposes the existence of the other, diametrically opposed thoughts and philosophies, which is called Oriental) always begins with Greece. Emphasis is placed on the variety and conflicts of the philosophical schools, the development of thought free from religious constraints, humanism, and the triumph of reason - all without reference to the ›Orient‹ whose contribution to Hellenic thought is considered to be non-existent.« (Amin 1989, 91)

This view of history assumes that Europeans took over Greek thought in the Renaissance and this thought comes of age in modern philosophy. The period of two thousand years separating »Greek antiquity from the European Renaissance are treated as a long and hazy period of transition« (ibid). Amin's understanding of this issue resonates with Martin Bernal's research demonstrating the fabrication of ancient Greece.

For European education and information systems the challenge is to engage in a wide ranging establishment of connections with other cultures and civilisations which are part of the fabric of contemporary European society, and also develop an understanding of its past which includes, Greece, Egypt and the Near Eastern connections.

The issue of Eurocentrism is not simply an issue of prejudices and errors which heighten xenophobia and chauvinism. Eurocentrism, according to Amin: »has replaced rational explanations of history with partial pseudo-theories, patched together and even self contradictory at times ... The Eurocentric distortion that makes the dominant capitalist culture negates the universalist ambition on which that culture claims to be founded.« (Amin 1989, 104).

The Enlightenment came not as a universal phenomenon, despite attempts to learn from other cultures, but as a narrowly defined European response to the obscurantism of Christianity.

There are obvious contributions that the academic, information and educational systems can make in the context of democratic egalitarianism which are also a feature of European societies. Such theoretical issues should have implications for what constitutes the common curricula and shared images in European schools and communities. Without such a curriculum and informational changes individual groups would demand separate political structures, schools and media systems for their own religious or ethnic groups. The rise of ethnic, culturalist and fundamentalist nationalisms in Europe at the present had to dire consequences for nation states as currently constructed.

References

Amin, S. (1989), *Eurocentrism*, London.

Bernal, M. (1987), *Black Athena: The Afro-Asiatic Roots of Classical Civilisation*, New Brunswick.

Castles and Kosack (1973), *Immigrant Workers and Class Structure in Western Europe*, London.

Castles, S., H. Booth and T. Wallace (1984), *Here for Good: Western Europe New Ethnic Minorities*, London.

D'Zouza, D. (1992), *Illiterate Education. The Politics of Race and Sea on Campus*, New York.

Denitch, B. (1990), *The End of the Cold War: European Unity, Socialism and Shift in Global Power*, London.

Gundara, J. (1990), »Societal Diversities and the Issues of ›The Other‹, in: *Oxford Review of Education*, vol.16, no.1.

Gundara, J. (1992), »The Dominant Nation: Subordinated Nations and Racial Inequalities«, in: Lynch, J., C. Modgil and S. Modgil (eds.), *Equity or Excellence? Education and Cultural Reproduction*, vol.III, London, pp. 67-77.

OECD/CERI (1989), *One School, Many Cultures*, Paris.

Said, E. (1993), *Culture and Imperialism*, London.

Panikos Panayi

Racial Violence in the Twentieth Century

I

All societies in all historical periods have experienced both racial intolerance and racial violence. However, both racial intolerance and racial violence have varied from one society to another. The manifestations of racial intolerance range from a simple refusal to enter into social and economic intercourse with a member of an out-group to the extreme of genocide. At the same time racial violence also varies from isolated attacks upon individuals to mass murder organised by the state. A variety of factors determine both the types of general racism which exist within a society and the ways in which this manifests itself both in a non-violent and violent way. The aim of this paper is to examine ways in which racism manifests itself and then to proceed to look at varieties of racial violence. The paper then asks why racial violence breaks out before examining why it manifests itself in different ways within different states.

We need to begin by focusing on racial intolerance generally and recognising that racial violence is just its most potent manifestation. We can divide varieties of racial intolerance into official and unofficial, and begin with the former. In the twentieth century, the existence of the nation state has led to the inevitable bureaucratization of racism, leading to the implementation of particular measures, which are structural components of the existence of the nation state, especially in its liberal-democratic form. The first of these components consists of immigration controls, whose existence mean that individuals not born within a country are not, in the case of western liberal democracies, offered the economic, social and political benefits of the native population.

127

The second structural component in the existence of the nation-state consists of nationality laws, which, again, are designed to exclude »foreigners« from the benefits enjoyed by natives. Using the example of Germany during the twentieth century, we can illustrate the ways in which nationality laws have remained from an autocracy, through a dictatorship and on to a liberal democracy, so that throughout these three regimes German citizenship has been determined by national origins rather than birth within Germany, *ius sanguinis* rather than *ius solis*, meaning denial of basic rights to second-generation immigrants born within Germany. The Nazi racial laws were an extension of nationality laws to suit Nazi racial goals (see Hoffmann 1992; Dawidowicz 1987, 78-101).

For the maintenance of nationality laws, the forces of law and order are used, varying from the SS in the case of Nazi Germany (Broszat 1979; Dawidowicz 1987) to the county constabularies and immigration officers of contemporary Britain (Supperstone and Cavanagh 1988). All police forces also have an ingrained racial bias in their everyday work, discriminating against members of minorities, a process which is usually helped by the judiciary (see Scarman 1981; Solomos 1989, 99-121).

Continuing with Government legislation, in extreme circumstances measures to control movement are introduced such as happened, for instance, against Germans in Britain during the First World War (Panayi 1991a, 47-59; Bird 1986) and Japanese Americans during the Second World War (Daniels 1975). Measures are also sometimes introduced which take away the property of the persecuted minority such as Jews in Nazi Germany as well as Germans in Britain during the First World War and Japanese Americans and Canadians during the Second World War (Panayi 1990; Sunahara 1981; Gilbert 1986).

Relocation is also a common response amongst governments towards minorities, especially in wartime, and can take various forms. In the first place it can simply involve forcing people to a specific geographical location, a classic example consisting of Russia under Catherine the Great during the eighteenth century with the formalisation of the Jewish Palle of Settlement created by one of her predecessors Tsarina Elizabeth (Baron 1964). A more common policy with regard to relocation, especially during the twentieth century, is the implemetation of internment, which has happened almost universally, practiced by both autocratic and liberal democratic states, especially in wartime (Panayi 1993, 7-8).

The state can also turn to violence. With regard to the forces of law and order we can point to the role of the police in the late nineteenth century Russian pogroms as well as the role of the German army and police forces in *Kristallnacht*, discussed below. Even more extreme, we can point to genocidal policies which obviously must have central government authority to work because of their scale.

Unofficial hostility goes hand in hand with official racism and can be state led in autocracies or can influence the Government in liberal democracies. We can point to various manifestations of popular racism. Most basically, a refusal to enter into social or economic intercourse with a member of minority, endemic in all systems of government, and difficult to measure (see Panahi 1980).

Economic discrimination is also widespread and this can manifest itself in the following ways. Firstly, in refusing to employ workers of a minority group. Britain during the 1950s would illustrate this situation, with black and Asian newcomers having difficulty in securing the sort of employment for which they were trained. Also in Britain during the 1950s as well as at the end of the nineteenth century there existed trade union hostility towards immigrants (Garrard 1971; Pilkington 1988).

Remaining with popular manifestations of racism, we can further point to press hostility which can also manifest itself in a variety of ways. For instance, we can mention media stereotypes which are essentially ever present (Hartmann and Husband 1974). In more extreme circumstances press campaigns can also develop over specific issues, a very good example being Germany immediately after reunification, where the press became obsessed with the threat of asylum seekers. Under conditions of serious insecurity within a state, especially one where racial images have been long standing, a conspiracy theory can develop as happened in interwar Germany although we need to bear in mind that antisemitic conspiracy theories existed throughout Europe during the late nineteenth and early twentieth centuries (Panayi 1994, 284; Cohn 1967).

Pressure groups can also develop as another manifestation of popular hostility and again we can give countless examples. For instance, Britain during the late nineteenthth century (Gainer 1972) or during the First World War (Panayi 1991a, 202) or, once again, contemporary Germany (Panayi 1994, 286). Racial violence might be seen as the most potent manifestation of unofficial hostility varying from the attacking of individuals to the total destruction of an entire community, discussed further below.

The relationship between unofficial and official hostility is extremely close. In autocracies the latter is fundamental in the manifestations of racial hostility. But in liberal democracies a more complex relationship between state and popular racism exists. In such cases we can see public opinion and the state feeding off each other and it often proves difficult to determine which leads the other.

II

Racial violence can be divided into four categories in the following order of severity. Firstly, isolated attacks upon houses and individuals which are universally present in the modern nation-state, although they manifest themselves at different times with different levels of severity as well as often being dependent upon geographical location within a country. We can examine the examples of Great Britain and Germany.

In Great Britain such incidents were probably endemic against nineteenth century Irish immigrants in areas where they were heavily concentrated such as Lancashire, London and Glasgow (Gallagher 1987; Neal 1988). Referring to the East End of London during the 1930s the historian Richard Thurlow has pointed to »the number of increased, unprovoked attacks upon Jews and Communists by young hooligans in the Stepney, Bethnal Green and Shoreditch areas during 1936« together with »the breaking of shop windows, the desecration of Jewish cemeteries and synagogues in the massive spread of antisemetic graffiti.« (Thurlow 1987, 110) In more recent British history we can point to a 1987 Commission for Racial Equality report on racial harassment in housing which demonstrated that during the previous 12 months 1 in 4 of the London borough of Newham's black residents had been victims of racial harassment, ranging from insulting behaviour to physical assault and damage to property. Furthermore, between 1917 and 1985 there were 63 racist murders in Great Britain according to Paul Gordon's research including 26 in 1981 (Tompson 1988, 171).

In Germany a similar situation has existed which deteriorated immediately after re-unification. In 1991 the extreme right in the Federal Republic committed more crimes than the extreme left for the first time ever. In 1992, 17 people were killed in racial attacks; the most serious and publicised incident occurred on 23 November 1992 when 3 Turks were killed in a arson attack in Mölln. Even worse was the killing of three women and two children by a firebomb in Solingen on 29 May 1993 (Panayi 1994).

A second manifestation of racial violence consists of riots against property and people. The important factor in this case is that large numbers of people are involved, in contrast to the previous category of racial attacks, where a few, usually anonymous, individuals are involved in sporadic incidents. In the case of the riots they break out against a background of recently increased xenophobia, which has developed against the more deep-rooted cause of the endemic racism of the nation state. The increase in xenophobia is caused by any one of a number of factors, considered below, including economic depression, political change, and war. The actual outbreak of rioting requires, further, a spark.

In Britain during the First World War riots broke out inspired by the press resulting in widespread violence affecting virtually every German property in Great Britain. On other occasions in Great Britain a riot has broken out in just one location such as Middlesborough in 1961 (Panayi 1991b, 139). In Brazil during the First World War we can point to riots against German property which broke out in April and October of 1917 (Luebke 1987).

Germany after re-unification offers an interesting illustration because of the question of whether the violence against asylum seekers consists of riots or attacks. In most cases they are the latter, involving just a handful of perpetrators. However, there are exceptions. For instance, the rioting against an asylum home in Hoyerswerda in September 1991. In addition, we can point to the attack upon a refugee hostel in Greifswald on 3 November 1991 involving the football fans of the East Berlin football club BFC. The worst violence of all occurred in Rostock in August 1992 and involved skinheads cheered on by local residents, with an ineffective local police force, meaning that the disorder lasted for a week (see Funke 1993).

The attitudes of the authorities plays a role in the destructiveness of race riots which break out. If they are slow to react, or, worse still, are implicated in outbreaks of disorder, then any disorder which does break out is likely to escalate. We can give several examples. First, late nineteenth and early twentieth century Russia which became saturated with antisemitism as we can see by the attitudes of the Tsars, the bureaucracy and the police which led people to believe that they could attack Jews with absolute impunity. Several major outbreaks of violence occurred. Firstly, that in 1881 focused especially in Odessa and Kiev. 45 Jews were killed in pogroms in 1903 affecting a variety of locations and then in 1905 a further 660 communities endured violence resulting in 1,000 deaths (Judge 1992; Aronson 1990; Klier and Lambroza 1992).

The role of the police and army in US racial violence during the first half of the twentieth century has also been called into question. In the East St Louis riots of 1917, for instance, violence »occurred in full view of armed soldiers who took no steps to halt the carnage« (Grimshaw 1963, 83). During the Chicago riots of 1919, which involved blacks and whites attacking each other, the police acted in a biased fashion in favour of the latter with regard to those they protected and those they arrested.

In the *Kristallnacht* pogrom of 1938, which took place against an increase in official anti-semitism in Germany, various facts point to a more direct complicity of various strands of authority. In the first place, after a Nazi party meeting with Hitler (on the night of the assassination of the German ambasador in Paris, Ernst von Rath, the spark for the disturbances), those *Gauleiter* who had been present told their local propaganda offices to strike out against Jewish businesses and homes. They also informed police posts to prevent looting but also to prepare for the arrest of Jews. In addition, members of the SA also took part in the rioting (Adam 1991; Read and Fisher 1991).

We can separate from the above what we might describe as the killing of individuals which ties in with the first subgroup of attacks upon individuals but has developed particularly in the USA in the form of lynching. Between 1886 and 1968 3,446 blacks and 1,297 whites were killed in US lynchings (Zangrando 1980, 5-8). If we wanted to define the characteristics of a lynching we would point to its ritualised nature, as events of this nature follow a particular pattern. Gordon Allport divided lynchings into two types. The first, which he described as »vigilante«, was carried out by a small band of individuals in a quiet manner. The second type, »mob lynching«, involved larger numbers of people and was more ferocious. In both varieties, the attitude of the authorities, is crucial, usually remaining out of sight, if not actually participating in events. Such activities are not completely unique to the USA (Allport 1954). We can draw a connection between lynchings and the attacks in our first category, especially if, as is often the case in the actions of youths involved in incidents within western European democracies, the intention is to kill, usually through use of a firebomb.

The most extreme form of racial violence in the twentieth century is genocide. This has the following characteristics. First, it involves the desire to exterminate all representatives of a particular minority. This is government policy which means that the state puts vast resources behind the extermination of members of a minority group. In some cases genocide is the central core of Government policy (see Dadrian 1975). The twentieth century has facilitated the process of genocide because of the development of methods of killing connected with technological changes so that the Nazi genocide was far more efficient than that carried out by the young Turks against the Armenians.

The above are the two major instances of genocide during the first half of the twentieth century. The Turkish massacre of Armenians during the First World War meant that, out of a population of 1.5 million Armenians who lived in the Ottoman Empire before the conflict, one million were murdered. The method of killing essentially revolved around deportation of the Armenian population from their homeland in eastern Turkey to Syria, with people either dying in large numbers on the journey (within trains or on foot) or perishing from exposure or starvation once they reached the Syrian desert (Kuper 1982).

More sophisticated and effective, because carried out by a more advanced state against a larger minority over a far greater geographical area, was the Nazi extermination of European Jewry during World War II which meant 6 million deaths or the annihilation of 67 per cent of the Jews in countries invaded by Germany, together with the killing of other minorities in the lower echelons of the Nazi racial hierarchy (Dawidowicz 1987, 480; Berenbaum 1990). As Zygmunt Bauman has pointed out, the effectiveness and efficiency of Nazi methods of killing is explained by the fact that bureacratic business methods were employed (Bauman 1989).

III

Having examined the manifestations of racial violence we can now ask why racial violence breaks out. In order to explain this we need to look at the following factors. First, if we accept the indisputable fact that nationalism has been the dominant ideology in the modern world, inextricably linked with state creation, we have to accept that racism inevitably exists in all states. However, the existence of an underlying racism can only explain small scale attacks upon individual members of minorities, who would be seen as legitimate targets by young males, who are invariably responsible for such incidents. Such individuals, who are more prone to carrying out violence of varying sorts than any other groups in society, would interpret the racism of the nation state, especially its media manifestations, as legitimising their racial attacks upon members of minority groups (Panayi 1994).

Rioting, meanwhile, only takes place against the background of an increase in racism within the dominant society of a nation state. A range of factors can lead to this increase in racism, which we can divide into socio-economic and political. With regard to the first of these, economic setbacks are fundamental in virtually all periods for the growth of racism. This has taken place throughout Europe. The classic example here is the inter-war years but we also need to mention the late nineteenth century and the 1990s. All of these periods witnessed racial riots in many parts of Europe, often on a nationwide scale, or at least affecting large numbers of locations (see Judge 1992; Aronson 1990; Klier and Lambroza 1992; Panayi 1993; Hockenos 1993).

Increases in immigration can be considered as another soci-economic factor which leads to a rise in racism and consequently racial riots. In this situation members of the dominant society perceive their social and economic position being threatened by newcomers, with particular concern shown towards housing and employment. Such fears are invariably wipped up by the press. A classic example of this situation is Britain during the late 1950s and early 1960s (Panayi 1991b). However, riots caused by the perceived socio-economic threat of immigrants are usually isolated and break out in particular locations because of factors particular to that location.

A variety of political causes can lead to an increase in racial violence, invariably linked, in some way or another, with the onset of political instability due to a profound change. We can first point to state creation. A good example here is Germany both from the 1870s until the outbreak of the First World War (Adler 1969) as well as contemporary Germany after re-unification. In both cases the euphoric atmosphere created by state formation led to a rise in both nationalism and xenophobia.

Changes in the system of government can also lead to a rise of racism. We can point to the Weimar Republic, the imposton of a liberal democratic system upon a country with little experience of democracy, but which harked back to imperial greatness which, in the perception of its opponents, had been destroyed by aliens (see Kolb 1988). But we can also point to contemporary Russia, again a situation in which a liberal democracy follows a period of imperial greatness in a country with an autocratic tradition.

War is as important as any other medium-term socio-economic or political factor in leading to a rise in racism. In fact, anyone studying the history of race during the twentieth century cannot avoid the conclusiuon that the worst persecution of minorities has occurred during wartime. Apart from genocide, illustrated by the Armenian genocide in World War I and the Nazi Holocaust in World War Two, states such as Britain and Brazil experienced some of their worst twentieth century outbreaks of violence during the First World War. The explanations as to why war leads to an increase in intolerance are many, but revolve around the increase in ostracisation of outgroups, facilitated by the seizure of control, directly or indirectly, by the military, as members of the dominant society gell closer together to fight the external enemy.

Another political factor which clearly leads to an increase in racism is the seizure of power by an overtly racist regime. The classic example here is the Nazis, who were, like the Young Turks who seized power in the Ottoman Empire in 1908, revolutionary, which meant that neither were bound by the constraints imposed upon political behaviour by the traditions of the state in which they seized power (Melson 1992); in both cases genocide followed. However, even in liberal democracies, the existence of overtly racist presssure groups and political parties influence the ruling party and create an atmosphere in which which violence is likely as the example of the Weimar Republic or 1990s Germany would illustrate (Broszat 1987; Leggewie 1993).

If we focus specifically upon rioting against minority groups, medium term factors simply increase the likelihood of racial violence breaking out. The increase in racism needs sparks for racial violence to break out. Against the backgound of an increase in immigration any one of a large number of incidents can spark off a disturbance, even as petty as an altercation over a restaurant, although more common are industrial disputes or sexual jealousies as numerous incidents in twentieth century Britain indicate (Jenkinson 1985, 46).

If nationwide riots break out against a background of rising racism caused by political factors, these can often be sparked off by an external event. We can give several examples. First, the assassination of Tsar Alexander II in 1881, which was followed by widespread pogroms, because of the perception that Jews had been responsible for the murder (Aronson 1990). Second, the sinking of the the passenger liner *Lusitania* in May 1915 by a German submarine off the coast of Ireland with the loss of over 1,000 civilian lives, which led to nationwide anti-German riots in Britain. And, third, the *Kristallnacht* pogrom in Germany in November 1938, sparked off by the assassination of the German amabassador in Paris. In all three of these cases in which a murder or murders were involved we can see the riotous reactions as a way in which members of the dominant society felt that they were returning blood with blood.

IV

How do we explain variations in racial violence from one state to another? Clearly, not every minority in every country endures the same experience, ranging from the isolated attacks which take place in most post-War liberal democracies to the genocide carried out by the Ottoman Empire and the Third Reich. We can offer a variety of explanations for the variation.

Firstly, a cultural approach, while carrying the potential for reducing explanations revolving around national stereotypes, can provide insights, as illustrated by Johnathan Steinberg's comparative study of antisemitism in Germany and Italy during the Second World War. In this volume the author stresses particular aspects of culture within these two states, especially the importance of obedience to civic virtue in Germany, compared with the »disorder, disobedience and *menefreghismo* (I-could-not-care-less-ism) of Italian public life«. The former meant that all orders within any bureaucracy tended to be carried out, while the latter meant an inefficient system operated. When the goal of a bureacracy is to carry out genocide, the former system has far-reaching consequences.

Some historians have taken an interactionist approach in their attempts to explain the severity of racial violence which breaks out in particular states. Frederick C. Luebke (1987, 217), for instance, uses this as an explanation for the differing responses of Brazil and the USA towards their German minorities during the First World War, with the former behaving in a more extreme manner, including the outbreak of nationwide riots on two seperate occasions. The basic arguments of interactionists is that a minority's refusal to assimilate increases the likelihood of racism and racial violence. However, we can dismiss this line of argument because the attitude of the dominant society is paramount, as the experience of European Jewries in the late nineteenth and early twentieth centuries illustrates. In this case German Jewry, as assimilated as Jews in any other European state, were the first to be dealt with by the Nazis. Subsequently, as the Nazis marched through Europe, levels of assimilation were meaningless.

The most important factors in determining the severity of racial violence within individual states are the system of Government which exists together with national traditions of intolerance, especially towards an individual minority. In times of instability, brought on by the socio-economic and political factors outlined above, racial violence becomes more likely.

For our purposes, we can divide sytems of Government into liberal democracies and autocracies. In the former, in times of stability, racial violence will be confined to small scale attacks, although when the socio-economic or political order is upset, then riots against a minority can break out. However, because of the rights of individuals guaranteed by liberal political systems, such events tend not to get out of hand, a development facilitated, especially during the twentieth century, by an all-embracing national media which focuses upon every perceived injustice within its borders. This applies especially to the West in the post-War years. However, just as important in liberal democracies is the fear of any disorder, which means that, whoever the perpetrators of violence are, the forces of law and order will suppress their activities.

Nevertheless, within liberal democracies, especially before the spread of a mass media in the post-War period, large-scale racial violence was usual, as the example of anti-black riots in the USA illustrates. In this instance the explanation lies in the all-embracing anti-black racism of American society and politics which could turn a blind eye to lynchings in the late nineteenth and early twentieth centuries. Furthermore, when blacks were perceived as having upset the *status quo* such as in Chicago immediately after the outbreak of the First World War, race riots could follow. In this case white society viewed newly arrived migrants from the south as competing for resources, while the self-confidence of former black soldiers, who expected a degree of emancipation in return for their fighting in Europe, also caused resentment amongst whites.

The US case is not unusual. In the case of Britain during the First World War the German minorities came under attack on a series of occasions. Again, we need to see these events against the background of the ubiquitous Germanophobia affecting all sections of British society while Britain fought a war against Germany. By the Second World War, however, a more mature British liberal democracy, which demonstrated some concern about the rights of minorities, insured that rioting against enemy aliens did not get out of control.

Autocracies, whatever their nature, be it monarchichal, fascist or communist, are, by their very nature, not controlled by public opinion and are therefore capable of resorting to more extreme forms of racial violence, often state led, which can culminate in genocide. The two examples of genocide considered in this article follow a similar pattern.

First, there exists a centuries long tradition of vicitmisation of a particular minority by the dominant society - Armenians in Turkey and Jews in Germany. Second, expectations were created during the course of the nineteenth century by the emancipation of Jews in Germany and the Tanzinat period in the Ottoman Empire, 1839-76, which called for the concept of equality between Muslims and non-Muslims. However, in both cases this was followed by a reversal, manifested in the rise of unofficial anti-semitism in Germany and an increase in state persecution of Armenians, resulting in pogroms on a massive scale before the First World War. The seizure of power of a revolutionary regime and a wartime situation and the effects of both of these developments, previously considered, are the final elements which made genocide almost inevitable in the Ottoman Empire during World War I and the German Empire during World War II.

V

As this essay has made clear, genocide represents the most extreme and potent form of racism. The nation-state, by its very nature in creating a dominant ruling group, is racist. This racism manifests itself in numerous ways, both official and unofficial, the former being far more important in autocracies, ranging from refusal to enter into social and economic intercourse to racial violence.

This racial violence varies from attacks upon individuals, endemic in most liberal democracies, to genocide, although a particular set of circumstances is needed for the latter to occur, especially the seizure of power of a revolutionary regime and a wartime situation. However, large scale racial violence can break out in any nation-state providing the correct intervening factors creating instability, together with particular sparks, develop.

References

Adam, U.D. (1991), »How Spontaneous was the Progrom?«, in: Pehle, W.H. (ed.), *November 1938: From ›Kristallnacht‹ to Genocide*, Oxford.

Adler, H.G. (1969), *The Jews in Germany from the Enlightenment to National Socialism*, Notre Dame, IN.

Allport, G.W. (1954), *The Nature of Prejudice*, Reading, MA.

Aronson, I.M. (1990), *Troubled Waters: The Origins of the 1881 Anti-Jewish Progroms in Russia*, Pittsburgh.

Baron, S.W. (1964), *The Russian Jew under Tars and Soviets*, New York.

Bauman, Z. (1989), *Modernity and the Holocaust*, Cambridge.

Berenbaum, M. (ed.) (1990), *A Mosaic of Victims: Non-Jewish Persecuted and Murdered by the Nazis*, New York.

Bird, J.C. (1986), *Control of Enemy Alien Civilians in Great Britain*, New York.

Broszat, M. (1979), »Nationalsozialistische Konzentrationslager 1933-45«, in: *Autonomie des SS Staates*, vol.2, 2nd ed., München, pp. 11-133.

Broszat, M. (1987), *Hitler and The Collapse of Weimar Germany*, Leamington Spa.

Cohn, N. (1967), *Warrant for Genocide: The Myth of the Jewish World Conspiracy and the Protocols of the Elders of Zion*, London.

Dadrian, V.N. (1975), »The Common Features of the Armenian and Jewish Cases of Genocide: A Comparative Victimological Perspective«, in: *Victimology*, vol.4, pp. 99-120.

Daniels, R. (1975), *The Decision to Relocate Japanese Americans*, Philadelphia.

Dawidowicz, L.S. (1987), *The War Against the Jews, 1933-45*, Harmondsworth.

Funke, H. (1993), *Brandstifter: Deutschland zwischen Demokratie und völkischem Nationalismus*, Göttingen.

Gainer, B. (1972), *The Alien Invasion: The Origins of the Aliens Act of 1905*, London.

Gallagher, T. (1987), *Glasgow: The Uneasy Truce*, Manchester.

Garrard, J.A. (1971), *The English and Immigration: A Comparative Study of the Jewish Influx, 1880-1910*, London.

Gilbert, M. (1986), *The Holocaust: The Jewish Tragedy*, London.

Grimshaw, A.D. (1963), »Three Major Cases of Colour Violence in the United States«, in: *Race*, vol.1.

Hartmann, P. and Ch. Husband (1974), *Racism and the Mass Media*, London.

Hoffmann, L. (1992), *Die unvollendete Republik: Zwischen Einwanderungsland und deutschem Nationalstaat*, 2nd ed., Köln.

Jenkinson, J. (1985), »The Glasgow Race Disturbances of 1919«, in: *Immigrants and Minorities*, vol.4, no.2.

Judge, E.H. (1992), *Easter in Kishinev: Anatomy of a Progrom*, New York.

Klier, J.D. and S. Lambroza (ed.) (1992), *Progroms: Anti-Jewish Violence in Modern Russsian History*, Cambridge.

Kolb, E. (1988), *The Weimarer Republic*, London.

Kuper, L. (1982), *Genocide: Its Political Use in the Twentieth Century*, London.

Leggewie, C. (1993), *Druck von Rechts: Wohin treibt die Bundesrepublik?*, München.

Luebke, F.C. (1987), *Germans in Brazil: A Comparative History of Cultural Conflict during the World War I*, Baton Rouge.

Melson, R.F. (1992), *Revolution and Genocide: On the Origins of the Armenian Genocide and Holocaust*, Chicago.

Neal, F. (1988), *Sectarian Violence: The Liverpool Experience*, Manchester.

Panahi, B. (1980), *Vorurteile, Rassismus, Antisemitismus, Nationalismus in der Bundesrepublik heute: Eine empirische Untersuchung*, Frankfurt a.M.

Panayi, P. (1990), »German Business Interests in Britain during the First World War«, in: *Business History*, vol. 32, pp. 244-258.

Panayi, P. (1991a), *The Enemy in in our Midst: Germans in Britain during the First World War*, Oxford.

Panayi, P. (1991b), »Middlesbrough 1961: A British Race Riots of the 1960s?«, in: *Social History*, vol.16.

Panayi, P. (1993), »Dominat Societies and Minorities in the Two World Wars«, in: Panayi, P. (ed.), *Minorities in Wartime: National and Racial Groupings in Europe, North America and Australia during the Two World Wars*, Oxford.

Panayi, P. (1994), »Racial Violence in the New Germany, 1990-1993«, in: *Contemporary European History*, vol.3, no.3.

Pilkington, E. (1988), *Beyond the Mother Country: West Indians and The Notting Hill White Riots*, London.

Read, A. and D. Fisher (1991), *Kristallnacht: Unleashing the Holocaust*, London.

Scarman, L. (1981), *The Brixton Disorders, 10-12 April 1981*, London.

Solomos, J. (1989), *Race and Racism in Contemporary Britain*, London.

Steinberg, J. (1990), *All or Nothing: The Axis and the Holocaust 1941-43*, London.

Sunahara, A.G. (1981), *The Politics of Prejudice: The Uprooting of Japanese Canadians during the Second World War*, Toronto.

Supperstone, M. and J. Cavanagh (1988), *Immigration: The Law and Practice*, 2nd ed., London.

Thurlow, R. (1987), *Racism in Britain: A History 1918-1985*, Oxford.

Tompson, K. (1988), *Under Siege: Racial Violence in Britain Today*, Harmondsworth.

Zangrando, R.L. (1980), *The NAACP Crusade Against Lynching 1909-1950*, Philadelphia.

Crispin Jones

Xenophobia and the Educational Construction of Europe

Introduction

In Cavafy's poem »Waiting for the Barbarians« (Cavafy 1961, 19), the rich city fathers waited at the gate of their city, waiting to surrender to the barbarians. The barbarians never turned up, leading to the ironic comment that without barbarians the city fathers might have a legitimation crisis. The feared outsider was the justification for many of the actions of the city fathers, and indeed the outsiders, the barbarians, fulfil a similar role in many modern states. Indeed, what is frequently conventionally defined as European and Europe in the schools of the European Union (EU), in contradistinction to the rest of the world, is a similar exercise to that of Cavafy's city fathers. Many living, learning and teaching within the EU, define themselves, their Europe and their »Europeaness« through the claimed inferiority and more certain fear of others defined as non European and living outside of Europe. But such definitional positions and exercises presuppose answers to an earlier set of questions, namely, where and what is this Europe, who are these Europeans and indeed, who are the barbarians?

How schools use these terms is vitally important, for if the terms are used as they have been traditionally used in education in most EU states, they will continue to be terms that exclude areas and peoples that have a right to be considered European.[1] The issue at stake here is the lack of recognition in school curricula of the contingent nature of both concepts. This paper attempts to demonstrate this contingency and does it through an examination of the academic underpinnings of some of the relevant subjects of the school curriculum in what is conventionally described as Europe, such as history, geogra-

143

phy, religious education and science. As these subjects use terms like Europe and European constantly, they help to shape, in the minds of young people as well as in their teachers, views of themselves and their position in and relationship to the world. And without an awareness of this contingency, such conventional definitions not only do not fit the facts, they help perpetuate chauvenisms, ethnocentricities, narrow nationalisms, anti-semitism and racism.

To assist schools in their task of counteracting such perspectives this paper seeks to put forward a view of Europe and the European that has been and continues to be constantly changing. Such a view of a changing Europe, almost a series of Europes, does not do definitional violence to the terms »Europe« and »European«. This is because, as this paper will argue, they have always been conditional terms, changing their meaning as the political and economic context within which the terms are located has changed over time. In other words, as with so many other aspects of education, it is important to understand the origins and provenance of current educational knowledge, policy and practice. In the context of this paper's concerns, this means a better understanding of the old Europes if sense is to made of the new and current one. And it is this new and current Europe that has to be at the focus of the school curriculum, not the old one. Furthermore, tracing the evidence put forward in this paper is itself part of the blueprint of a new European curriculum that better reflects current European realities.

However, the paper is not putting forward a postmodern relativistic agenda for combatting racism and xenophobia within European schools. It is arguing that the modern agenda is not discredited but should be seen as more complex than has hitherto been the case. As Giroux puts it:

»Modernism is far from dead - its central categories are simply being written within a plurality of narratives that are attempting to address the new set of social, political, technical and scientific configurations that constitute the current age.« (Giroux 1991, 63)

In other words, plurality and complexity have been a constant feature of European societies; it has now become an urgent task for schools to recognise this state of affairs.

The Changing Map of Europe

As a scientific term, »Europe« is a convenience only. Geographically, it is a continent by convention and should better be known as being part of the Eurasian land mass.[2] Biologically, the zoogeograpical area that includes conventionally defined Europe is the Palearctic and, like the Eurasian land mass, extends from Iceland to Japan (see Campbell and Lack 1985, 145-148, 429-430; Cramp et al. 1977 onwards) In other words, Europe is a scientific vanity.[3] It is a vanity that extends even to our maps, with a distorted Europe at the centre of a diminished world as in Mercator's famous projection. It is also a vanity with a long history as its origins reveal.

The starting point for any such examination of origins has to be the origin of the term »Europe« itself. It is of Greek origin, already being used before the 5th century BC to distinguish mainland Greece from the islands. By the 5th Century BC, the concept was refined to distinguish the Greek world from the non-Greek world that lay to the East.[4] In other words, the term Europe was being used to distinguish »our land« from »their land«. It has continued to be used in this way down to the present: Europe is »our« territory in contradistinction to that which is not »ours« or which is non-European. The problem is who is »us« and what is »ours« and who is »them« and what is »theirs«.

The subsequent growth or development of Europe as is frequently taught in schools is very much a process of looking at the past through the spectacles of the present. The great empires of so called European history, as taught about in schools within the EU, were seldom in the same place or contained the same peoples. The Roman Empire was a Mediterranean empire rather than a European one: indeed, the comparative neglect of Mediterranean studies is very much a feature of a dominant North West Protestant European scholarship that is almost completely divorced from the Mediterranean.[5] The consolidation of the Frankish Empire under Charlemagne was not so much a delineation of Europe but a delineation of Christendom, seen very much as being in territorial and religious conflict with the new and expanding religion of Islam. Interestingly, a religious map of Christendom in the early Middle Ages would very roughly correspond with the current dominant image of Europe, although the differences are not without contemporary significance.[6]

Although this medieval image of Europe is surprisingly similar to many more modern ones, it corresponded to a political/religious reality for a surprisingly short period of time. If a map of Christendom in 1360 looks like a modern, stereotypical map of Europe, by the end of that century the map had begun to change rapidly as the Ottoman Turks moved westwards beyond the Bosphorus. Their expanding empire soon included much of the Balkans, reaching to the gates of Vienna, with religious and demographic consequences which continue to dominate the politics of the area, as this Turkish and Islamic presence has continued to the present day. However, this particular European empire is seldom in the school history books of the EU. It is still often presented as the alien presence that Europe defeated and threw back, as at Vienna, when in fact it was seen at the time as more the defeat of Islam by Christianity. Indeed, much of the educational and curricula discourse about the concept of Europe within the states that now make up the EU has continued to operate by excluding, ignoring or misrepresenting this reality.[7]

This is not the sole example, however. Other boundaries of Europe have remained, and continue to remain obscure. A classic example of this is the position of Russia. Is Russia in Europe or not? If it is, is all of Russia, to Siberia and beyond, or is it Russia West of the Urals, the most common boundary used today? This issue has vexed Russian politicians and intellectuals since the time of Peter the Great. For example, the Russian Slavophile, Danilevsky, argued in the 1860s for a clear division between an Orthodox Russian dominated Slavic Eurasia and a Latin Christian Europe (cf. Balace 1991; Delrot 1992). These and similar views were still influential in pre-1917 Russia and, indirectly, may still influence the politics of both Russia and the Balkans to this day.[8]

These examples demonstrate that Europe is very much a moveable geographical and historical feast. It would appear that use of the term Europe was, and still remains an excluding category masquerading as an objective spatial referent. However, for obvious practical reasons the term Europe will continue to be used as a convenient label in classrooms, lecture theatres and in everyday discourse, but students should be made more aware of the term's semantic history. Part of that awareness lies in the recognition that the term is still used in a wide range of ways and meanings. In other words, the one single and agreed definition has always been and continues to be an illusion. For example, the World Bank uses the category »Europe and Central Asia« to avoid a boundary drawing issue, drawing lines around countries of similar income levels, such as one might call *isoeconomies*, rather than clear lines around operational regions of the globe. Under this scheme, adopted by the World Bank amongst others, within Europe, the Isle of Man and Greece rub shoulders with former states of the Soviet Union such as Moldova (World Bank 1993, 28-29, 125 seq.). Such examples help demonstrate the definitional plurality and flexibility that is needed in a rapidly changing world. In educational terms, they add to the uncertainties that schools traditionally find difficult to handle but which increasingly they will have to face.[9]

Where are the Europeans if not in Europe?

If discussions about Europe's boundaries have frequently been used to exclude, the term European has an even more exclusive history. In English for example, the Oxford English Dictionary (Murray 1933) gives a comprehensive, and most interesting definition of »European«. The dates of first usage are equally interesting, coming from the period when the European domination of the globe commenced. Three related meanings are given:

1. »Belonging to Europe, or its inhabitants.« (First used in 1603.)
2. »Taking place in, or extending over, Europe.« (First used in 1665.)
3. »A native of Europe.« (First used in 1632.)

In the 1972 Supplement (Burchfield 1972) a further meaning is added, relating to the third one, interestingly enough also coming from the seventeenth century, this time from 1696. This fourth definition states that a European is a »person of European extraction who lives outside Europe: hence, a white person, esp. in a country with a predominately non-white population.« (Emphasis added.) By the time of the second edition (Simpson and Weiner 1989), only the definitions 1. and 2. mentioned above survived.[10] These changes are fascinating, and reflect an increasing sensitivity about the power of the term in question. (They also indicate that national intellectual institutions are not above self censorship.) In relation to this paper, they reveal that in the English language at least, the term European was synonymous with only the white population of Europe, with even that problematic term (white), being seen as self evident. The interesting shift in perception that these definitions reveal is that from seeing a European as a person living in a Christian state, to that of a white person living in the same. In other words, not only has the shifting nature of the European boundary been forgotten, but so has the fact that there has been a constant non-white European presence (see Fryer 1984; and Shyllon 1977).

Despite such a complex etymological and demographic history, school history books and lessons have not always taught how mixed the population of Europe has always been. What has been most often taught is that there is a clearly definable group of people to whom the descriptor »European« can be attributed, as opposed to other groups of people living within Europe who may be described as »foreigners«. Of course, it is legitimate for a state or superstate like the EU to define its non-citizens as foreigners, but it is not logical and legitimate to define citizenship through principles of exclusion that rest solely on stereotypical perceptions of putative national identities. For how a state defines its nationals or citizenry is crucial, as is the portrayal of such status in the curriculum.[11] In other words, who is or was German, who is or was Spanish, who is or was English?

The history of Europe over the last few hundred years shows how difficult it is to answer such questions in ways which all citizens consider just. At a very obvious level, a citizen is often considered a person born within the boundaries of a state and/or a person descended from a recognised citizen of that particular state (commonly citizenship by blood and/or birth). However, Europe's history, particularly its recent history, has been bedeviled by the confusion between a national group and a national boundary, the two rarely coinciding. Many politicians would claim otherwise, unfortunately, and two major European communal wars this century, as well as the current violence within the former Yugoslavia, confirm the power of such »natural« perceptions.[12] For example, at the beginning of the French Revolution, the revolutionary Danton, who had earlier coruscated Bourbon territorial aggrandizement, reiterated the view that France had »natural boundaries« within which, presumably, French people lived or had the right to live. He claimed: »The limits of France are marked out by nature. We shall reach them at their four points; at the Ocean, at the Rhine, at the Alps, at the Pyrenees.« (quoted in Doyle 1989, 200)

Even then, it was not clear whether some groups of people living within these boundaries were French, the obvious examples being the French Jews. Yet, many key concepts relating to human rights derive from this era, an era preoccupied with the relationship between the state and the citizenry, with both key terms being seen in restricted terms. In their discussions, the politicians and (mainly essentialist) political philosophers of that time failed to resolve crucial areas of debate over the extent of state power over groups and individuals, debates which have bedeviled most states subsequently. And, of concern to education, the rights of children remained obscure, the more so as there had only recently been significant changes in the social construction of childhood as a result of the writings of romantic philosophers such as Rousseau.

More recently, but still within that Rousseauesque paradigm, the 1989 UN Convention on the Rights of the Child provides an internationally agreed set of principles that give children not just the right to survival but also rights to protection and to personal development free from discrimination.[13] Thus, *de jure* if not *de facto*, most states should formally approve of the centrality of a perspective that espouses civic (including educational) rights for all children, including children from minorities who may or may not be defined by that state as the children of citizens. These rights include ones in respect of their education, insofar as that is provided by the state.

Despite such exhortations by international organisations, citizenship and being European remain problematics. The many nationalities and/or groups contained within modern Europe and its constituent states are often ignored or submerged. At the national level this is done through the creation and propagation of national stereotypes and at the European level by a further set of stereotypes that ape the national ones. Such myths of national state identity and European identity are, in fact, partly a codification and legitimation of the dominant group(s) social and economic arrangements and partly a reflection of dominant concepts of the nature of Europe and its citizens (see Jones 1992). Thus, the manner in which the term »European«, is propounded in the curricula of many EU states, could well have the following characteristics:

1. a view that within Europe there are European languages (like French and German) and non-European languages (like Turkish and Arabic);
2. an agreed set of economic arrangements, mature capitalism, of which the EU is one international facilitator;
3. a common European history, although of course one with agreed national emphases and variation;
4. the belief that the religion of Europe is Christianity, with all its denominational variation. Other religions, such as Judaism or Islam, may be present but they are not essentially »European«;
5. a belief in a common European philosophical and political perspective, based on democracy, rationality and tolerance.

However, none of these assertions stand up to any detailed empirical scrutiny. Like the boundary issues explored earlier in this paper, they are all based on operational, contingent definitions. Some are ideal typical models with little purchase on social reality, such as the belief that Europe should be distinguished by its tolerance. Others are simply incorrect, as is the case with the belief that Christianity, a middle Eastern religion like Judaism and Islam, is somehow »more European« than the other two. In other words, many Europeans do not share these characteristics.

The issues that arises for education from this confusion are complex and difficult to handle. One way forward is to accept (and teach about), not just the contingent, plural nature of Europe and the plural nature of the states within it but also the acceptance of the concept of individual plural identities (or decentred subjectivities) for individuals at both the national and international, European level. As Stuart Hall puts it: »The fully unified, completed, secure and coherent identity is a fantasy. Instead, as the systems of meaning and cultural representation multiply, we are confronted by a bewildering, fleeting multiplicity of possible identities, any one of which we could identify with.« (Hall 1992, 277)

Within most EU states, such plural identities have been accepted at the level of practice if not at the level of policy (or academic theory), although seldom in any systematic way. In Britain, for example, there has been long acceptance of certain traditional national identities such as English, Scots, Welsh and Irish. More recently, there has been acceptance of other minorities, such as Jewish people, Gypsies/Rom and other travelling people.[14] A similar, more contested acceptance has been given to various black British groups.[15] It is important to note that acceptance of such plurality can have both positive and negative social consequences, more often the latter. Such national complexity is not accepted by all in British society and is one of the key factors in the continuation of racism, anti-semitism and other »ethnonational« discrimination in Britain. Similar patterns of plurality exist in most other EU states, although details will differ, often quite markedly. Education, with the support of other social agencies such as the mass media, still has a great deal to do in introducing and explaining such perspectives to children and young people.

But even before this first task,- the explication of the complex and plural nature of each EU state is completed, a similar task has to be undertaken in respect of plural identity at the EU level. Staying with the British example just put forward, that same person could also, if s/he wished, be European and African. Other groups of British citizens could be European and Indian, even European, Indian and African. In other words, schools need to put forward the perspective that a European is someone who sees him/herself and/or is seen by others as belonging to a contingent, operationally defined Europe, whose life takes place in such a Europe, and who is indeed, a »native« of Europe. In other words, the whole definitional debate needs to become fluid and perhaps, more importantly, has to enter into the curricula of Europe's schooling systems. This is because such a pluralistic European identity would contradict much in the existing curriculum.

Educational Consequences, Educational Aspirations

Thus, the terms Europe and European are more complex than is often seen in the textbooks used in schools and colleges within the EU and in the way such education systems prepare both students and teachers in relation to teaching both in and about Europe. So, in the same way that intercultural education attempted to make national systems look again at what they did in relation to the multicultural society they served, so it also has the added task to look again at the broader European context within which state systems are located.[16] The consequences of such a new intercultural perspective are many and will, of course, vary within individual state contexts as well as over time. For the curriculum for example, just as ethnocentricity has to be combatted and countered in the curriculum so must a false eurocentricity. Much of the debate about a eurocentric curriculum argues for an international dimension to be laid against a European one. What has to be clarified is the boundaries of such a European curriculum, as well as its content.[17]

Two key curriculum areas in this respect are the geography and history curricula. In relation to geography, the earlier part of this paper, in its discussion of the concept and positioning of Europe, sets out a potential agenda for teaching about the geography of Europe. It also sets a potential agenda for the history curriculum, for perhaps it is within the history curriculum that the hidden hatreds of Europe linger on most insidiously as some of the statements that have come from participants in the break up of the former Yugoslavia indicate. Similarly, in Northern Ireland, where the hatreds of history are seldom hidden, Catholic and Protestant children learn alternative histories, depending on their community affiliations, such affiliations being increasingly supported by residential segregation.[18] Suppressing such partial and xenophobic histories is not enough, however. Indeed, suppression is seldom an effective pedagogical or didactic strategy. For example, the current rise of anti-semitism, fascism and racism across Europe may show how unsuccessful the education service has been in teaching about Europe's past.[19] More to the point, it would seem that the Holocaust, perhaps the key to an understanding of contemporary Europe, is still not given the curricula space and treatment that it deserves.[20] Clearly, the teaching of history in the former states of Yugoslavia failed to give many people the skills with which to deal with the rise of ethnic particularism. Indeed, in respect of this, the response of many within the EU to the Muslim/Christian violence has been one of puzzlement about the presence and long standing survival of Islam within Europe.[21]

If schools within Europe have, in general, failed to teach the full range of histories that have made it,[22] the teaching of and/or about religion has done even worse. Within the teaching of and/or about religion there are even more obvious opportunities for the conscious or unconscious repetitions of old antagonisms, misconceptions and even hatreds. The concept that there are three major world religions in Europe, Islam, Judaism and Christianity, would still be seen as bizarre and wayward by many who organise education systems within the states of Europe.[23] Continuing with the same theme, how many EU states support or accept the presence of Muslim schools within their formal education system? To illustrate this point, although the law is clear in Britain, in that Muslim schools are, under the same conditions as Christian and Jewish schools, entitled to state support, none has yet been so funded, despite numerous applications.[24]

As Edward Said had commented, albeit in relation primarily to literature, itself another critical curriculum area in relation to these issues, »fictional identities are the weapons of cultural war«.[25] School definitions of Europe and Europeans are currently being used in a similar fashion. If not subject to constant critical examination, EU schools will continue to contribute towards Europe's becoming a narrow, self-regarding and excluding group of states on the periphery of Asia and Africa. Such a view also means that a narrow eurocentric and xenophobic curriculum is likely to continue to be the norm rather than the exception in the education systems of Europe.[26] And this in turn will contribute little to the combatting of the racism, anti-semitism and xenophobia that plagues the EU and its schooling systems.

This definitional issue then, far from being an arid intellectual exercise, is crucial to a perception of a genuinely intercultural education for European states. If Europe's borders are recognised as being fluid, as indeed they are, and if a European becomes an including rather than an excluding category, as it should, then some essential first steps are taken in providing an appropriate political context within which an intercultural educational debate can take place.

Notes

1   And include others, e.g., Israel competes in the Eurovision Song Contest (!). A fascinating area for definitions of Europe is that found in the small print of travel insurance, where distinctions between Europe and the rest of the world are rarely in agreement and often include countries (e.g. some North African states) that reflect the imperatives of tourism rather than geopolitics.

2   The term continent is merely an operational division, with no scientific authority, hallowed by long usage in schools and elsewhere. It is doubtless useful but it is not scientific. If it is to be maintained, it has to be related to real divisions of the Earth's surface, such as those proposed by plate tectonics. However, one of the main divisions of the globe that this branch of science puts forward, the lithospheric plates, while having African, Antarctic, South American, North American, Indo-Australian and Pacific plates, has no European plate, simply a Eurasian plate, reaching from Spain to Japan. In other words, geology has some difficulty in relation to Europe, because it has no need of it.

3   Science has not always been so dispassionate. The nationalistic debates about the pre-eminence of German science in the eighteenth century shows how scientists can be swayed by xenophobia *within* their field (Schneider 1989).

4   The information here comes from the entry on »Europe« in *Encyclopedia Britannica* 1947.

5   The work of Martin Bernal (e.g. Bernal 1987) is an important attempt to look in a new way at this issue.

6   The major difference was in part of the Iberian peninsula, where, under Moorish rule, Moslems, Jews and Christians lived in a multicultural society which the rest of Christendom feared and hated, whose memory has been almost forgotten in the collective European consciousness and which is rarely given a positive mention in the history books used in the education systems of Europe. Another difference would be where the Crusader states of the Middle East (Antioch, Edessa, Jerusalem, Joscelin, Tripoli, etc.) would fit in to Europe.

7   The classic example of this would be the contemporary debates about Turkish entry to the EU.

8   The relations between Russia and Serbia (both Orthodox in historical terms) are different from the relations between Russia and the other states of the former Yugoslavia. For a comment on this, see Marr 1993.

9   Cosmology, particle physics and chaos theory would suggest that general unifying theory (GUT) and similar certainties are not to be readily found (Gleick 1987;

Overbye 1991). As Stephen Hawking put it »Why is it we remember events in the past but not in the future?« (Quoted in Overbye, op.cit., p. 377.)

10 A new third one had appeared, referring to the new European institutions, first used in 1952.

11 The term citizen is preferred to national here, although it usually refers to adult status. The term »national« links in with concepts of the oxymoronic »nation state« and is not preferred as a consequence.The term »inhabitant« is also not used, as it confers no status save that of location.

12 As this paper was being written, as a further example, conflict between Slovakian Hungarians and the Slovakian government seemed imminent.

13 As of January 1994, the Convention had been ratified by over 126 states. UNICEF claimed its proper implementation would cost $25 billion a year; this is roughly about the same amount of money spent on wine in Europe each year.

14 The acceptance does not yet seem to have been extended to New Age Travellers.

15 Of course, Hall's multiplicity of identities would include other aspects of an individuals identity besides their race or ethnicity. These might include sexual orientation, class, disability, religion, language or gender.

16 See, for example, the work of the Council of Europe in this area (e.g. Jones and Kimberley 1986) as well as recent issues of the *European Journal of Intercultural Studies*.

17 In Science for example, the Ptolomaic cosmological system is often taught as a European contribution to scientific knowledge. Equally, his map of the world is often taught in Geography as one of the first European attempts to map the world. Yet Ptolomy was, by some of the definitions explored earlier in this paper, an African. Greek Alexandria in Egypt was one of the centres of scientific thought for nearly eight centuries. But where was Alexandria and who were the Alexandrines? Trying to claim it »for us« (whoever »us« are, or, indeed, »them«) seems a ridiculous act of educational xenophobia.

18 In many ways, this segregation has been a less violent form of »ethnic cleansing«. On a more positive note, the work of educational institutions like Lagen College in Belfast, that make a real effort to bridge the gap between the two communities should also be mentioned.

19 This may be unfair as comparisons cannot readily be made. It could equally be argued that things could be a good deal worse if it had not been for the efforts made in schools, colleges and other educational institutions.

20 At secondary school, the writer's children studied both the 1914-18 and the 1939-45 wars. The causes and the horrors of war were well explored; the Holocaust was given hardly a mention. The same was true when the writer was at secondary school. Yet anti-semitism was a feature of school culture for both generations.

21 It is useful to point out that the current European disgust in relation to »ethnic cleansing« within the states of the former Yugoslavia seldom mentions that this Christian/Moslem antagonism not only has long historical roots but has contem-

porary precedents, as in Cyprus following its United Nations supervised partition in the mid 1970s and the Northern Ireland example given earlier in the paper.

22 A good British example of such hidden history is revealed in Peter Fryer's excellent history of blacks in Britain (Fryer 1984). Another English example would be Shyllon (1977).

23 Of course there are secular education systems within Europe, even secular constitutions. However, the Christian churches are still perceived as being the normative religious manifestation in just about every state. Bosnia-Herzegovina may yet be the first European state where this is not the case, though such a possibility was looking more unlikely as this paper was finalised.

24 The last government enquiry into the area, the Swann Report (DES 1985), argued against new state funded religious institutions while accepting those already operating. This issue did, however, formally divide the committee in that there was a minority opinion dissenting from this view.

25 Edward Said, talking about his book *Culture and Imperialism* in a BBC 2 TV programme *Arena*, 12 February, 1993.

26 Such a state of affairs is, of course, not confined to Europe. It appears to be a feature of dominant groups of states elsewhere in the world. For example, the concept of Central America, it could be claimed, was brought into being to exclude Mexico from North America, in a remarkably similar way to the treatment of Turkey in the European context.

References

Aronowitz, S. and H. Giroux (1991), *Postmodern Education*, Oxford.

Balace, F. (1991), »Russian nationalism from Tsarist imperialism to the present day«, Paper presented to the European Seminar on the Nationalities Question, Beneux, Belgium, April 1991.

Bernal, M. (1987), *Black Athena: The Afroasiatic Roots of Classical Civilisation*, vol.1, »The Fabrication of Ancient Greece 1785-1985«, London.

Burchfield, R. (ed.) (1972), *Supplement to the Oxford English Dictionary*, vol. 1, Oxford.

Campbell, B. and E. Lack (eds.) (1985), *A Dictionary of Birds*, Calton.

Cavafy, C. (1961), *The Complete Poems*, transl. R. Dalven, London.

Coulby, D. and C. Jones (eds.) (1992), *The World Yearbook of Education 1992: Urban Education*, London.

Cramp, S. et al. (1977 onwards), *Handbook of the Birds of Europe, the Middle East and North Africa: The Birds of the Western Palearctic*, Oxford.

DES (1985), *Education For All*, The Swann Report, London.

Delrot, J. (1992), *The Nationalities Question - From Versailles to the Present Day*, Strasbourg (Council of Europe).

Doyle, W. (1989), *The Oxford History of the French Revolution*, Oxford.

Fryer, P. (1984), *Staying Power*, London.

Giroux, H. (1992), »Postmodernism and the discourse of educational criticism«, in: Aronowitz and Giroux (1992).

Gleick, J. (1987), *Chaos: Making a New Science*, London.

Goodman, D. and C. Russell (eds.) (1991), *The Rise of Scientific Europe 1500-1800*, London.

Hall, S. (1992), »The question of cultural identity«, in: Hall et al. (1992).

Hall, S. et al. (eds.) (1992), *International Journal of Intercultural Studies*.

Jones, C. and K. Kimberley (eds.) (1986), *Intercultural Education: Concept, Context, Curriculum Context*, Strasbourg (Council of Europe).

Jones, C. (1992), »Cities, diversity and education«, in: Coulby and Jones (1992).

Marr, A. (1993), »The case for trying to bully the bully«, in: *The Independent*, 25 March 1993.

Murray, J. (ed.) (1933), *The Oxford English Dictionary*, Oxford.

Overbye, D. (1991), *Lonely Hearts of the Cosmos: The Quest for the Secret of the Universe*, London.

Schneider, H.-G. (1989), »Nationalism in eighteenth-century German chemistry«, in: Goodman (1991).

Shyllon, F. (1977), *Black People in Britain, 1555-1833*,Oxford.

Simpson, J. and E. Weiner (eds.) (1989 ongoing), *Oxford English Dictionary*, Second Edition, Oxford.

World Bank (1993), *The World Bank Annual Report 1993*, Washington.

Robert Ferguson

Racism and The Mass Media: Struggling with Normality

The horror of racist violence is not something to be treated lightly. The excesses of mindless nationalism, the resentment and fear of outsiders, the persecution, intimidation, and sometimes murder of ethnic minorities, all take their place in a catalogue of human misery and suffering which is part of late twentieth century life. The crucial difference between this and earlier centuries, however, may or may not be that things are worse now than they have ever been. There have been in the past pogroms, massacres, chauvinistic excursions which sought to colonise and exploit vast areas of the globe. And, of course, there has been that chilling reminder of the depths to which modernity can sink with the holocaust (see Bauman 1989). It is not surprising, then, that concerned individuals, organisations or academic communities wish to concentrate upon such abominations in order to try to understand what is happening at the local, regional and global level.

What distinguishes the present from the past most significantly is the fact that today television brings reports of events to what is virtually a global audience within a very short amount of time. There is not the literal or metaphorical space for the messenger to travel over land and sea with the news of a fresh disaster or atrocity. Today the audience may be there as it happens. In the press in most parts of the world it is possible to read of these same (televisual) happenings no more than twenty four hours later. Wars, murders, racist attacks, are part of the seemingly endless flow of media messages[1]. It is hardly necessary to point out, however, that the events of which we may hear or read are mediated accounts of what has happened, and these mediations need to be carefully studied in order to clarify their formal organisation, the principles upon which they are based, and the interests likely to be served by the way in which such messages offer up their meaning. The key point for the moment is the recognition that what we know (and in this context »we«, means the vast majority of the media audience), is based almost entirely upon media messages.

On the one hand the messages of which I am writing may be sensationalised in the tabloid press or treated with a version of intellectual and analytical rigour in the broadsheets; on the other they may be sent out in sound bytes and image clusters like bursts from an omnipresent electronic machine gun along the radio and television airwaves. The result of this media deluge, this perpetual discourse of violence and hatred, is to normalise such matters. Not in the sense that they are accepted by audiences as just a part of life, but in the sense that they have become a late twentieth century material and psychological hazard. Something to be avoided if possible and tolerated with some stress. By the same metaphor, they are also happenings about which one can do little or nothing, because hazards are dealt with by the professionals.

In a break from writing this piece, I have been watching »Euronews« on cable television. In five minutes I have seen - without any commentary, because they have a section entitled »No Comment« - Palestinian youths in Gaza in running battles with the Israeli forces. After some rock throwing and lobbing of teargas grenades, one young boy was shot in the leg. He dropped like a stone and then began to scream in agony. I stared at his image, numbed by the intensity of his pain. Within a couple of minutes there was another sequence filmed in Pakistan. It showed a truck full of troops and a single man not in uniform who had, for some reason, been arrested. As the sequence began, and as if aware of the presence of the camera, one soldier slapped this man hard around the head. In the next shot the man was shown, cowed, being dragged from the army truck by his hair. More followed of people with little or no food in Bosnia; then South Africa; then Angola. The whole sequence took no more than five minutes.

Within this tapestry of cruelty and hardship one also finds images of overtly racist violence. One thing, however, is sure. Although these recurrent sequences of brutality may offer details of how a person looks who has been shot, or the physiognomy of the starving and dying, they provide no way of making sense of what is going on. We live in a world where what were once referred to as »real relations« are merely hinted at through phenomenal forms. The abundance of instantaneous imagery which is on offer is no guarantee that any insight will be gained into the underlying causes, the power relationships, the political positions assumed by all those »participants« in acts of violence. A great deal of the reportage of violence which we receive falls on our heads like the water on a wet rag placed over our face to stop us breathing. There is no respite, no pause in the »flow«. The contemporary means of dealing with intractable problems is to change channels.

Given this concentration on the reportage of certain[2] violent acts, it is not surprising that seminars concerned with violence look to those acts, the way they occur and how they are reported in order to provide data for discussion and debate. It is not the purpose of this paper to argue against such research. It is necessary and can be elucidating. What will be argued here, however, is that the violent activities and chauvinist excesses which occur and are reported on as part of daily life are rather like the visible part of an iceberg. If this metaphor is sustainable for long enough to explore certain discursive and ideological possibilities, then the bulk of this great floating mass will have to be perceived as underwater and hence not immediately apparent. It is not, however, buried in our unconscious. It is merely out of sight. For the purposes of this paper, that great mass of ideological ice upon which violence, xenophobia, nationalism and racism can be sustained, will be designated as *normality*.

The concepts of normality and the »natural« are of considerable significance in relation to the construction and sustenance of ideological positioning. Following Barthes (1957, particulary the essay »Myth Today«), this paper suggests that naturalisation is the process by which certain social relationships, often of power and subordination, are made to seem natural rather than being the result of the complex interaction of groups and individuals, ethnic groups and genders, classes and power blocs. Representations of normality, or the invocation of a discursive structure of normality, are used again and again in the media in order to provide ballast for views and representations which are, upon further consideration, highly question-able. Normal life is that which can be summed up in the common sense phrase »it's only natural«. The construction of »otherness« is, unsurprisingly, something which stands in symbiotic relationship to the discourses of normality. Chauvinistic and xenophobic behaviour towards the outsider, the stranger can thus be not only justified, but made to seem natural. From these relatively simple beginnings, a whole range of popular discourses can arise and flourish. Such dis-courses, at least from the viewpoint of the »Natural Englishman«, justify the retention of the crassest racist stereotypes in the name of »our« normality. The second part of this paper will consider in some detail the ways in which such discourse might be constructed.

There is very little about normality in the literature about the me-dia and issues of racism and violence. The emphasis tends to be on concepts of deviance, and how they are treated or represented by the media. Just as a newspaper editor might tell one that a good story does not come from reporting that thirty thousand anti-racists went on a demonstration where there was no violence and much goodwill generated, so the media researcher and theorist might decide that researching the normal would be unbelievably boring and possibly academically and intellectually unrewarding. Debates about the na-ture of ideological domination have tended to centre on discussion of whether or not audiences are being manipulated or are »making use« of media messages for their own ends. The former position has found a large number of sympathisers linked with what has become known as the »effects« tradition in media research. The latter position has become more significant in recent years, and has been argued with some persuasiveness by De Certeau, who writes of the »silent, trans-gressive, ironic or poetic activities of readers (or television viewers) who maintain their reserve in private and without the knowledge of the ›masters‹« (Certeau 1984, 172). This is a generous and a possible reading of some audiences in some socio-cultural settings. Another, and parallel reading might be more appropriate for many contempo-rary European audiences. This would conceptualise media audiences as amorphous bodies which somehow seek stability (homeostasis) in the messages they receive and consider many communicators as pro-fessionals who seek to maintain stability in the messages they construct. Such stability is premised upon the maintenance of established relations of power and subordination in society, so messages which undermine that stability are likely to be curtailed or rejected. Despite possible disquiet at developments in one's vicinity, or nationally and internationally, the best course of action is to be sure not to rock the boat. The world, after all, has enough troubles, so one should keep one's head down and not muddy the waters. Indeed, it is possible that the link between political inactivity and the process of normalisation is most often given discursive form through the use of such metaphoric strategies by both the producers and the consumers of media messages.

This paper wishes to argue for a detailed and patient engagement with representations which serve to confirm ideological positions, mainly through appeals to common sense and a notion of normality. The example which has been chosen here is one which relates to an occasion when a public figure - in this case a government minister in the UK - publically voiced racist sentiments which are usually left to the relative privacy of the bar or the meal table. The voicing of such discourses of racism and power, it will be argued, has a critical role to play in the maintenance of what might be called the »discursive reserve«. What this suggests is that there is available in social and cultural formations a range of rhetorical and linguistic reference points which are identified and passed from individual to individual and group to group. These reference points do not require subtlety of argument or clarity of exposition and they are usually invoked through the process of implicature. This concept is derived from the work of the philosopher H.P. Grice. »An implicature is a proposition emerging from something that is said, but not actually stated by the words uttered, nor logically derivable from them. It must therefore be a product of the relationship between utterance and context; and a vital part of context would be the knowledge and motives of the speaker and addressee« (Fowler 1986, 106). This concept of implicature will now be linked in an analysis with the construction of »normality«.

The example chosen relates to a speech made on Thursday 4 February 1994 by Mr.Michael Portillo of the British Conservative Party, and a newspaper column written by a fellow Tory, Mr.Alan Clark, some days later. Mr.Portillo had been speaking to a gathering of students at Southampton University when he launched a virulent attack on the corruption of (unnamed) foreigners. His speech was widely reported in the British media and elicited, amongst other things, the response from his colleague Mr.Clark which will be analysed below. The core of Mr.Portillo's argument was that Britain was the most honest country in the world. Foreigners did not rate so highly in Mr.Portillo's estimation: »Outside of this country the standards of public life are way below what goes on in this country. If any of you in this room have got an A level it is because you have worked to get it. Go to any other country and when you have got an A level you have bought it or because you were a friend of a minister.« (sic) (The Guardian, 5 February 1994)

The construction of this argument is based around gross and unproblematic generalisation. The students to whom Mr.Portillo was speaking may or may not have accepted his statement as a serious commentary on »other« countries. Through the concept of implicature, however, it is possible to understand Mr.Portillo's comments as redolent with the discourse of British middle class white racism. Understanding implicature is about understanding how to fill in blank spaces, be they literal or metaphorical. Mr.Portillo' speech was, then, widely reported. Some newspapers suggested, correctly in my view, that Mr.Portillo's political credibility was under severe strain as a result of his ill-judged remarks. For others, as we shall see, Mr.Portillo was a man of integrity. The piece written by Clark which will now be analysed is probably more important in ideological terms than was the original speech.

Alan Clark has a weekly column in the right wing *Mail on Sunday*. On 6 February 1994, he chose to devote the whole column to a discussion of Mr.Portillo's speech. In so doing he erected a paradigmatic argument justifying the soft and hence »normal« dimension of white British racism. It is an argument built around an upper middle class-based judgement of »foreigners«, and one which serves to sustain deeper and more worrying judgements about otherness.

Under the photograph of Mr.Clarke and his name - there to signify his personal column, the piece is headed »A sorry ›gaffe‹ blown out of all proportion«. This title establishes the general modality of the article. It is based around invocations of what »we« all know to be the case. The unpleasant inferences scattered throughout are offered up with an air of bonhomie and bravura. Indeed words from »other« languages seem appropriate here. The use of the word »gaffe« in inverted commas is itself either ironic or grossly misjudged, coming as it does from the French! But the phrase »sorry gaffe« is very much a piece of upper middle class English chattiness. To speak of a »sorry mess«, a »sorry gaffe« or a sorry anything is to place the situation described in the world of public school education or after dinner chat. This is confirmed by the remainder of the title - »blown out of all proportion«, for which, from a position inside the ideological framework of the *Mail on Sunday*, one might read »made into something much more significant than it should have been to anyone with half a grain of common (English) sense«.

Mr.Clark thanks God that Mr.Portillo is around. This is not an act of religious devotion. Its is another piece of class rhetoric, inviting silent discourses of reactionary fervour in the reader. Thank God that Mr.Portillo is around so that somebody at least can tell the truth about these bloody foreigners! He praises Mr.Portillo for two other speeches made earlier in the month. Clark uses very English descriptive terms such as a »shower« to describe the British Establishment. The connotation of the term »shower« is generally that of a disorganised and disreputable group of people. It is also used, as with the adjective »sorry«, as a means of colloquialising and euphemising unpleasant or potentially offensive judgements. By demonstrating that Portillo has been critical of the Establishment, Clark seeks to vindicate the former's judgement of »foreigners«. In this way the discourses of racism and chauvinism can be offered as no more or less than common sense judgements by reasonable men.

Clark, however, is in no mood to compromise with the critics of Portillo. »Since when has it been a gaffe«, he wants to know, »to say what everyone knows to be true«. Portillo had suggested that outside the sanctity of the United Kingdom, people were corrupt and bought their qualifications. No country was named by him. Clark does not adress this allegation directly. Instead he rounds on alleged bureaucratic procedures and the corruption of officials in France, Italy and Greece. He equates, bizarrely, this alleged corruption with xenophobia - probably that of the corrupt officials, but this is not clear. By this time in the argument it does not really matter. Clark then turns his venom on those »closet liberals or worse« who are suspicious of nationalism. He has moved away from Mr.Portillo's scurrilous allegations and into the discursive modality which allows for the (re)construction of Great Britain and those who dare to criticise her. In order to so he has to introduce some fifth columnists in the form of liberals and high-minded commentators. These unidentified persons are then linked to the humiliation of Britain. It is of no consequence that Clark has by now moved into a new and more vicious discursive mode. He is, metaphorically at least, foaming at the mouth: »So it does not matter to what humiliation Britain is subjected, the recommended response is always the same - roll about on the ground and wave your paws in the air«. The reader has been taken a long way from the speech of Mr.Portillo. Clark moves with ease from the visit of Gerry Adams to the USA, to unintelligible but sombre warnings about North American society and its »urban concentrations of power on Eastern and Pacific seabords which are violent, rootless, and prone to hysteria«. A brief diversion into Tory politics and the article has come almost full circle.

Mr.Portillo, according to Clark, is someone who can articulate ideas and who should be listened to in the name of Tory unity. It is time to administer to the reader the final rhetorical blow. Clark admits that »what Michael Mr.Portillo said might have seemed, from the lips of the Foreign Secretary indecorous. But he is a junior member of the Cabinet and he was talking to a student meeting«. The choice of the word »indecorous« is important here. Once again it is a word with a good middle or upper middle class pedigree. It carries with it connotations of lacking propriety or good taste. It is from the same discursive repertoire as terms such as »sorry gaffe«. Such terms are a cover for vindictive thought and malicious discourse. They also serve to impart an air of normality to what might otherwise be exposed as jingoistic and reactionary claptrap.

Mr.Clark's logic has not yet reached its point of exhaustion. He reminds his readers that what might have seemed »indecorous« from the lips of the Foreign Secretary can hardly be deemed so when it comes from the lips of a mere junior member of the Cabinet. Not only that, but he was talking to an audience of students. Presumably this gives license to any junior Cabinet member to let his words and thoughts run riot. What's wrong with a little xenophobia, racism and chauvinism when talking to a group of students cries Clark's discourse from between the lines? Any sympathetic reader of Clark's column, and it is for them that he writes, might now be waiting for some kind of climb down or move towards reconciliation with Mr.Portillo's critics. But it is not to be: »Now we have been told he is ›sorry‹. So am I. There are few spectacles so distasteful as that of one who has *told the truth* being compelled to apologise.« (italics added). In this final comment there is the self-righteous indignation of the reactionary who reserves the right to spread his views as »normal« thinking.

This brief analysis has been offered in order to demonstrate just one way in which xenophobic and chauvinist ideas can be constructed as both normal and desirable. Clark's column is not a sophisticated piece of rhetoric, but it demonstrates very adequately the general line of approach adopted by those racists and chauvinists who insist on remaining stubbornly normal. The context of their discourse is that it usually operates most powerfully on ideological home ground. Clark is preaching to the converted, but such preaching is very important to maintain morale amongst beleaguered conservatives, whether or not they vote for the Conservative Party.

The limitations of space have made it necessary to concentrate here on a single example of newspaper journalism. The final section of this paper will attempt to identify other ways in which the »normal« and invocations of normality, with their context of potential intimacy or discursive closeness, facilitate the circulation, nurture and practice of racism and xenophobia. It will also be argued that behind the invocation of normality there lurks the promise of violence which will come from those who wish to preserve normality at all costs. These invocations may come from the relative anonymity of newspaper editorials, or from the mediation of the speeches and comments of public figures. One way of theorising this situation is through the concept of hegemony put forward by Antonio Gramsci (1971), but this is less appropriate when one is trying to understand the intimacy and directness characteristic of many media messages, particularly when they are dealing with issues of racism and chauvinism. Media messages address their audiences in the language of the everyday and require a theorisation which recognises that everyday life has become the apolitical centre of the mediazation (see Thompson 1990) of culture. Making media sense of the outsider through the discourses of racism and xenophobia is something which is done by appeals to that (usually national) lifestyle which, allegedly, existed once and which is now potentially under threat. There is no need to define such a lifestyle in any detail. The less said the better. The »past« for the xenophobe is sacred and to be guarded as a precious memory. Normality must invent the »good old days«, whether these take the form of street parties and the exercise of community spirit or the Great Empire which was once the civilising force in an alien world.

There is also, to conceptualise implicature slightly differently, the frequent use in racist and xenophobic discourse of what might be called the »nod-and-wink« approach to issues relating to »race«, nationalism and xenophobia. Clark is an expert at such inferential argumentation. His technique of bemoaning the fact that one can no longer speak the truth about issues and (Other) people is one which is replicated on occasion in bus queues, in right wing newspaper editorials and in some bars where alcohol loosens the tongue. Such replication is not easily quantifiable and would be both costly and morally and ethically questionable to research[3]. Sometimes it is necessary to turn to the world of the dramatist and the film maker to hear what the researcher cannot collect as data for analysis. The status of dramatised or »fictional« evidence is, understandably, problematic. The more problematic alternative, however, is that research will have to become synonymous with spying and informing. Everyday life and the »normal« are two of the most inaccessible facets of our social existence. It is easier to research our rituals and our celebrations than the mundanities of our quotidian existence. Yet it is with the latter that we may find the ideological cornerstones upon which the social edifices of chauvinism and xenophobia are erected.

It may be that »normality«, upon closer analysis, will be identified as much of a fiction as any other generalising concept designed to explain the operations of daily living. But that does not mean that the media cannot and do not recycle this concept in order to make ideological appeals through other fictional constructs such as »the national interest« or »our tradition« (see Hobsbaum and Ranger 1983). In this way there is a direct route through the normal to the alleged need to protect a fictional sense of identity to practices which are anything but fictional. It is upon the complacency in the behaviour of those who inhabit the world of the normal that the violence of those who have left the domain of verbal discourse for that of physical action can survive or thrive. This is not to suggest that racist violence and xenophobia can be reductively attributed to the ways in which normality is constructed and maintained. It is, however, to suggest that it is crucial to problematise our notions of normality in order to better understand how the concept may serve to legitimise existing relations of power and subordination in societies.

This paper has put forward some tentative suggestions which seek the possible roots and sustenance of violence and xenophobia in concepts of normality. It has been suggested that the study and research of the horror of violent acts is important, but may be misleading. One of the most uncomfortable realisations for those who see themselves as responsible and »normal« citizens of their country (and perhaps of the world), is that we are all implicated in that violence. Violence and xenophobia can be explained and sometimes justified through appeals to normality. Those who wish to better understand how and why this might happen would do well to focus their research upon quiet residential areas as much as run down inner cities, upon the honeyed persuasiveness of grey suited pundits of the normal as much as the angry and dispossessed. It would be naive to suppose that such a refocussing of academic attention would render up sufficient or final explanation of racism and xenophobia. But it would be short-sighted and willful negligence if researchers did not recognise that the toleration of racist violence and xenophobia has to be related to the lifestyle and ideological predispositions of those who live in societies where child abuse and domestic violence co-exist with moral outrage at the outsider and the Other.

It is to media representations of normality in relation to the above issues that we, as academic researchers, may turn to unravel more of the ideological puzzle which is the backdrop for racist and xenophobic behaviour. But we must do so in the knowledge that we are implicated in and may be complicit with the ›world‹ which we investigate.

Notes

1 The concept of »flow« has been invoked by Raymond Williams in relation to television programmes as a means of identifying the apparently seamless continuity by and through which television messages are made constantly available in may of the industrialised countries. There is the endless pressure to »place« issues and then move on. Of course, a similar argument could be made in relation to the recurrent presence of the daily press, although newspapers are unlikely to achieve the immediate international audience of television news. See Williams (1974).
2 A notable and perhaps understandable absence here is the graphic presentation of domestic violence. The absence on screen of violent acts in the home can easily lead an audience to forget or underestimate the prevalence of such acts in our societies.
3 There is no reliable research methodology which will allow the »noormal« to be studied without, in the process being de-normalised. The only possibility left, apart from living reflectively in a state of normality, is spying!

References

Barthes, R. (1957), *Mythologies*, Paris.

Bauman, Z. (1989), *Modernity and the Holocaust*, Cambridge.

Certeau, M. de (1984), *The Practice of Everyday Life*, London.

Fowler, R. (1986), *Linguistic Criticism*, Oxford.

Gramsci, A. (1971), *The Prison Notebook*, Lawrence and Wishart.

Hobsbaum, E. and T. Ranger (eds.) (1983), *The Invention of Tradition*, Cambridge.

Thompson, J. (1990), *Ideology adnd Modern Culture*, Polity Press.

Williams, R. (1974), *Television: Technology and Cultural Form*, London.

Uli Linke

Fantasizing About Violence: Memory, Alterity, and Identity in German Political Culture

Episodes of Violence in Post-Cold War Germany

According to a *New York Times* report from October 1993, »A wave of anti-Semitic and xenophobic violence has claimed 24 lives over the last year and a half (in Germany), with the bulk of the attacks inspired, if not directly ordered, by militant nationalists and neo-Nazi groups ...« (Whitney 1993, A1).

A surge of firebombings, directed particularly against Turkish immigrants and eastern European refugees, has been reported since 1989: 4,147 violent crimes against foreign residents in Germany were recorded in 1992, of which 550 were arsons (Archiv für Sozialpolitik 1993a, 31). Nationalist violence displays a remarkable continuity in cultural form, relying on symbols significant to German culture: Rightist militants, in their attempt to annihilate the ethnic other, make use of fire, which is in Christian (and Nazi) symbology a sign of overcoming, a possible transformation into a new period. It is remarkable that the same repertoire of symbols and images is invoked as a medium of violent protest by the political left: By setting fire to large shopping centers, which were despised during the seventies as products of capitalist culture and consumption (and historically as the property of wealthy Jews), members of the Red Army Faction returned to the violent tactics of the generation that preceded theirs - »though, of course, they conceived of themselves as fighting for the exact opposite cause, and their appeals were no longer linked with anti-Semitism« (Borneman 1992, 256). This synchrony of memory and violence, and the persistence of these historically problematic symbols in the repertoire of the political left is the subject of my investigation.

Dissociation/Denial/Negation

»(A)fter a long period of playing down the violence ... Chancellor Helmut Kohl and other leaders have taken a sharper tone of condemnation: »The damage that neo-Nazis have done to our reputation in the world cannot be described drastically enough« (Whitney 1993,).

A series of arson attacks against eastern European refugees were reported from the vicinity of Bamberg, Upper Franconia, in February 1989. During the first incident, two firebombs were hurled against a housing complex occupied by fifteen refugees from Hungary and Poland. As reported in the news media, like *Die Tageszeitung*, for instance, »Memmelsdorf residents react with indifference to last night's occurence; the catholic priest points out that after all one asylum-seeker costs the government 2,300 marks each months. The refugees live in fear ... 24 hours after this attack another Molotov cocktail is thrown against the door of a residential project at the outskirts of Bamberg. This former shelter for the homeless also houses refugees, primarily from eastern Europe ... The police, after the last arson attack, ... refuse to talk about a right-wing movement in and around the city of Bamberg ... (Instead) Police even consider a family quarrel as a possible motive. A policeman, delegated to protect the homes, does not want to exclude the probability that the refugees started the fire themselves in order to gain public attention.« (Siegler and Ennsle 1989, 5)

In December 1988, the nineteen-year old Josef S. was arrested in connection with the firebombing of a residence in Schwanndorf, northern Bavaria: the inhabitants, three Turks and one German, were killed by the fire. Josef S. confessed and admitted to the act of arson »out of rage against foreigners.« The man was known to local law enforcement officials because of his previous involvements with the rightist organization *Nationalist Front*. Several thousand mourners march in silent protest. According to news reports, »Schwanndorf's mayor does not see it necessary to attend the demonstration. For him, there is ›no reason for such a declaration.‹ He does not participate for fear of giving the impression that ›here in our town is a stronghold of neo-Naziism and that one has to fight against such tendencies.‹ ...There is, according to the judicial press secretary Guerrein, no evidence that links Josef S. ›to the members of a rightwing radical group or youth organization.‹ ... Police and the prosecution cultivate their version of the perpetrator as ›a loner without political affiliation.‹« (Siegler 1989, 5)

Acts of violence against immigrants are sometimes enhanced by the actions of law enforcewment officials. For instance, in late August 1993, in the town of Lotte, near Osnabrück in northern Germany, a twenty-four year-old Turkish man was attacked and savagely beaten by rightist militants. After the Turkish man lost consciousness, a black swastika was painted on his forehead. The severely injured young Turk was hospitalized. Four days after the incident, police and prosecutors could not confirm that the Turkish man was a victim of rightist violence. On the contrary, they charged him with conspiracy and participation in »the fabrication of an unlawful act«. The results of the investigation remain inconclusive (Archiv für Sozialpolitik 1993b, 32).

Collusion/Participation/Complicity

The resurgence of violent nationalism can be documented in other contexts. Reporters for the German weekly *Die Zeit* describe a celebration of election results by right-wing Republicans at their party headquarters in Cham, Bavaria: »There they hovered with their obese bodies in their folk costumes, red-faced with rage and fixated eyes and shouted ... When the reporter blocks the view of the guru (party leader), someone in the back calls out ›Beat it or else you'll end up in Dachau‹. Similar outbursts were directed against the small crowd of brave protesters outside the beer hall. ›Parasites!‹ ›Gold-bricks!‹ ›Pollack lovers!‹ they are called ... ›To the gas with them. The cancerous growth must be gassed‹, a man hisses in passing.« (Grill et al. 1989, 17)

In late October 1992, an arson attack destroyed an unoccupied building in the town of Dolgenbrodt, near Berlin; the building was scheduled to become a shelter for political refugees. Now prosecutors are investigating reports that the residents of this German town raised money to pay rightist youths for burning the shelter. The investigation, as reported by *The New York Times*, reveals that just before the incident, »(S)everal dozen Dolgenbrodt residents met in a local tavern to discuss the pending arrival of asylum-seekers. According to press reports, some of them expressed fear that the refugees would be Gypsies who, having nothing to do in the placid village, would turn to house-breaking and other crimes.

Several nights later a group of youths on motorcycles ... drove by the hostel. One youth threw a firebomb, and the hostel burst into flames ...

(Almost 6 months later, police finally detained a suspect) He later confessed and told them that he had been paid for his participation... The money (for the firebombing) is said to have been secretly collected from the 250 townspeople.« (Kinzer 1993, A1, A6)

By August 1993, almost a year after the incident, the nineteen year-old suspect begins to deny his participation in the firebombing, but admits that others - having received »logistic support« from the village population - had taken the money. While rejecting the accusation of popular conspiracy, the mayor of Dolgenbrodt, Ute Preissler, cofesses: »We were not particularly sad when our problem was temporarily resolved (by the fire)« (Archiv für Sozialpolitik 1993c, 32).

Reproduction

In Berlin, leftist and alternative protesters, voicing their opposition to the nationalist resurgence, tend to conjure the following formulaic slogans (*Der Spiegel* 1989, 30):

»Turks in, Nazis out«
»We rip open/tear up the Republican's asses«

Immediately after the January 1989 elections in Berlin, anti-establishment activists and members of the Green/Alternative party assembled in protest. Their anger was directed against the militant right-wing party of Republicans, which had unexpectedly gained eleven seats in the Berlin Senate. Alternative protesters organized nightly demonstrations, where they diplayed banners expressing their political sentiments: One banner showed a clenched human fist smashing a swastika (hitting it dead center, fragmenting it). Another banner displayed a human skeleton made of cloth and paint. It was accompanied by the written slogan »hit/smash away/annihilate (hack) the brown filth« (Linke 1989, fieldnotes). Variants of this slogan appeared in protest chants, on stickers, and as graffiti (ibid.). Other examples included such catch-phrases as »Death to fascism«; below the text were painted two gallows from which dangled the SS sign and a swastika. Similar fantasies of violence appeared in formulaic statements like »Smash the Reps to bits!« »Hack the Nazi's heads with shovels, until they crack«. »Hit the Nazis on the neck, until their throats crack«.

One Saturday evening, in January 1988, in Schriesheim near Heidelberg, six young men (four of them skinheads) entered a shelter for political refugees and savagely beat two Indian men with wooden sticks, insulted and threatened the other residents, and then left unrecognized. Police arrested them several days later.

»Days before the beginning of the trial (almost a year later), a flyer by an ›anti-fascist action group‹ circulated at the universities in Mannheim and Heidelberg. It encouraged ›attendance at the Nazi trial‹: ›Don't give an inch to the fascists!‹ ›Hit them/beat them where ever you meet them‹. ›Foreigners stay, drive the Nazis away!‹« (Reuss 1988, 16)

Memory

In Troschenreuth, a village in Upper Franconia, the nationalist Republican party received more than half of the electoral votes. Here, the far right has a simple majority.

Yet in February 1989, as reported by *Die Zeit*, »After the Berlin elections, the (spray-painted) slogans: ›Nazis out!‹ and ›Thwart the early beginnings!‹ were clearly displayed on a wall in the center of the village. They have remained there until today and provoked Dettenhoefer's son (the son of the nationalist village leader) to draw oblique historical comparisons. ›That's just how it got started back then, when people began to defile the synagogues‹. (According to the reporter) He says this in all innocence, an open, good-natured young man, nevertheless a rabid neo-Nazi.« (Grill 1989, 15)

The Interpretation of Narrative Violence

Anthropological interpretations of the coercive mechanisms of power have tended to regard the occurence of violence as a-typical, abnormal events, as a form of action or behavior that inevitably disrupts the continuity of intentions, the regularity of behavior, on which causal, historical or structural accounts are based. However, in some cultural contexts »violence is constitutive of social order and social identities through the elaboration of narratives and political symbols that provision the ongoing political process« (Thornton 1988, 3-4). It is precisely because people routinely represent violence to themselves in terms of causal schemas that politics can appear to use violence instrumentally. What it uses, however, are the rhetorical schemas which people construct in order to understand violence and give it meaning (Feldman 1991; Thornton 1990a, 1990b).

But it is not only the interpretation of violence that is intrinsically cognitive and symbolic. Although violence relies on the use of implements, as Hannah Arendt (1990) observed, and acts of violence are perpetrated on others by the use of such implements, these tools of violence are not necessarily physical. Violence, as suggested recently by Pierre Bourdieu (1989), can also be symbolic and narrative. Acting below the level of consciousness, narrative violence may be concealed, sometimes invisible or undetected, but makes its presence felt in quasi physical form.

As a symbolic medium, violence plays an important part in the formation of contemporary German identity. If we take Anderson's notion of the nation as an »imagined political community« (1992), then images of violence are among the principal themes which structure the German imagination. Common to all discourses about being German is the centrality of narrative violence. Violent fantasies memorialize German history as an agent of political identity. Among rightist nationalists, violent images and practices reaffirm German self-identity by invoking partial memories of a once negated past to restore its promise of power and racial supremacy. Among leftist activists, narrative violence is an equally important vehicle in the construction of political identity. Through their fantasies of violence, members of anti-establishment/alternative movements have constructed patterns of linkages - genealogies - of events and roles that link their interpretation of a contested present to cultural memories of a contested past.

I intend to explore this assertion and then broaden the discussion of German political identity to include processes of national identity formation. I will examine German notions of selfhood and alterity in the post-cold war era by exploring the violent imagination of German popular culture.

Schemata of Violence

When analyzing the rhetorical schemata or narratives of violence which incite the imagination of the political left, the following assessments can be made. German anti-establishment activists tend to promote the use of fantasized violence as a medium for political contestation. A range of highly charged image schemata, focused on death, silencing, and physical brutality, typified by the swastika, SS sign, gallows, Nazi rhetoric, and death camps, are appropriated as anti-symbols and are transformed into a language of resistance against the German state.

These fantasies of violence, marked by a language of death and annihilation, with its evocation of simple brutality, ranging from an advocacy of expulsion to murder by strangulation and bludgeoning, permeated all levels of Green/Alternative politics in Berlin. In the course of my research in 1988 to 1989, and again in 1990, I uncovered such fantasies in the domain of political agitation, in the rhetorical speech-styles of propaganda and campaigning, in the contexts of organized protest, in the articulation of conflict at the party's grassroots level and in committee meetings. Never, however, did I observe the use of such fantasy material at the level of public ideology or parliamentary representation, where instead the global goals of democracy, peace, women's rights, and environmental protection were promulgated. How can we explain the prevalence of such fascistoid fantasy material at the local level? And how does it contribute to the formation of political identity among anti-establishment activists? How does the violent content of the German popular imagination affect Germans' self-image and their perception of the Other? To what extent do such images affect German notions of post-cold war peace efforts?

The most prominent image schemata appeared in the form of the swastika, SS sign, gallows, and the color black. The political mobilization of these symbols permits the evocation of the past: the swastika, for instance, is appropriated as an icon of German history. It stands as a sign for the Nazi regime: the totalitarian state, the party, the police and military as well as other administrative agencies of the fascist state. The icons of German history stand for institutional violence and institutionally enforced violence: the dehumanized, faceless, sanitized perpetration of brutality.

In the oppositional rhetoric of the Green/Alternatives, the swastika, as the other icons, is mobilized as a metonym, signifying the congruence of the fascist regime and the contemporary German state with its enormous police force and right-wing political spectrum. Fantasies of violence, directed against the political »other«, are thereby not merely historicized, but reproduced as templates for action and identity. Transformed into an anti-symbol, the swastika is integrated into a key scenario (Ortner 1973), in which the use of violence is legitimated and tangibly »embodied«: the clenched fist, signifying the »muscle« of the Green/Alternative membership, resists and crushes the iconographic emblems of Nazi institutions.

Through a reversal of these depictions of »embodiment«, the violent content of the key scenario, with its message of death and brutalization, is intensified. The use of a generalized social category, such as »Nazis«, unlike the iconographic evocation of the past, promotes recognition of membership and agency. The term »Nazi«, unlike the swastika, stands for the human (rather than the institutional) perpetrator of genocidal cruelty. It thereby permits/invites the equation with other contemporary agents: the »bulls« (i.e. police officers), the »Reps« (i.e. Repulican party members), »fascists«, »neo-Nazis«, and so on. In the political slogan, the social and historical reality of the »Nazi« is made tangible by his physicality of presence -- he is »embodied«: the textual references envision »Nazis« with heads, necks, throats or mouths, sometimes genitalia, to which acts of violence can be applied. In these key scenarios, the fantasizer assumes a disembodied presence: violence is inflicted through technical contraptions or instruments (e.g. Arendt 1990): the gallows, the shovel, the clenched fist. The fantasy is focused on the act and consequences of violent behavior: crush, crack, croak, smash, hack, kill. The implied brutality of Green political fantasy is shocking because of the casual invocation of murder (and the rhetorical absence of emotional affect).

Memory and National Identity

Although such fantasies of violence appear to be at odds with the pacifist ideology of the Greens, the narrative vehicle by which they are expressed - a combination of invocation and dissociation - is a pervasive one in contemporary German culture. Since World War II the construction of a German national identity has been mediated by the reconstitution of collective memory. The legitimacy of the West German state (Federal Republic) was built upon a dual consensus: the rejection of fascism and the rejection of a socialist solution (Maier 1989). The regime was defined by what it was not. Reunification in 1990 further exacerbated this pattern of historical amnesia and remembrance. The thematic focus of German political identity was (and is) therefore one of dissociation from the past. German collective identity relied on motifs of negation and opposition. Yet while historical contiguities were officially denied, images and events from the past continue to be invoked culturally.

The resiliance of fascistoid material was mentioned by the linguist Victor Klemperer in 1946, who was disturbed to see the unselfconscious and uncritical reproduction of Nazi thinking by means of verbal templates: »The language of the Third Reich seems destined to survive in several characteristic idioms; these have burried themselves so deeply that they seem to become a permanent property of the German language« (1946, 2). Klemperer's appears to have been correct, and anti-Semitism and the fantasized brutalization of others are inextricably rooted in German ways of speaking.

References to the death camps permeate everyday language: a boring situation or event elicits the formulaic response »it ought to be gassed« - made extinct (e.g. »*Es ist zum Vergasen*«). Another variant of this gruesome idiom, in common use in contemporary Germany, describes the consequences (the endurance) of an exhausting, repetitive task, executed »up to the moment of gasification« (e.g. »bis zur Vergasung«). The utterance refers to someone carrying out an action to the point of extinction or utter futility (Dundes 1987, 27, n. 12).

The imagery of genocide also surfaces as a metaphor: a smoke-filled, crowded pub is termed »a densely packed gas chamber« (e.g. »*Gaskammervoll*«) by a reporter for the Berlin daily *Die Tageszeitung* (Kapielski 1988). The news editor, accused of carelessness by the rest of the staff, responds: »I really don't feel like defending this man's infantile garbage. I don't know whether I would have deleted the word from the text, because I don't know whether it is good or evil, and I don't have any associations there. I don't concern myself with German history« (Riedle 1988, 8).

The ensuing editorial debate about the abuse of metaphoric language is sarcastically dismissed by another staff member (Droste 1988, 9) who calls such inquiries the »final solution of the *Duden* question« (e.g. »*Endlösung der Dudenfrage*«): *Duden* is the German word for »dictionary« and it rhymes with *Juden* which is the German term for »Jews«. In this instance, historic memory in an attempt to oppose the editorial board's decision to impose greater restrictions on the writers' »verbal spontaneity and humor« (Jhering 1988, 79). Media images of genocide are thereby not only invoked as figures of speech, but used instrumentally as commodities.

In a similar case, in 1989, a leftist news magazine reports the historical movement to purify or cleanse the German language from words of foreign origin (Konkret 1989), which led to the publication of the Germanistics dictionary, the so-called *Duden*. The critical debate about this nationalist publication (owned by every German household) entered the revisionist currents of German popular culture under the heading »*Dudenrein*« - literally »dictionary cleansing«. Here the word play alludes to the gruesome attempt by National Socialists to make Germany »Jew free«. The verbal reference reminds us that Jews in Germany were treated not as humans but as a dirty problem to be solved or eliminated. In this instance, ethnic cleansing is metaphorically equated with the purification of language. In such rhetorical instances, the memory of the Holocaust is diffused and trivialized by the routinized verbal encounter. Inserted into the cultural vocabulary, the language of violence has become part of the German repertoire of speaking.

Fantasies of extermination and Nazi violence are also projected onto narrative encounters which dramatize acts of genocide through the symbolic medium of play-acting. One such event took place during an air show at a U.S. military base in the Rhine Palatinate in Germany (e.g. Schrep 1983, 72-73; Lange-Feldhahn et. al. 1983, 207, 209). Anti-establishment protesters staged the occurence of a nuclear holocaust by simulating mass-death. When the U.S. military police finally intervened, the event turned into a form of dramatic poetry in which members of the German audience played out familiar roles, becoming participants in the physical brutalization of their political opponents. One spectator, a man with a small son, proclaimed that he wanted to »rip the heart« from one of the protester's bodies. Another shouted that the activists »should be run over with a tractor«. A man to his left, who until then had been contentedly chewing on a hot dog, suddenly poured his cup of beer over a young woman lying on the ground, and began to shout »Blood! Blood! Blood! while rythmically stomping his foot up and down. A female spectator, while kicking and spitting at the protestors, screamed: »Beat them to death, beat them all to death!« As the peace protesters were loaded onto the waiting military trucks, another man proclaimed: »And now into the gas with them!« In this collectively sustained performance, fantasies of violence are used for cognitive ends: The symbolism of the event renders explicit cultural memories of genocide and, at the same time, deflects the historicity of violence which it attempts to legitimate.

The same patterns of invocation and displacement are revealed by so-called »Auschwitz« jokes and video games. In these narrative contexts, the sordid and vicious details of the extermination of Jews in such concentration camps as Dachau, Buchenwald, and Auschwitz are remembered and made the subject of humor and entertainment. In several of the jokes and games, the death camp reality is appropriated as a key scenario with contemporary human targets: Turkish immigrants (who symbolize the ethnic »Other« in post-war Germany) are incorporated into the German repertoire of violent fantasy. Thereby, the annihilation of Jews is historicized, whereas the threat of victimization is directed against Turks (Albrecht 1982; Linke and Dundes 1988; Nierenberg 1984). The same fantasy is promoted by concentration camp video games: »The player must manage the camp, selling gold fillings, lampshades and labor to earn enough money to buy gas and add gas chambers to kill Turks« (*New York Times* 1991, A 10). According to one version of this game, called *The Arien test*, the players' racial purity is established by killing Jews in concentration camps and by eliminating others of mixed ancestry in combat at the eastern front. The successful conclusion of the game produces the text: »Sieg Heil. The state needs men like you« (Freudenreich 1989, 13). In each of these cases, the violent content of the fantasy is objectified through its historicity, and German self-identity is constructed through the fantasized annihilation of the »Other«.

Violence as a Key Scenario

Such racist templates constitute the broader context of cultural attitudes within which German political identity is formulated. As John Borneman (1992) recently suggested, the concentration camps, particularly Auschwitz, have become a key symbol around which guilt, Germanness, and identity cohere in the national imagination of the post-war German state. I argue, moreover, that such violent templates exist not merely as representational or summarizing symbols; they function more dangerously as key scenarios: through the invocation of historical brutalities from a contested past (as by the left) and the use of narrative violence as an element of cultural memory (as by the right), political activists assert their cultural identity, while at the same time re-enacting (according to unarticulated formulae) the cultural sequences of fantasized violence aimed at annihilating the cultural or political Other. In contemporary Germany, where such fantasies are once again acted out literally, and where immigrants, refugees, tourists, and even foreign athletes have increasingly become targets of racist violence, we witness the transformative power of such key scenarios: symbolic (narrative) violence has become ritualized practice and continues to reproduce templates of violence that are incorporated into the German popular imagination to replenish its repertoire of violent fantasy.

References

Albrecht, R. (1982) »Was ist der Unterschied zwischen Türken und Juden? Antitürkenwitze in der Bundesrepublik Deutschland«, in: *Zeitschrift fur Volkskunde,* 78, pp. 220-29.

Anderson, B. (1992), *Imagined Communities: Reflections on the Origin and Spread of Nationalism.* London.

Archiv für Sozialpolitik (1993a), »Jeder ist uns der Nächste. Zwanzigster Teil einer unvollständigen Chronik der Gewalttaten gegen Ausländer im wiedervereinigten Deutschland«, in: *Konkret* (January)1, pp. 30-31.

Archiv für Sozialpolitik (1993b), »Jeder ist uns der Nächste. Teil einer unvollständigen Chronik der Gewalttaten gegen Ausländer im wiedervereinigten Deutschland«, in: *Konkret* (October)10, pp. 28-32.

Arendt, H. (1990), *On Violence*, Chicago.

Borneman, J. (1992), *Belonging in the two Berlins: Kin, State, Nation*, Cambridge.

Bourdieu, P. (1991), *Language and Symbolic Power*, Cambridge.

Der Spiegel (1989), »Die neuen Deutschen. Einwanderungsland Bundesrepublik (I): Fremdenfurcht verändert die politische Landschaft«, in: *Der Spiegel* 43 (7), pp. 26-50.

Droste, W. (1988), »Tazionalsozialismus. Die Fortsetzung des Holocaust mit liberal-humanistischen Mitteln«, in: *Die Tageszeitung* (November)14, p. 9.

Dundes, A. and Th. Hauschild (1987), »Kennt der Witz kein Tabu? Zynische Erzählformen als Versuch der Bewältigung nationalsozialistischer Verbrechen«, in: *Zeitschrift für Volkskunde,* 83 (1), pp. 21-31.

Feldman, A. (1991), *Formations of Violence: The Narration of the Body and Political Terror in Northern Ireland*, Chicago.

Freudenreich, J. (1989), »Verfahren wegen Volksverhetzung. Judenvernichtung als Computerspiel«, *Süddeutsche Zeitung* 34, (February 10), p. 13.

Grill, B. (1989), »So normal, so stinknormal«, in: *Die Zeit* 8, (February 17), p. 15.

Grill, B., M. Haller, K. Kruse, H. Luehrssen and R. Merkel (1989), »Alte Parolen, neue Parteien. Gegen Asylbewerber, Gastarbeiter und Aussiedler: Heil ohne Hitler?«, in: *Die Zeit* 8, (February 17), pp. 13-17.

Jhering, von B. (1988), »Sprachkünstler auf hohem Seil. Stoiber, Kohl und die *taz*: Sprachliche Entgleisungen oder neuer Antisemitismus?«, in: *Die Zeit* 49, (December 2), p. 79.

Kapielski, Th. (1988), »Klassenloser Luxus. Auch der Dschungel ist schon zehn Jahre alt«, in: *Die Tageszeitung* (October 17), (reprinted November 14), p.9.

Kinzer, St. (1993), »Did a town in Germany pay a firebug for attack?«, in: *The New York Times* (August 25), A1 and A6.

Klemperer, V. (1946), *Lingua Tertii Imperii. Notizbuch eines Philologen*, Berlin.

Lange-Feldhahn, K., Cl. Duppel, A. Pfaff and I. Reick (1983), »11. 11.1981 -- Ausbruch (?) aus dem Irrenhaus«, in: *Friedensbewegung: Persönliches und Politisches* (K. Horn and E. Senghaas-Knobloch, eds.), Frankfurt/Main, pp. 202-217.

Linke, U. and A. Dundes (1988), »More on Auschwitz Jokes«, in: *Folklore* 99 (i), pp. 3-10.

Maier, Ch.S. (1989), *The Unmasterable Past: History, Holocaust, and German National Identity*, Cambridge.

New York Times (1991), »Video game uncovered in Europe uses Nazi death camps as theme«, in: *New York Times*, International (May 1, 1991), p. 10 A.

Nierenberg, J. (1984), »Ich möchte das Geschwür loswerden. Türkenhass in Witzen in der Bundesrepublik Deutschland«, in: *Fabula* 25, pp. 229-40.

Ortner, Sh. (1973), »On key symbols«, in: *American Anthropologist* 75 (5), pp. 1338-46.

Reuss, E. (1988), »Prozeß gegen junge Rechtsradikale: ›So richtig Lust hatte keiner‹. Warum schlugen sie Asylbewerber krankenhausreif?«, in: *Die Zeit* 49 (December 2), p. 16.

Riedle, G. (1988), »Richtigstellung. Zur Beschäftigung mit der Geschichte«, in: *Die Tageszeitung* (November 14), p. 8.

Schrep, B. (1983), »Totschlagen, alles totschlagen«, in: *Der Spiegel* 37 (33), pp. 72-73.

Siegler, B. (1989), »Schweigemarsch gegen Ausländerhaß«, in: *Berliner Tageszeitung* (January 16), p. 5.

Siegler, B. and D. Ennsle (1989), »Ausländerfeindlichkeit in der Bischofsstadt«, in: *Berliner Tageszeitung* (February 18), p. 5

Thornton, R.J. (1988), »Time, Context, and the Interpretation of Violence«, Unpublished manuscript.

Thornton, R.J. (1990a), »The Peculiar Temporality of Violence.« Rutgers Center for Historical Analysis. Unpublished Manuscript.

Thornton, R.J. (1990b), »The Shooting at Uitenhage, South Africa, 1985: the context and interpretation of violence«, in: *American Ethnologist* 17 (2), pp. 217-36.

Whitney, C.R. (1993), »Germans begin to recognize danger in neo-Nazi upsurge«, in: *The New York Times* (October 21), pp. A1 and A6, column 1.

Katherine C. Donahue

Race, Racism, and Culture in France

Introduction

Violence and aggression are frequently seen as stemming from bio-logical, natural causes, shared by humans with many other non-human primates and mammalian species in general. Aggression among members of non-human primate species in the wild has become increasingly well documented; Jane Goodall's observations of chimpanzees at Gombe Stream, Tanzania, in the 1980s led her to rethink some of her earlier assumptions about aggression among chimpanzees living there, not only that of males, commonly thought more prone to aggression than females, but also of mother-daughter pairs, observed killing infant chimpanzees. Recently, Wrangham has described social behavior of juvenile male chimpanzees which seems to closely resemble that of gangs of juvenile human city dwellers, out for a night, surveying the territory, and attacking when the opportunities seem right. Baboons, as described by Strum and others, are known for their aggressive ways. Gorillas, on the other hand, despite their size, strength, and teeth, may be less inclined to aggression than their chimpanzee relatives, although this may be due to their particular social relationships. Recently, Margaret Power (1991) has contested the view of chimpanzees as aggressive, dominance-seeking animals, arguing that Goodall's and other observations of aggression were caused by artificial feeding situations; both chimpanzees and human beings living in »immediate return« foraging situations are, according to Power, egalitarian and non-aggressive. There is still a great deal to be learned about the connection between violence and social order among both humans and non-human primates. It appears, however, that humans share much behaviorally with many of their

187

primate relatives. The question still remains: how much of this violence is due to nature, how much to nurture?

If the literature on the anthropology of war is correct, violence and aggression among humans may be learned behaviors (see Fry 1992). Aggression and warfare, it has been argued, seems to be correlated with social formations such as states, and according to Robert Carneiro, may indeed lead to state formation. Douglas Fry describes the situations among the Mexican Zapotec in which aggression is enculturated in one town, but is not enculturated in another town.

Aside from any particular natural causes of violence (hormonal reactions, testosterone levels, if these indeed are sufficient causes), it appears that violence has a cultural, symbolic, component, particularly when choices are made about the particular category of person against whom that violence is directed. Particular persons, or categories of person become targets of violent attacks. In the United States, domestic violence, violence directed at someone within the household, is frequently directed towards women; racial violence has been directed toward people of African, Chinese, and Korean origin, among others; whites get attacked; there are attacks specifically directed toward gays and lesbians. Each of these types of victim reflect some form of difference from the attacker. How do the attackers perceive their targets? What sort of model or category might be used for such designation?

In France, as elsewhere in Europe, violence against the person has been directed against »foreigners«. These people, often referred to as »immigrants«, some of them recent arrivals, some not, reflect their difference from citizens of the »host« state through skin color, clothing, religion, and/or language (see R.D. Grillo 1985, for a discussion of the differences in meaning between »immigrés« and »étrangers«). These cultural differences serve as symbolic markers of otherness. Cultural markers become symbols of difference and the bearers of those symbols the targets of violence. It is these targets to which one speaker referred when she said that she was ras le bol, fed up, with the immigrants (M.C., personal communication, May 1989). The metaphor is actually one of a bowl, full to over-flowing, which has lead to over-consumption. No more can be admitted, whether to the stomach or to the state.

Membership in states is maintained and constructed through inclusion and exclusion. While the French state claims to promote concepts of tolerance of difference, the political and legal system, the broadcast and print media, mediate membership and transmit concepts of who belongs in the state, and who does not. In what follows, violence is seen as a form of communication taking place in a context of symbolic construction linked with aggressive interaction. This violence, then, intersects both nature and culture.

In order to pursue this line of argument, I turn to some of the work done by Geertz (1973), Victor Turner (1974), Ortner (1973) on models, root metaphors, and key symbols respectively, and more recently by Fernandez, et al. in: *Beyond Metaphor. The Theory of Tropes in Anthropology*. My argument then moves to a discussion of metaphor and action, the formation of violence, its production and reproduction, and the meaning of these violent acts.

Symbol and Metaphor in Human Thought

The late 1960s and early 1970s were a heady period in American linguistic, structural and symbolic anthropology. Folk categories, such as those for firewood and animals, were being analyzed and described (see Tambiah 1969); dialectical opposites, both raw and cooked, natural and cultural, were discussed and digested, albeit a bit later than they were in France (Levi-Strauss 1969); Victor Turner was working on »root metaphors« (1974) and Sherry Ortner on »key symbols« and »key metaphors« (1974); Clifford Geertz, meanwhile, brought to our attention the concept of »models of« and »models for« action which we and all actors carry in our heads. From this work came the concepts of »performative« symbols which Turner discusses so well in *Dramas, Fields and Metaphors* (1974), for instance in his analysis of the events leading up to the martyrdom of Thomas Becket.

More recently, Thomas K. Fitzgerald (1993) has combined the insights of anthropology, psychology, communication theory, to analyze the metaphors of personal identity; Anthony D. Smith of the London School of Economics has explored the construction and symbolism of national identity; in which he discusses ways in which ethnic origins, religion, language, and shared symbols, all constructs of culture, are combined to provide a sense of nationhood.

Symbol and Metaphor in Human Action

It is this performative concept, as well as Clifford Geertz's models of and models for action, which have led to subsequent works, such as those published in the Fernandez volume (1991) *Beyond Metaphor. The Theory of Tropes in Anthropology.* Metaphors and metonymy, using comparisons or parts-for wholes, aid us in a formation of categories. Stating that »You are an brick«, or »You are my right hand« help us to identify the position or role which people play. Similarly, stating that »They are all animals« (metaphor) or »They don't eat pork« (metonymy) help us to place people in cultural categories, implying style of living and food taboos which are symbols of religious beliefs.

The argument over the wearing of the foulard by Muslim schoolgirls is an example of such use of symbol and metaphor. The foulard, the headscarf worn by Muslim girls, became a symbol of the Muslim way of life. It was a metonymic symbol, one which stood for a whole religious and cultural group, living in France, a nation which several hundred years before had formalized the distinction between church and state, which distinction then, according to French logic, meant that religious symbols should not appear in a branch of the state, the school. Furthermore, the state itself creates the categories for inclusion and exclusion, in legal construction of the rights to citizenship, primarily on the basis of citizenship by blood jus sanguinis, due to birth to people themselves French citizens; and birth on French soil, jus soli. As with most nation-states, those who live on French soil without the proper proof of citizenship according to one or another of these principles runs the risk, eventually, be being deported, unless the proper waivers and paperwork are acquired. Citizenship acquired by virtue of blood and soil is itself citizenship acquired through symbolic production; for what is the relationship between blood and rights to citizenship?

Symbols are powerful as rallying points for action; they can gal-
vanize a crowd, they can be good to think about and good to act on,
they provide something to fight and die for. The tattered flags in the
church of Saint-Louis-des-Invalides, not far from Napoleon's Tomb,
are touching evidence of this sentiment.

Robert Darnton (1985) describes in *The Great Cat Massacre* the
meaning of the killing of the cats by printers' apprentices in Paris
during the late 1730s. This massacre of cats reflected the mentalite of
the workers, angered at their conditions. They turned to torturing
cats, a practice found throughout France during the medieval and
early modern period; this practice embodied ideas of revenge on
masters who could afford to feed household pets better than the
workers were; (it also embodied ideas about women and their sen-
suality, less germane to Darnton's subject at hand, a workers' revolt,
but saying much about ways in which women were viewed in early
modern France). The cat was, in Victor Turner's term, a multivocalic
symbol, or a metaphor for the many things to which cat-torturers
were opposed; authority, females, masters, mistresses, wealth; and
the cries of dying cats let this opposition be heard by the true targets
of the workers frustration and anger.

Formations an Production of Violence

As Feldman (1991, 5) says about Northern Ireland, »though the
conditions of this conflict can be traced in part to the relations of
production, the reproduction of antagonism takes place in other
spaces and materialities. In turn, as much as ethnicity symbolizes in
part an inequitable cultural division of labor that has precipitated
communal violence, I have found that violence can effect autonomous and retroactive interventions in the construction of ethnicity.«

Ethnicity and race are cultural constructions. They do not flow
naturally from the body, nor do these categories spring from the head
of the bearer, with signs that say Muslim or Jew or Algerian. No,
they have been created, in some cases through thousands of years of
mediation, or self-ascription, or oppression. The oppression of Jews
in Germany was, made horribly manifest by the imposition of the re-

quirement that Jews wear a symbol meant to point them out as Jews, on their clothing. Others choose to wear a symbol of their affiliation, be it religious (the *foulard*), or cultural (other articles of clothing, such as a fez).

Signs and symbols can be placed on the body; skin color comes »naturally«. Yet that too varies, and the meaning we attach to skin color is often assigned by the beholder, not always by the bearer. Color, clothing, language, accent, use of dialect, religious expressions borne on the body, all provide the viewer with what they think are clues to identity.

Feldman speaks of the »politicized body«, and says that the »body made into a political artifact by an embodied act of violence is no less a political agent than the author(s) of violence. The very act of violence invests the body with agency« (1991, 7). The attacks on members of the »other side« then become, in a sense, the very act of »writing on the body«, leaving symbolic imprints carrying meaning.

Far from an over-intellectualization of aggressive, seemingly irrational and animalistic acts, the product of steamy hormones and pure bloody hate, the systematic violence perfected by groups such as the IRA or the Protestants, or the German neo-Nazis, or the French against seemingly non-French foreigners, are an expression of something much more complex and somewhat less biologically driven. These are to a large extent symbolic acts of force directed at some constructed other, determined through religious, land, race, class, or ethnic boundaries.

Inclusion and Exclusion: Field Work

During the week, in the central shopping district of Montebéliard, a town in eastern France, the busy streets thin out towards noon. Last minute purchases of bread are made for the noon meal. The office workers and store employees hurry home as steel gates come rumbling down over shop entrances. By 12:15 the streets are almost empty except for the North African factory workers and me. The North Africans are on their noon hour from the nearby Peugeot plant, but don't want to stop for expensive lunches. Nor do I, so I eat a piece of bread and hide behind my newspaper. The North Africans wander around, or sit on the steps near the fountain, smoking and talking together quietly. We are all strangers here. We have no apartment or house close by, where we can go for lunch.

The newspaper, a regional one, has news articles about local towns and gatherings of the elderly, or the firemen, or of some event for school children. An article about permanent residents from North Africa catches my eye, and a recent conversation over lunch in a restaurant with some French friends comes back to me. A few years ago, said one, you never saw men with prayer rugs over their shoulders in the streets. Now you see them more and more. Now the towns in the outskirts of Montebéliard have many such men, he continued. It is the Peugeot plant that attracts them here. But why can't they be more French?

These quiet scenes belie the recent experiences of immigrants living in Europe, in particular in France, Germany, and Spain. These two experiences are but two aspects of the contentious shared pool of experience which illustrate the complexity of the apparent »rising tide« of racism in France, the appeal of Jean Le Pen and his Front National, the perceived increase in immigration into France, the conflict and misunderstandings over the wearing of scarves by young Muslim schoolgirls, the beatings of North Africans in various cities in France, the death of a young North African while in police custody, the desecration of Jewish cemeteries, the deportation of a Turk who does not have the proper papers, the difficulties of assimilating North Africans into the French Army.

What are the French reacting to when they join the Front National in Marseille or shoot a North African in Reims? What indeed do North Africans mean when they shout »racists« in the aftermath of the acquittal of a store-owner from a charge of murder of a North African? (See *Le Monde*, 15-16 November, 1992, 8.) Are these tensions due to actual differences in »race«, in perhaps their biological differences? Or are they due to class differences, as in their economic, educational, or social backgrounds? Or are they due to differences in culture, for instance in the fact that North African women cover their heads, and men stop work to pray to Allah?

It is easy to say that the fact of this difference, that even though many may speak French, but they are not French, and don't look French, is enough to make them targets for attacks on the »Other«. It is easy, too, to say that the main reason for these attacks is economic; that numbers of the French see these immigrants as threats to the economic order in that jobs as well as social services go to these immigrants. As with many matters of the construction of the human social fabric, the situation is at once more complicated, and yet capable of being unravelled in order to understand its constituent parts. These are, after all, constructs of humans, who are almost endlessly capable of construction of shared identities and numerous boundaries over which others are not supposed to cross.

The attacks on immigrants are reported in the French and foreign press in discussions of the rise of racism in France, and it is difficult to untangle issues of »race«, from those of »culture«, »class«, »ethnic relations«, and »migration«. Mixed into this web of construction are issues of citizenship and nationality. What, in fact, does it mean to be French? Who has the right to be French? How are such issues decided? Who will remain non-French, even while living on French soil, and born in France?

In this paper, »racism« will be seen as an aspect of what at times becomes, in France and elsewhere, a violent debate about national identity, in which physical and cultural differences, or »racial« and »cultural« attributes are used as visible symbolic markers of difference; of difference which connotes a threat to self-appointed protectors of the »host« state either through perceived usurpation of jobs and opportunities or through perceived inadequacies in intelligence, in proper behavior or apparent inability and ineligibility to be part of the body national.

In this analysis of race and culture in France, I will discuss some statistics on past and present migration into France, present some of the arguments made since the French Revolution about construction of rights to French citizenship, and then proceed with an analysis from an anthropological, holistic, point of view, of perceptions of race, class, and culture as they are expressed and played out in the region of Montebéliard. In that discussion I will draw on several informal interviews I had with residents of Montebéliard in January of 1992.

Migration to France

»A great deal is learnt about a country through its treatment of foreigners. The census, its definitions, the handling of the figures are also the image of a society and its moods« (Singer-Kerel 1991, 281-282).

The English-language literature on migration in Europe in general and in France in particular is large and is represented by the work of Castles and Kosack (1985); Freeman (1979); and more recently by Miles and Singer-Kerel (1991). Migration statistics, although they usually represent official numbers and may undercount the number of actual immigrants, do allow for some understanding of trends and flows of migration. According to Singer-Kerel (1991), France has been the second largest importer of foreign labor after the United States since the early nineteenth century. This, she suggests, is because of the ever declining birth rate, the slower pace of the Industrial Revolution than in Great Britain, great emphasis on agricultural production, and continuing nationalism, in which immigrants were viewed as useful for such things as cannon fodder (Singer-Kerel 1991, 279).

While the popular press leaves the impression that migration into France, both legal and illegal, is at higher levels than ever, migration statistics do not bear out this assumption. Singer-Kerel reports that in 1931 foreigners comprised 6.58% of the total population, 7.40% of the labor force. In 1975, foreigners were 6.54% of the total population, and 7.28% of the labor force (in both instances, less than in 1931). In 1982, foreigners comprised 6.78% of the total population (2% more than in 1975) and only 6.62% of the labor force (66% less than in 1975) (Singer-Kerel 1991, 292). Therefore, according to these statistics, the total population of foreigners rose from 1931 to 1982 by only 2%, and in the labor force the percentage of foreigners has actually fallen, from 1931 to 1982, by 78%. These figures may well not reflect accurately the number of illegal immigrants (clandestins)

195

which are reportedly entering, in particular from West Africa, to live in crcwded rooms in areas around Marseille and elsewhere (reportedly 300,000 of them in 1985; Husbands 1991, 182), but the figures do show that, officially speaking, the portrayal of a rising tide of immigration is a somewhat suspect construct of reporting in the popular press, among members of the *Front National* and its adherents, and in the general consciousness of the French.

However, in the case of North Africans, there appears to be general consensus that during and after the Algerian War, close to a million repatriates, French who had lived in Algeria, came to France. Another half-million *harkis*, Algerians who had fought side by side with the French, and French Muslims, also entered France during the early 1960s (Husbands 1991, 172-173).

Who has The Right to be French?
The National Construction of Rights

Harlem Desir, leader of the group *S-O-S Anti-Racisme*, in an interview with the French journal *Le Debat*, quoted Napoleon as saying: »The children of foreigners who are established in France have the French spirit, French habits, the attachment which each one bears naturally to the country where (he) was born.« (Harlem Desir 1990, 53; translation mine).

The national census of 1851 was the first to ask specifically about the presence of foreigners in France (see Silverman 1991). In the 1880s a legislative debate centered on whether a tax should be imposed on foreigners in order to protect jobs of French workers. In 1889 a Nationality Code was established, and by the end of the nineteenth century the French educational system established its own unique way of insuring that all children attending school, either on the French mainland or in colonial outposts, would be instilled with a French identity, a system which has tended to be reproduced to this day (see Silverman 1991, 335-336; see also Citron 1987, for a critique of French history texts; see Anderson 1983, for a discussion of the history and development of nationalism). (I was told by a Parisian architect of Lebanese origin that he thought the French educational system was indeed the genius of the French creation of identity; through the education system all school children, of whatever origins, became French; personal communication, G.J., May 1991).

The Evian Agreement, in 1962, gave rights of citizenship to Algerians in France, except political rights. Children of these Algerians, born on French soil, are considered to be French citizens (under the concept of *ius soli*), even if they are not French under the concept of *ius sanguinis*, French by »blood« inheritance. Children of foreign-born parents, after five years of residence in France, have had the right to become French citizens. Recent legislative proposals (1986), since abandoned, focused on whether the Nationality Code should be changed so that children of foreigners born on French soil would have to wait until the age of eighteen and formally ask for the right to become citizens (see Bernstein 1990, 104).

Race, Class and Culture

In January of 1992 I spent two weeks in Montebéliard in order to finish some research on census material begun two summers earlier. While there, I discussed »race relations« in America and France with several residents. It appeared, one person thought, that the situation was somewhat similar in both countries: »There are now more North Africans in the area than there used to be. They seem to be different from the Lebanese. They are perhaps less intelligent than the Lebanese. It is economic reasons that create the problems; there are not enough jobs. They have a different religion and habits, which make them different from the Poles, Italians, and former Yugoslavs, who are Europeans. The people of the Maghreb of North Africa have not risen as much as the Lebanese or American blacks.« (M.E., personal communication, January, 1992).

An acquaintance of this person has a daughter who lives with a North African. The North African is all right, she says, but his mother is impossible. However, the North African is probably living with the French woman, says my informant, because it will help him get better benefits, ultimately of citizenship.

197

A retired worker from Peugeot, living on a pension in a house in Montebéliard and with a second vacation house in the south of France, was more direct. »The North Africans, I don't like them«, he said. »They all come here just for the benefits.« (C.A., personal communication, January, 1992).

The conversations wove together a number of reasons for their feelings about foreigners; they included differences in race, which appeared to include skin color and basic assumptions about the origins of these people, that people from Algeria and Morocco, particularly the Maghrebiens, were of a different race; differences in culture, in particular because of both Arabic dress and language and because of the practice of Islam; as well as certain indications about their taking a part of the economic pie which wasn't rightly theirs, through laying claim to French social security benefits.

Symbolic Construction of Identity: Social and Spatial Considerations

Since the 1960s, anthropologists such as Lévi-Strauss, Victor Turner, Fernandez, Geertz, Eva Hunt, Ortner, etc. have given much attention to the meaning, construction, use, and manipulation of symbols. While not necessarily all of the same school, their interpretations of meaning systems have had a wide impact on social and linguistic anthropology. More recently, interest in dialogue, narrative, discourse, textual analysis, and the problems of writing about »The Other« has permeated anthropological conferences and literature. Concepts of »multivocality«, of »many voices« speaking from many perspectives, or of single symbols which have many voices (Turner 1991) are utilized frequently.

More recently, Margaret Rodman, in an article in the *American Anthropologist* (»Empowering Place: Multilocality and Multivocality« 1992, 640-656) has pulled together an intriguing argument using concepts of »voice« and »place«. »Place, like voice and time, is a politicized social and cultural construct«, she argues, and »multilocality as well as multivocality can empower place conceptually and encourage understanding of the complex social construction of spatial meaning« (Rodman, 640).

In a paper I presented at the *American Anthropological Association* annual meeting in 1991 (Donahue 1991), I argued that the use of space in the town of Montebéliard reflects the way in which the inhabitants of the region think of themselves, either as owners and controllers of certain spaces during the celebration of Bastille Day (the French dancing to accordion music in the center town square) or as marginalized members of the society (the West and North Africans in the side streets, playing, listening, and dancing to West African music).

The question of »who controls this place?« is apparent in much of the discourse about race, citizenship, and culture carried out in Montebéliard in particular and in France in general. Napoleon's view that somehow children born in France, on French soil, inherit a spirit and feeling of Frenchness is still embodied in the French education system. If one absorbs the concepts of Frenchness through French textbooks, the system helps make one French. The textbook becomes a mediator for the instillation of spirit of the place. However, control of Frenchness still corresponds approximately to control of space and place, and it is still the case that many North Africans are consigned to living in high-rise apartment blocks in the banlieue, the suburbs of cities and towns such as Montebéliard. It is they who walk the streets of the central shopping district of Montebéliard during the noon hour, since it is too far to get back to their apartments from the Peugeot plant to have a good French lunch.

The complex social construction of spatial meaning which Rodman describes is not unlike the complex social construction of regional and national identity which has been operating at least since the nineteenth century in Europe and in some cases earlier.

Nation-states by the nature of their construction and inclusion of various peoples move through phases of incorporation and integration of different regions, regional peoples, and languages, as was the case in the construction of the French nation from the seventeenth century, during which Louis XIV moved to extend and reinforce the boundaries of France as he saw it. Various attempts since then by regions to detach themselves from France have never been very successful (Brittany, Besancon, for instance).

By the early nineteenth century both romanticism and nationalism served to create concepts of the spiritual quality of »Frenchness« of which Napoleon spoke earlier in this paper; that there was something in the French soil and the French air which, breathed in, made one French. This quality, this je ne sais quoi, cuts across class boundaries but creates a French culture in the minds of those who partake in it; and perhaps those who observe it. Until fairly recently, it was the French educational system which helped to create this common culture, which for a while could even cut across »racial« divisions too. But now that the French are feeling pressed, the observable symbolic markers which help to differentiate those who are not »French«, such as color and cultural appartenances such as dress, including girls' headscarves, help to identify those who are not as closely connected to the French national corporate body.

The state which extended its borders during a colonial period, and which declared many of those subject peoples to be French, has helped to create the situation now in hand. With »decolonization«, former colonial peoples have come to the metropole, and the French state now tries to regulate Frenchness through legal battles over such symbolic issues as the headscarves, or the attempt to impose the requirement to declare that you do indeed want to become a French citizen at the age of majority.

It is necessary to say that the state is a construct of people, and it is people who manage the affairs of state. Much as has happened in America in the last hundred years, and in South Africa, residents of France are drawn into the debate about being French, or foreign, and all who live there, and who create public policy, begin to define themselves in terms of who they are, or are not. This construction of identity is, at base, just that; a construction, linked through language and thought to the symbolling and imaging powers which we all possess, and worked out in various areas of human life, in economic relations and class divisions, through conflict and negotiation.

Conclusions

Rather than argue that violence stems from our animal instincts, separated from reason, the result of some atavistic sense and emotion, I have argued that instead it is useful to turn this concept on its head. What if, instead, violence is actually a cultural construct, determined and directed by cultural categories, boundaries, and symbolling activities? There is increasing evidence that animals, both non-human primates and other mammals, indeed other non-mammals such as birds, may be capable of far more symbolic activity than Western-trained scientists had ever thought possible. Since not all animals are uniformly violent or aggressive, it is possible that such violence arises in particular situations. Economic constraints or overcrowding have been suggested, yet even such situations do not always lead to violence. State societies do seem to produce and reproduce violence in defence and maintenance of boundaries, in creation of nation-states. The creation of others, such as ethnic groups leads to such boundary creation, and to exclusion from participation. Violence leads to such creation of ethnicity and difference, and helps to insure separation. Violence leads to the construction, production, and reproduction of cultural categories.

References

Anderson, B. (1983), *Imagined Communities*, London.

Bernstein, R. (1990), *Fragile Glory. A Portrait of France and the French*. New York.

Castles, St. and G. Kosack (1985), *Immigrant Workers and Class Structure in Europe*, London (2nd ed.).

Citron, S., (1987), *Le Mythe National: L'Histoire de France en question*, Paris.

Darnton, R. (1985), *The Great Cat Massacre*, New York.

Desir, H. (1990), »Interview«, in: *Le Débat*, no. 61, pp. 42-58.

Donahue, K.C. (1991), »Town, Region, State: The Construction of Social Identities in Montebéliard, France«, Paper given at the

American Anthropological Association Annual Meeting, Chicago, Illinois.

Feldman, A. (1991), *Formations of Violence*, Chicago.

Fernandez, J. (1991), »Beyond Metaphor: The Theory of Tropes in Anthropology«, in: *Anthropology*, Stanford.

Fitzgerald, T.K. (1993), *Metaphors of Identity: A Culture-Communication Dialogue*, Albany.

Freeman, G.P. (1979), *Immigrant Labor and Racial Conflict in Industrial Societies. The French and Bristisch Experience 1945-1975*, Princeton.

Fry, D.P. (1992), »»Respect for the Rights of Others is Peace«: Learning Aggression versus Nonaggression among the Zapotec«, In: *American Anthropologist*, 94(3), pp. 621-639.

Geertz, C. (1973), *The Interpretation of Cultures*, New York.

Grillo, R.D. (1985), *Ideologies and Institutions in Modern France*, Cambridge.

Husbands, C.T. (1991), »The Mainstream Right and the Politics of Immigration in France: Major Developments in the 1980s«, in: *Ethnic and Racial Studies*, 14(2), pp. 170-198.

Miles, R. and J. Singer-Kerel (1991), »Migration and Migrants in France«, in: *Ethnic and Racial Studies* 14(3).

Ortner, Sh. (1973), »On Key Symbols«, in: *American Anthropologist*, 75(6), pp. 1338-1357.

Power, M. (1991), *The Egalitarians, Human and Chimpanzee: An Anthropological View of Social Organisation*, New York.

Rodman, M. (1992), »Empowering Place: Multilocality and Multivocality«, in: *American Anthropologist*, 94(3), pp. 640-656.

Silverman, M. (1991), »Citizenship and the Nation-State in France«, in: *Migration and Migrants in France*, Miles, R. and J. Singer-Kerel (eds.), Special issue of *Ethnic and Racial Studies*, 14(3), pp. 333-349.

Singer-Kerel, J. (1991), »Foreign Workers in France, 1891-1936«, in: *Migration and Migrants in France*, Miles, R. and J. Singer-Kerel (eds.), Special issue of *Ethnic and Racial Studies*, 14(3), pp. 279-293.

Smith, A.D. (1993), *National Identity,* Reno (Nevada).

Tambiah, S. (1969), »Animals are Good to Think and Good to Prohibit«, in: *Ethnology*, 8(4), pp. 423-459.

Turner, V.(1974), *Dramas, Fields and Metaphors*, Ithaca, NY.

Roger Hewitt

Adolescence, Racism and Violence in South London

Background

The course of adolescent racism in London over the past twenty years has been characterised by (1) a sharpening of the distinction between ethnically mixed urban locations on the one hand and very predominantly white urban locations on the other; (2) a sustained but limited influence from neo-fascist organisations; (3) a gradually articulated hostile response to anti-racist policies in schools and other contexts; (4) a sustained participation in racial violence; (5) a continued sense of loss of sources of cultural identity amongst white working-class youth. This ad hoc collection of features is less unsystematic than it may seem.

The sharp rise, during the late 1970's and early 1980s, in the percentage of the population of African-Caribbean origin that was under the age of twenty, plus a particularly effervescent period of Caribbean popular cultural production, provided one of the bases of black/white youth solidarity in certain working-class areas of the capital, as well as in other cities in the U.K.. A localised, community-based anti-racism grew up amongst young people in many urban areas at that time, and inter-racial friendship, together with much conscious and unconscious cultural cross-influencing, became commonplace. As Gilroy and Lawrence put it, »In many areas the culture and politics of working-class youth exhibits a seamless and organic fusion of Black and White sensibilities« (1988, 141). This was culturally evident in the realms of musical affiliation, dress and language use, where both the direct and indirect impact of black adolescent speech forms was evident amongst working-class whites. Neither was this restricted to the mixing of white and African-Caribbean influences. In areas

where Turkish and Asian families had settled, similar, if less spec-
tacular influences could be seen (Hewitt 1986; Jones 1988; Sebba
1994; Rampton 1995).

In these predominantly inner-city areas, the older, strong lines of
insulation between cultures became eroded and transformed, creating
an urban sociocultural landscape that was quite different from that of
previous generations, of whatever ethnicity (Hewitt 1991; Hewitt
1995). While the inner city was still being characterised by some
policy makers, academics and journalists as a location of »racial tension«, it was in fact being transformed, so that while it was still true
that many older white people, especially in the traditional working-
class neighbourhoods, clung on to many of the ancient hostilities, the
younger generations of whites found themselves increasingly at odds
with their parents' generation. They had different social experiences
from their parents, and partook in a different, vigorous and rapidly-
developing multi-ethnic urban culture.

Where this was not so was within white enclave areas in the inner
city, particularly those parts of London, such as the docklands, where
traditional white working-class communities had lost their economic
base. Here, conununity closure, sometimes exacerbated by insensitive
local authority housing policies, continued to be articulated around
discourses of race and nation. Violent assaults on minorities and
various forms of racial harassment were, and continue to be, endemic
in the vicinity of such enclaves.

Similarly, from the late 1960s onwards, suburban areas, traditionally a site of middle-class settlement, became, along with the
»new town« developments in many parts of the country, a site of
white working-class relocation from the inner city areas, and a sign
of new social mobility. As ethnic minority families came to settle in
what had previously been exclusively white inner city neighbourhoods, suburbs and new towns became the destinations of »white
flight« where working-class and middle-class racial discourses
merged. Thus by the 1980s, although levels of racial harassment in
ethnically mixed areas were numerically higher than elsewhere, it
was often the predominantly white areas - enclaves, suburbs and
»new towns« that were experienced as the most dangerous for minorities and proportionately the level of harassment and assault were

extremely high (Wrench, Brar and Martin 1993; Hewitt 1992, 1996; Gordon 1990).

If these demographic and cultural trends were one relevant dimension of the racism that effected adolescents over this period, the politics of the racist political organisations was another. Neo-Fascist activism in the U.K. has been constant, if always limited in scale, since the 1930s. However, in the late 1970s and early 1980s, both the National Front and the openly Nazi »British Movement« made successful attempts to link racist politics to a skinhead youth cultural style, and to enlist the support of white youth. South London was especially prominent with respect to recruitment to racist parties and groups during this period, including suburban areas. One strategy that was used by racist activists was to simply state the connection in stickers reading »Skins Hate Wogs«. Another was to appeal to white male adolescents as victims of police unfairness. Thus, at a time when skinhead gang violence was at a peak, one leaflet distributed on the streets in the south east of the capital in 1979 showed a white boy being arrested by the police. It read: »This boy wishes he was black« and went on to assert that police gave preferential treatment to black youth. Such deliberate attempts at forging a necessary association between the skinheads and the far right were successful and racist political marches into the 1980s were characterised by a strong skinhead presence. Earlier phases of skinhead youth culture had not only been far less directly associated with racist politics but had actually been developed through a strong relation to the new urban black presence in music and dress codes (Hebdidge 1979). The early 1980s mark the high tide of the powerful symbolic association of skinhead style with racism and racist violence in the U.K. which was later to become part of the »natural« symbology of neo-fascism across Europe.

A third strand in the context of adolescent racism, was the gradual articulation of a white »backlash« to anti-racist and multicultural policies as articulated through local government. This was evident primarily through the adult white population, but also had resonances amongst the young, From the 1970s onwards, local government gradually came to reflect the presence of ethnic minorities through the implementation of multicultural, anti-racist and equal opportuni-

ties policies in schools, housing, leisure services and other departments, the creation of special units for racial equality, and the elaboration of various committees and posts having as their brief the interests of the different minorities. Developments of these kinds were
occurring over the same period in many parts of London and in other
cities in the U.K. (Ball and Solomos 1990; Gilroy 1992; Solomos
1993). These developments were both established and contested
within a local politics transected not only by party lines, but also by
the emergent political formations within the various ethnic communities.

There were two distinct phases to the backlash to these processes.
The first was part of an onslaught by the Conservatives on left-wing
local government, where resistance to the policies of central government during the Thatcher years were often most evident. In a conver-
gence of different sets of political interests, during the 1980s many
Labour local authorities were attacked through the right wing press
and other channels, for a »loony leftism« that anti-racism in particular came to symbolize. The budgets of politically active local authorities were cut and gradually the number of local authority units
specifically dedicated to ethnic minority community issues, including
racial harassment, dwindled almost to zero.

While »town hall anti-racism« was also not without its critics on
the left and from within an anti-racist perspective (Macdonald; Gilroy), a second wave of popular white »backlash« has also become
evident in some areas, which takes as its concern not only local government equal opportunities policies, for example, but also putative
police and media over-attention to racial incidents including racist
assault. Events in the London Borough of Greenwich, in the south
east, are characteristic of this trend. In 1991 a sixteen year old black
boy was murdered by a gang of white youths in Thamesmead, a
large, predominantly white housing estate bordering the river
Thames. Following the murder a march was held organised by local
black and anti-racist groups particularly concerned with the activities
of the British National Party (BNP), the most prominent of the racist
political groups currently active in the U.K., which had established a
headquarters and »bookshop« in the London Borough of Bexley, just
beyond the Greenwich border. The media attention received by these

events, including a television programme and a number of features in national newspapers, generated a great deal of resentment amongst whites in Thamesmead, who believed they were being characterised as extreme racists by association. At the same time the claim was repeatedly made that assaults on whites by blacks were ignored by the police and the media whilst those by whites on blacks were always characterized as racist regardless of their nature (Hewitt 1992). This apparently trivial and local belief is in fact widely articulated and takes a variety of forms. It is interesting to note that it is also a version of the »unfairness to whites« theme evident in the British Movement leaflet of the late 1970s cited above.

The »unfairness« theme functions especially to deflect the need to address the issue of racial harassment and assault, especially in those parts of London where levels of racial attack are highest. According to police statistics, the London Boroughs of Tower Hamlets and Newham in the east end, and Greenwich in the south east have the highest levels of racial incidents in the capital (Metropolitan Police Performance Information Bureau). In each of these areas the theme of »unfairness« to whites is commonly articulated *across* social class lines. The case of Greenwich, dubbed by the press »the racist murder capital of the UK«, is particularly illuminating.

Greenwich - A Case Study

Lying in the south east of the capital, the London Borough of Greenwich (LBG) extends from the inner city districts on the south side of the Thames, opposite the east-end docklands, southwards and eastward to the more affluent suburbs. Of the total population of 208.000, 117.000 inhabitants live within the waterfront wards, some of which have male unemployment levels of above 30%, reaching over 40% in some months. Overall unemployment stands at 14.9%, and over the last thirty years the area has seen a dramatic decline in manufacturing jobs available, from 33.000 in 1966 to just over 6.000 today (Source: Department of Employment). The local economy is severely depressed. Average earnings in Greenwich are low even for those in employment. In April 1993 average male earnings were £90.

per week lower in Greenwich than in its neighbouring inner city boroughs to the west. (Source: New Earnings Survey 1990 - 1993) A
recent study, Breadline Greenwich 1994, showed that 26% of Greenwich residents lived in households with an income of less than
£5.000 pa. in 1993.

Immigrants from what was then called the British Commonwealth
began to arrive in the early 1950s when people from south Asia -
mainly Jat Sikhs - also began to settle in small communities in parts
of the borough. Gujerati small traders and Sikh artisans from East
Africa followed in the late 1960s. According to the 1991 census,
4.2% of the population (32.1% of the ethnic minority population) describe their ethnic origin as Indian, Pakistani or Bangladeshi. By the
early 1980s people from the Caribbean constituted another distinct
minority and now comprise 2.5% of the population (19.7% of the
ethnic minority population). Other groups, from Vietnam and Somalia and other parts of Africa, also make up the borough's 12.8%
ethnic minority population. The remaining 87.2% are white.

Today the ethnic minority population is most strongly represented
in the wards to the north and north east of the borough, where the
percentage of minorities ranges from 20% to above 30%. These figures (drawn from 1991 census data) do not include many of the 8.000
refugees living in Greenwich, since the number of refugees, especially those from Somalia, has grown considerably over the past four
years. The wards in the south and in parts of the west are very predominantly white, with ethnic minority populations as small as 2.5%
- 5%. Many of these white majority neighbourhoods contain low-rent
housing estates that were developed by the council during the 1920s,
1930s and 50s. An initially well-meant but ultimately discriminatory
housing allocation policy designed to nurture community through
kinship - the »sons and daughters« policy - which continued until
very recently, resulted, however, in such estates remaining almost
exclusively white. The distinctly »white« areas constitute a social
mixture of redbrick, working-class homes and suburban mock-Tudor
middle-class residences. The appearance is often pure suburban, the
reality more complex. These areas have been the site of some of the
worst instances of racial violence in the borough.

While the precise breakdown of racial incidents varies from year to year, the 1994/5 annual report of the Greenwich Action Committee Against Racial Attacks (GACARA), a monitoring group sponsored by the borough Council, provides tables showing that in the year from June 1994 to May 1995 there were a total of 265 racial attacks within the borough, 39.6% of these being against African Caribbeans and 32.8% against people of Indian, Pakistani and Bangladeshi origin, with the remainder divided mainly between the various refugee groups such as the Vietnamese and Somali communities. Approximately 75% of all racial assaults took place on or near to the low-rent public housing estates provided by the local housing authority. These assaults were in addition to other racial incidents such as threats of violence, racist abuse, graffiti, damage to property, etc. Even the monitoring unit of the police division serving that part of the borough containing the highest number of ethnic minority people recorded and investigated four hundred racial incidents of varying degrees of seriousness during 1994.

While the largest *number* of racial attacks in Greenwich occur in those neighbourhoods with the largest ethnic minority population, proportional to the size of the minority populations in particular wards, neighbourhoods which are very predominantly white but with high levels of deprivation also feature conspicuously. These white majority areas were also the location of the most serious cases of violent racial assault. The murder, by stabbing, of the black teenager Rolan Adams 1991 mentioned above was followed by two more, those of Rohit Dugal in 1992 and Steven Lawrence 1993, in each case by gangs of white male adolescents in the age range 16 - 23 years. Indeed the ward in which the last two of these murders were committed ranks amongst the highest on the Poverty and Social Deprivation Index for Greenwich but is flanked on several sides by other predominantly white wards ranking the lowest.

Despite the above average levels of unemployment, low earnings amongst some groups, and poor housing quality in some wards, social and economic conditions in the borough as a whole are by no means the worst in London and can not be equated in any simple or direct way with the borough's high levels of racial assault and harassment. A number of London boroughs have far worse profiles in all of these respects but without such high levels of racial harassment. Neither can the correlation be made on the smaller scale of ward and sub-ward level. A number of factors are likely to be at work against the backdrop of social and economic conditions. These may include, for example, community relations derived from the specific demographic and historical features of the white and minority communities, promoting racism differentially across a range of social bases family, adolescent peer-group, work place, school etc. They may also include the processes by which wider ideological issues become articulated within the local political order.

In addition to these features, it is also of significance that the headquarters of the extreme racist organisation, the British National Party (BNP), is located just a mile or two beyond the Greenwich border. This organisation has links with other European white supremacist political groups and with similar groups in the U.S.A.. Race-hate stickers and posters produced by the U.S.-based »White Aryan Resistance« and by an openly Nazi group based in Lincoln, Nebraska, have appeared in recent times on the streets of Greenwich. The BNP also has strong links, and to some extent an overlapping membership, with terrorist organisations in the U.K., particularly with a British terrorist organisation, »Combat 18«, which has been responsible for a number of vicious attacks on ethnic minorities, on academics and professionals working in the race field, and on various political opponents. The BNP has been publicly active in Greenwich since establishing its headquarters in 1991 and has put up candidates for election in local Council elections in Greenwich and elsewhere in London - including once successfully, if only temporarily, just over the Thames in Tower Hamlets in 1993.

Racism amongst White Adolescents

Adolescent racism in the LBG has been recorded since at least the early 1970s when immigrants from the New Commonwealth were even fewer in number. By the late 1970s recruitment to racist political organisations, such as the National Front and the British Movement, and informal affiliation to those groups, was particularly prominent amongst young people in the borough and was closely associated with skinhead youth-cultural style. There were many skinhead gangs in the area at that time and the LBG was the site of the most successful national recruitment to the neo-nazi British Movement. In addition to skinhead racist politics, there was also a strong strand of quotidian racism that eschewed both political association with racist political groups and skinhead stylisties. This was less visible but may constitute the more enduring type of racism in the borough, growing, as it appeared to do, out of working-class conununity closure and embedded within a long history of local class identity formation (Roediger 1991; 1994). Woolwich, the administrative centre of the borough, was an important town in the early development of the co-operative and labour movements in the south of England around the turn of the century and subsequently (Crossick 1979; Hewitt 1986).

The recent upsurge in racist activity in the borough bears traces of both of these histories, although skinhead style *per se* is for the most part absent. Racist graffiti in the borough commonly demonstrates a symbolic allegiance to the BNP, although actual membership and activism amongst young people is low. In the predominantly white areas recent graffiti includes »Kill All Blacks«, as well as the insignia of political groups, »BNP«, »NF«, »KKK« and on defiled gravestones in the parish church-yard, a drawing of a masked skinhead in Nazi salute beside the inscription: »BRITISH ARIAN RACE AND NATION«. Other inscriptions give a less ideologized message: »WATCH OUT COONS, your now ENTERING ELTHAM«.

Other public evidence of popular racism resides in the large number of racist jokes that are in circulation amongst young people, as well as school-yard rhymes, particularly about Pakistani and Indian shopkeepers. There is also a virulent strain of »nigger jokes« similar in kind to those still circulating on the internet and emanating from Michigan (*The Guardian:* April 30th, 1994) There is no evidence of any direct connection to the internet source, but the kind of humour is certainly recognisable. It serves to project black people as cultural anti-matter and appears to link into the crediting of black people with bestiality and the origins of AIDS.

While formal recruitment of the young to racist political groups very low, in certain parts of the borough the initials of racist political groups, such as the BNP and the NF, are consistently used by young people to map out a territory as distinctly a »white area«. While it would be a mistake to account for adolescent racism by reducing it to the expression of some form of territorialism, either innate or learned, very clear articulations of territoriality are evident in both what young people say about issues of race and ethnicity, and of how certain neighbourhoods are marked out with graffiti of different kinds. Although this may seem to share something of the characteristics of, say, football club fan tribalisms which are also often mapped onto a territorial base, to reduce it to just another manifestation of this aspect would be to misconceive the nature of racism and its ability to integrate with various sociocultural processes. Probably of far wider significance is the way in which local community itself has been eroded in recent years, especially insofar as this has a bearing on the life trajectories of young men - the primary perpetrators of racial violence.

Locality, community, neighbourhood combine geographical, social and imaginary elements in ways which function differently for different groups. For young men from working-class areas in particular, and to a lesser extent for young women also, conununity has meant something very specific at the economic level: a network of kinship and friendship associations that can provide an informational resource with resect to jobs, training, housing, buying and selling, and other activities within the »black economy«. This informal economy, particularly with regard to employment and training - with fathers, uncles, brothers etc. - within a relatively stable ecology of small businesses in such domains as the construction and transport industries, has been drastically eroded, particularly since the near collapse of the housing market. Where once formal and informal apprenticeships would have come on-stream for boys even from their early teens onwards, now not only has the old formal apprenticeship system been abandoned but the web of contacts and associations that provided the basis for informal tutelage has been decimated. Where once negative attitudes to schooling and to the »need to prepare for the world of employment« as it was characterised within secondary education, were regularly vindicated by the ability of young men to find jobs and training through their own *informal* associations, now the old »school refusing« attitudes persist but are no longer supported by any independently-fuelled material success. Male adolescents are left with the rhetories and attitudes of previous generations, but time, and the economy, has moved on leaving them stranded. »Community« has let them down as material provider and exists now as »locality«, with boundaries but with little internal social coherence. These boundaries are, of course, readily racialized.

It is here in particular that the »white backlash« evident in middle-class discourses as much as working-class ones becomes especially salient. Here, the voice of white working-class adolescents seeking to drown out the protests of the black minorities with regard to the racism they experience, articulates with the racialized struggles over the local political order conducted by parts of the middleclass local electorate. Both a party-based and non-party articulation of the view that »too much attention« is given to minority issues, serves to combine with other voices in the *discourse of unfairness* that forms a serious obstacle to the redress of racial harassment and assault.

All of these local processes have been particularly relevant to the bifurcation of adolescent »race relations« in south London in general in recent years. On the one hand white enclaves have developed a consistent and sometimes virulent strain of racism that is especially focused amongst the young. On the other hand a newly emergent, multicultural and commonly evident cultural hybridity have come to dominate the inner city socio-scape, infusing social relationships, especially amongst the young, with a new flexibility and potential creativity. To the latter may be attributed a kind of spontaneous and culturally encoded anti-racism inherent in the very lack of vigilance along potential cultural and social boundaries. To the former mnay be attributed its reverse: an obstinate racialization of social and geographical boundaries, a forlorn re-iteration of moribund attitudes and rhetories. Both exist within the same set of crude economic indicators unemployment and wage levels, etc. - and both suffer from much the same degree of social insecurity. But while the cultural and social mixing of inner city life both reflects and contributes to the global trend towards flexibility, change and the flowing distribution of cultural elements through numerous diasporas, the boundary vigilance of the enclave cultures reflect a hopeless, backward-looking order that is imprisoning the young in a spiral of cultural vacuity. Violence in general and racial violence in particular is one of the most obvious manifestations of this condition.

Thus although racial violence amongst adolescents in south London has maintained consistently high levels over the past twenty years, the social, economic and cultural conditions that have produced these have not remained the same. Furthermore, as the severity of racial attacks has worsened in some areas, elsewhere good »race relations« have developed in parallel, creating an implicit critique of purely economistic accounts of racism and its spread. (The »riots« in many British cities in the early 1980s, it will be remembered, witnessed, in a way quite unanticipated by the sociologies of both race and youth, black and white adolescents side by side against the police. This black and white »brotherhood of despair« was attributed to »unemployment« with the same readiness that »unemployment« is also trundled in to simplistically explain racism itself.) Hope, in this situation, resides, therefore, not in structural miracles but in superstructural energy. The very fact of cultural variation in the manifestations of racism and racial violence lend a certain urgency and optimism to new strategies for countering adolescent racism through mass youth anti-racist movements, through imaginative youth work programmes, and through a relentless commitment to inter-cultural and anti-racist educational programmes.

References

Ball, W. and J.Solomos (1990), *Race and Local Politics*, Basingstoke.

Crossick (1979), Crossick, G. (1978), *An Artisan Elite in Victorian Society: Kentish London 1840-1880*, London.

Gilroy, P. (1992), »The End of Anti-Racism«, in: Donald, J. and A. Rattansi (eds.), *»Race«, Culture and Difference*, London.

Gilroy, P. and E. Lawrence (1988), »Two-tone Britain: white and black youth and the politics of anti-racism«, in: Cohen, P. and H. Baines (eds.), *Multiracist Britain*, Basingstoke.

Gordon, P. (1990), *Racial Violence and Harassment*, London.

Hebdidge, D. (1979), *Subculture: the Meaning of Style*, London.

Hewitt, R. (1986), *White Talk Black Talk: Inter-racial Friendship and Communication Amongst Adolescents*, Cambridge.

Hewitt, R. (1991), »Language, Youth and the Destabilization of Ethnicity«, in: C. Palmgren, K. Lovgren and G. Bolin (eds.), *Ethnicity in Youth Culture*, Stockholm.

Hewitt, R. (1992), *Sagaland: Youth Culture, Racism and Education; A Re-port On Research Carried Out in Thamesmead*, London.

Hewitt, R. (1996), *Routes of Racism: The Social Bases of Racist Action*, Stoke.

Hesse, B., D. Rai, C. Bennett, M. Lone and P. McGilchrist (1992), *Beneath the Surface: An Enquiry into Racial Harassment in the London Borough of Waltham Forest*, London.

Jones, S. (1988), *Black Culture White Youth*, Basingstoke.

Macdonald, I. (1989), *Murder in the Playground: the Report of the Macdonald Inquiry into Racism and Racial Violence in Manchester Schools*, London.

Rampton, B. (1995), *Crossing: Language and Ethnicity Among Adolescents*, London.

Roediger, D. (1991), *The Wages of Whiteness: Race and the Making of the American Working Class*, London/New York.

Roediger, D. (1994), *Towards the Abolition of Whiteness*, London/New York.

Sebba, M. (1993), *London Jamaican: Language Systems in Interaction*, London.

Solomos, J. (1993), »The Local Politics of Racial Equality«, in: Cross, M. and M. Kelth (eds.), *Racism, the City and the State*, London.

Wrench, J., H. Brar and P. Martin (1993), *Invisible Minorities: Racism in New Towns and New Contexts*, Monographs in Ethnic Relations No.6, Centre For Research in Ethnic relations, University of Warwick.

III.

Descriptive-Empirical Studies

Ralf Bohnsack

»Episodical Community of Fate«
and Youth Violence:
A Qualitative Analysis of Hooligan Groups

Since sociologists began taking deviant and violent behavior of young people as a topic of empirical research (Thrasher 1927, Shaw 1930), two features have always been emphasized: the episodic character of juvenile delinquency (among others: Matza 1964) and the importance of the peer group in this context. There exist nonetheless, as has been commented upon in past years, no theoretical models explaining the episodic character[1].

As we were able to show in our study this is dependent mainly on the fact that the specific problem of the adolescent development in young workers, the group appearing most often in the crime statistics, has until now hardly been taken into consideration. The reason for this in the area of criminology, is that the labeling-approach, which can be very fruitful when taken on a paradigmatic-theoretical level, limits itself in the discussion in Germany to an analysis of the agencies of social control[2]. A remarkable gap is also to be seen in social research on juveniles in the area concerning adolescent development of either young workers or young adults from »less well educated« population groups. This is true too for those studies specializing in the phenomenona of youth violence[3]. Also to be seen in this regard is the central role played by the peer group in the emergence of deviant behavior in young people and more importantly, in the readiness to commit violence. This has been empirically verified but remains theoretically poorly explained.

These particular theoretical weaknesses are due primarily to the fact that the importance of the practice of collective behavior in regards to the process of socialisatoric interaction has, untill now, hardly been taken into consideration. Howard S. Becker already had put the practice of collective behavior in to the center of empirical analysis in his study »Outsiders«. He emphasized, »Instead of the deviant motives leading to the deviant behaviour, it is the other way around, the deviant behaviour in time produces the deviant motivation« (Becker 1963, 42).

The practical accomplishment of everyday activities beyond or below utilitarian motives and intentions has gained a new and central importance in the current theoretical discussion (from the »praxeological epistemology« of Bourdieu to the category of »practical consciousness« according to Giddens 1984). A valid methodical access to the practice of activity accomplishment is required for a successful application of these concepts. This access can be gained through the methodologically based procedures of the qualitative or »reconstructive« social research (see Bohnsack 1993).

Using the concepts of »*habitual activity*« and »*habitual concordance*«, which we have been developed in our empirical analysis, we worked out processes of socialization and of the emergence of »habitual elements of style« in peer groups.

Central to our study are groups of Hooligans from the former East and West Berlins, which were compared with rockbands, with an inconspicuous group, and with a group of potentially violent leftist youth from the former East Berlin[4]. One of the reasons for doing this was to avoid the premature identification of the peculiarities in orientation and conspicuous biographical features of the young workers as being constitutive elements of a »criminal career«, but rather to establish them in general theoretical design of socialization in peer groups of young workers.

It is then possible to work out in comparative analysis the unique biographical conditions which lead to specific practical actions in the adolescent development, such as violent behavior. It can be shown that, the much discussed thesis of milieu-specific desintegration, although not false, is too general and one dimensional.

As our results show, experiences of milieu-specific desintegration or of »habitual insecurity« are dealt with in very different ways. Of great importance here is, among other things, how far communication within the family goes toward provision of conditions for (meta-)

communicative coping with orientation problems and for the development of personal identity.

Theoretical Foundations, Methodology and Methods

According to Becker, one of the founders of the labeling-approach, the analysis of the definition processes of the agencies of social control was still connected with the analysis of the daily practices of those, whose activities these definitions are focused on[5]. These areas are currently dealt with in isolation without sufficient reference to each other. Criminology in Germany deals, as mentioned earlier, mainly with the analysis of the everyday activities of the agencies involved in social control.

In prominent german studies about youth violence on the other hand, the systemic importance of the potential for deviance and violence due to the intervention through these agencies and through isolation pressure from the general public is given insufficient consideration. Generally one finds an *»objectivistic«* access to social reality in these studies. This means that »objective« social reality is dealt with as a phenomenon analysed seperately from the »subjective« experience. So, for example, Heitmeyer (1992) differentiates »potentials of desintegration« from »experiences of desintegration« whereby the former are considered objective and thus not open to empirical examination, which is only applied to the latter, the *»experiences* of desintegration«. It is also found in studies like those by Heitmeyer et al. (1992), which represent themselves as »qualitative«, that this aspect, qualitative analysis, is often equated with the analysis of the »subjective«. Here we find that, through this »key epistemological difference« (Matthes 1992) between »objective reality« and »subjective experience« in the process of empirical research, a tacit presupposal takes place concerning what those being studied can experience or in which framework an empirical analysis of these experiences is to take place. This categorical framework is then not thoroughly theoretically explicated and, more importantly, the milieu-specific preconceptions of the researchers themselves become integrated in its conceptualization of that framework. In doing so a privileged access to social reality is claimed without it having been methodologically legitimated.

In the sociology of knowledge developed by Karl Mannheim, in discourse with among others, Marx and Durkheim, this »key epistemological difference« (and the objectivism attached to it) has become obsolete. This is due to the fact that social »existence«, social positioning finds its place not outside of the experience of those being studied, but from the onset can only be constituted through the mutual aspects of the biographical experience of the practical actions, of the socialization history, and in general of common fate. And it can only then become empirically tangible. Mannheim (1982) was especially interested in not limiting the analysis of collectivity, of collective representations to its being done in terms of their »reification« as in the sense of Durkheim. Belonging to the same milieu, to the same generation for example, means then integration in a common nexus of experiences, in a»conjunctive experiential communitiy« or in a »conjunctive experiential space« (Mannheim 1982, 194). An analysis of social environment in this sense always means an analysis of (collective) biographies, of common »sediments of experience« (for this conception of milieu see also Bohnsack 1993).

Those sharing conjunctive experience need not neccessarily live together as a *group*. Using the »nexus of generation« as a conjunctive experiential space as an example, Mannheim has shown, that it is formed by a common sediment of experience, based on common experiences of particular historical events and developments in the practical action. And this without direct communication between those connected through these common experiences and belonging thusly to the same generation. But these generation- and milieu-specific *collective experiences* and orientations are *articulated* in a comprehensive manner only when those having these experiences in common come together, for instance, in peer groups.

The empirical access to the process of coming to terms with experiences and problems and to the process of socialization in the peer group presupposes a detailed reconstruction of the discourses during which the articulations took place. Because of this we prefer the method of group discussion (see Bohnsack 1996) in addition to that of the »narrative interview« and participant observation. The analysis is based on new methods of text interpretation (see Bohnsack et al. 1995 and Bohnsack 1993).

In our study, which was financed by the DFG (Deutsche Forschungsgemeinschaft)[6], we dealt with intensive case analysis of more than 60 peer groups. The results reported here are based mainly on four cases from the Hooligan Scene in Berlin. These cases were submitted to a comparative analysis as follows; one group belonging to the Hooligan hardcore in the former East Berlin, one consisting of peripheral members of this group, one consisting of the girlfriends of the hardcore members, and one consisting of Hooligans from the former West Berlin. The hardcore group from a satellite town on the edge of the former East Berlin was, as mentioned earlier, compared with other groups of young workers from the same district[7].

In favor of a presentation of our results, I will now go no further into the explication of the theoretical and methodological backrounds of our research, which are based in the Chicago School, the labeling-approach and the sociology of knowledge by Mannheim, particularly the »documentary method« (see Mannheim 1952a, Bohnsack 1992 and 1995)[8].

First some general remarks on the adolescent development in young workers. In so doing I would also like to refer to the results of an earlier study[9].

General Features of Adolescent Development in Young Workers

There appear with the passage from school to job and the first experiences relating to working life problems concerning orientation and the meaning of life. This causes the young people to experience more or less a crisis, mainly because they are so little prepared for this transition. In order to understand this it is necessary to look more carefully at the specific structure and temporal character of young workers biographical orientations and prospects in life. These are little influenced through a practical orientation in regards to an institutionalized pattern of training and career. Of much more importance is an orientation in reference to the more intimate aspects of environment-specific life, such as the neighborhood, the quarter, the affinity with their experiential spaces of a common daily life and the cyclic activities connected with them.

The challenge of the search for habitual concordance presents itself everywhere where an uninterrupted integration into such communities, such »habitual concordances«, into the milieuspecific everyday activities is missing. The search is not primarily theoretical or reflexive, but is realized, and this is crucial to understanding it, through spontaneous practical actions, in other words through *actionisms*. There where a commonality of the history of socialization is only partially present, it is, so to speak, produced. Commonality produced in this way, be it that of making of music, or that of fighting, connects through its development of a history of social interaction, even if this is episodical. This is due to the common experiences of depending on each other, of confronting danger, and of a »collective effervescence« in the sense of Durkheim.

An understanding of these processes of socialization based in collective actionisms presupposes an ambitious theoretical conception of the practice of action, which although it is not to be understood as primarily intentional and therefore rule or norm oriented, is none the less regular[10].

The socialisatoric interaction is grounded in the practice of and the search for habitual concordance, through the means of actionism. The rock groups in the study serve as an example of a specific type of collective actionism. I would like to now refer to them before later taking up the Hooligans.

Seeking for Habitual Concordance: The Rock Groups

In regards to the rock groups we can speak of an »aesthetic actionism«. The attempt at the development of collective elements of style, sometimes with a minimum of musical or technical training, is not a product of intention or one resulting from theoretical ideas or designs. Researchers questions concerning theoretical or reflexive intentions in their own music productions were always firmly denied or answered ironically.

Habitual concordance results from the process of »making« itself, and leads, if hindered, to a new constellation within the group or to a move to another group. The change in groups is in this respect not accidental or chaotic but rather one that follows the inherent laws of development through trial and the development of a collective habitus. Collective actionism is the medium which allows for testing how far and in what respect the personal elements of style may be condensed and intensified into a collective style. This creats an orientation framework and thereby security regarding decisions in daily life, for instance in the search for a partner. This environment-specific way of dealing with the problems of adolescence appears, therefore, to be immanently »rational« and can not be characterized, for example, as a »magic« solution, even though ritually produced and thusly far removed from any intentional rationalism[11].

The concern here is much more one of establishing a positive understanding and concept of ritual action, which is missing in sociology (see criticism by Douglas 1970). This again is due to weaknesses in the theoretical and methodological conceptualization of practical action.

The collective and ritually produced actionism of music production as a medium for the search for aesthetic-stylistic orientation presupposes a relatively high level of organization and communicative coordination, these being based on a trusting reciprocity of perspectives.

This though appears precarious in the Hooligans, the other groups that we intensively studied.

Episodical Community of Fate: The Hooligans

Collective actionism as observable by the hooligans assumes hat might be called planlessness, this being not the organizational form seen with the band but rather one of the »mob«, as the youths themselves put it. The football riot is paradigmatic for the mobilization of the »mob«. The activities of the »mob« are organised in a rudimentary, hierarchical way by well known and »fight proven« identification figures, who are always looking for the »fight« (the english term is used by the german youth) and this preferably with other hooligans. The fight has primarily the function of entanglement in the compulsions of a »situative actionism«. It is the self initiating and unanticipatable dramaturgy in the fight situation, with its trajectory like nature, and the resulting dependence of the fighters that constitute an elementary form of collectivity, an episodal community of fate. We find similar phenomenons, though under other conditions, in sports or among combatants at the front.

The personal identity, with its premise of freedom from bodily harm, retreats behind the focus on collective actionism and becomes reconstituted, also in its group specific attributes, through this and through the resulting episodical community of fate. The momentum of the process defies utilitaristic control and produces »secondary motives«[12].

The subordination of personal identity as well as its newly produced form in relation to the group point out the precarious nature of the previous biography and identity.

The aim at the same time is that of severing the ties to the everyday existence, to be somehow catapulted, at least on the weekend, out of the everyday and the workaday. »To switch off from life«, »to break the rythm« are the metaphors that the youths use to describe what we call »episodical negation of everyday existence«[13]. The actionism gains its function through the emergence of an episodical community of fate while at the same time serving as an episodical negation of everyday existence. A utilitaristic orientation towards victory over the opponent or even to his destruction takes it place at the rear. It is rather, at least among Hooligans, a readiness for gradually formed and lasting friendship (»Freundschaftsbereitschaft«), formed through the fight and through beating on each other (»Sich Klatschen«), that is the aimed for, as paradox as it may seem.

The Precarious Character of Rules and the Reciprocity of Perspectives

It is based on this understanding of the fight, of the rules of fairness (the »fair fight«) then that the rules of reciprocity are gradually established. They are extracted from the narrations and descriptions by the Hooligans and formulated finally in an comprehensible fashion. It is through these rules of fairness, their own fightworthiness and the resulting comradeship (»Kameradschaft«), that the hardcore members; i.e. identification figures, of the group distinguish themselves from the »mob« and establish their claim to leadership over it. Therein lies the importance of the initiation of learning processes regarding rules and reciprocity for this particular peer group. The rules of reciprocity remain precarious when the encounters involve other than Hooligans. In contacts for instance, with »leftists«, the rules of fairness are paid little attention. The youths are well aware of this discrepancy.

The precarious nature of the reciprocity of perspectives[14] can also be observed in the establishment of intimate relationships between the Hooligans and their girlfriends, with whom we also carried out a group discussion. A habitual concordance on the level of situative actionisms is here too the precarious basis, which shows itself in »getting a crush« or being »randy«. If this basis no longer exists then there occurs a radical reversal into »disgust«.

Communication Within the Family

The analysis of biographical interviews allows for insights into the background of the history of socialization. Firstly regarding the family; the difficulty as regards the history of socialization does not lie in the fact that the families, seen from the outside, are no longer intact. This particular problem is observable not only with the Hooligans but in the other groups as well. It is not for example the suicide of the father or the divorce of the parents as such which present a problem. It lies much more in the silence surrounding the father's suicide or the divorce that has already taken place. Assurance of continuity on the reflexive level is needed where there has been a break, often related to the loss of milieu-specific security, in the continuity of family life. This can take place on the level of a communication in particular about the individuals childhood history in relation to the family. It is significant that references to this type of communication are missing from the biographical interviews with the Hooligans. Such an *»elimination of the family-related childhood history«* becomes especially apparent in a comparative analysis with the rock groups where detailed narratives about childhood are to be found. This loss of communicative understanding in the families of the Hooligans is found not only in cases of *compulsory authoritarian interaction* (»the total pressure«) but also the socialization mode of »unconditional permissiveness« (»everything was served to me on a silver platter«). An experiential space for communicative bargaining about principles and borders is unlikely to develop in either case.

Provocation and the Experience of Society as a Total Institution

It is the non-open communication that has become a problem for the young people. And the provocation in public is a reaction to the experience of such non-open communication. The aim of provocation is to establish which (moral) principles and destinctions »actually« or »really« are behind the actions of others. This does not occur though through some sort of understanding concerning rules and principles but rather through the use of actionism to force the other to take a position. It concerns a »character contest« as Goffman (1972) has called it.

Emblems and stylistic presentations are also chosen for their provocative nature. The young people during the »GDR« times for example presented themselves as fans of the Berlin Football Club (BFC), which in those days was known as a »Stasi Club« (Stasi=State Security Police), in order to provoke those opposed to the Stasi. At the same time they had adopted the Skinhead outfit in order to shock the real fans of BSC or as it was, the Stasi itself. During »GDR« times the young people from »East Berlin« concentrated their provocations on testing those who they considered to have a »double standard«, on testing the the »squares« (Spießer) and the »narrow minded« (Schichtler). Double standard here means among other things, that hidden behind an emphasis on efficiency and discipline there lies political conformity (in school for instance). This is an essential part of of the »total pressure« experienced by the youth. Society appears then as completely institutionalized. »Society is like the army« is what is said in the group discussion, with the english term »army « being used.

Double Stigmatization - Imprisonment and the Consolidation of the Hooligan Career

It was just this double standard that was used to strike back against the youth and their provocative reaction to the double standard and the »total pressure«. The provocation was not only disciplinarily stigmatized and criminalized but simultaneously politicized in a way that was at the time unpenetrable. This double stigmatization created alienation and a trajectory of marginalization. As in the case of Arno, one of the hard core members of the East Berlin Hooligan scene, who, as a consequence of having been involved in a village brawl at the age of 16, not only was labeled a »youthful violent offender« but also as »an opponent of the state«. As a result he was sent to a maximum security prison rather than a juvenile hall of detention. In connection with further provocative confrontations with the authorities he took the description »rightist« and eventually »nazi« as used by others and used them as a stylistic reference to himself. As he says in the biographical interview; »at the time of the second trial at the latest you say to yourself: ›okay so you're calling me a nazi, then I am one, so what do you expect, anyway?‹ Yeah, to shock all those people, just sitting there«.

At a certain point of alienation there appears a provocative self incrimination. It is here the last remaining possibility to preserve elements of autonomy and self determination, and also therefore of dignity. This has already been recognized by David Matza (1964). The »turning point« or tearing down of the wall (»Wende«) was not seen as a trigger for orientation crises but as an opening of the way for the potential enactment of already existing orientation crises. This potential occurred because of the temporary paralysis on the part of the agencies of social control, because of the so called »control vacuum« and because of the new legal situation.

The situational actionisms and provocations of the Hooligans are hardly understandable within the framework of political conviction, ideologies, or theories. They are much more, as we have seen, political self presentations and emblems in the service of provocation and situational actionism, and the resulting episodal community of fate. This means then, that when the situational actionism loses its funtion due to progress in the adolescent development ,it suddenly appears »totally senseless« to have been such a »rightest idiot«. That is what is heard at the age of 19 in a group on the fringes of the Hooligan scene; at the end therefore of a crisis filled phase of adolesent development, a phase that we found in various forms in all groups of young workers. We labeled it the »phase of negation«. The Hooligans in the hardcore, on the other hand, although older, have still not completed this phase. The reasons for this become clear when the two groups are compared in respect to their socialization histories. Although reports about delinquent behavior are similar in both groups, only members of the hardcore have prison experience. These experiences of inprisonment, in particular those of coerced sexual relations with other inmates, are characterized in group discussions as an extreme loss of personal integrity and identity. These experiences become even more important when considered in regard to the socialization history in that they consolidate the attitude that fighting is the basis for development of sociality and belonging rather than communication based on the acknowledgement of perspective, of personal identity, and of the uniqueness of the person. At the same time in the group discussions the prison stay becomes a central proof, a privileged experience with which the hardcore members explicitly legitimize their claim to leadership. All of this binds them to a Hooligan career.

It is thusly the official stigmatization, taken over as provocative self identification as rightist or as nazi, and also the consequences of imprisonment that are decisive, not only in the intensity of the Hooligan career, but also in the hinderance or prevention of its discontinuation.

Notes

1 See critically: Mariak and Schumann (1992), also Peters (1985) The »episodal« character of juvenile delinquency also has been pointed out with respect to GDR society by Lekschas et al. (1983) Young males, especially working ones, are overrepresented in a specific age-group (»Heranwachsende«: late adolescence, 18-21 yrs.) in the statistics of the police and justice. They are convicted 2 1/2 times more often than the average population.

2 Schumann (1994, 242) remarks: »When critical criminologists deal with violence, then preferably with the discourse about it, not with the activity itself«.

3 98.8% of criminal offences and violent offences against foreigners were categorized as *group-offences* (in the representative study of Willems et al. (1993)).

4 The groups of young female workers are not in themselves a topic of research in our study on Berlin. Integrated in our research, however, there was a group of Hooligan girlfriends. One of the rock groups and one group with strong family ties had in each case a young female member.

5 The access to the level of practical action was dealt with by Becker in a convincing way but there was some confusion concerning the theoretical-categorical definition. In a later edition of »Outsiders« an added chapter 10 could still only insufficiently clarify the issue. It is necessary to differentiate fundamentally between *communicative* (intentional) and *habitutal* action.

6 The precise title of the project is: »Entwicklungs- and milieutypische Ausgrenzungs- und Kriminalisierungserfahrungen in Gruppen Jugendlicher«. For a more comprehensive report of the results see: Bohnsack/Loos/Schaeffer/Städtler/Wild (1995).

7 Comparative analysis gains in importance when seen in terms of our method not only on the basis of its production of concepts of typification, but also in the sense of a methodical control of the »bonds of standpoint« concerning the (social environment- specific) perspective of our own interpretations.
The »positions bonds« (»Standortgebundenheit«) of interpretation in the sense of Karl Mannheim (1991) means, seen methodologically, the dependence of interpretation from the (experiential bonds) comparative horizons of the interpreter. Methodical controls of these horizons can be accomplished by empirically grounded and thus controllable comparative analysis of different (empirical) cases (see also Glaser/Strauss 1967).

8 On the methodological and methodical background of our research, the »documentary method« in: Bohnsack (1993), about the theoretical framework: Bohnsack (1995).

9   These results from our research about juvenile peer groups in the small city and town are also part of the compartive analysis; in the sense of a »maximum contrast«.

10 So the categories of »practical consciousness« as in Giddens and the category of »habitus« as in Bourdieu, although we do not fully agree with these conceptions. For a critical review of the conception of habitus in the sense of Bourdieu see Bohnsack (1993).

11 In this respect our analysis taken in the framework of the sociology of knowledge is different from that of the Birmingham School (CCCS) or from the concepts of some of its representatives. Productions of style have been characterized by some representatives of the Birmingham School as »magic solutions«, comparing them with the horizons of a historical solution of contradictions in society in a functionalistic perspective (see Clark 1976). The empirical reconstructive research of Willis (1977) in comparison appear immanently rational, as does Giddens' (1984) reinterpretation of the works of Willis.

12 What Neidhardt (1981) worked out concerning the self-dynamics of the »absurd processes« using the example of a terrorist group is also relevant here, although under different circumstances.

13 Elements of such an »episodal negation of everyday existence« have also been described by Buford (1991).

14 Here every case of the taking over of perspectives of others is precarious in the sense of »universe of discourse« as in Mead (1934) and of the »constitutive rules« as in Piaget (1984). Though even the »cooperative reciprocity« in the sense of of Youniss (1984) in interaction with strangers appears precarious (in the sense of Piaget: »the rules of coordination«).

References

Becker, H. S. (1963), *Outsiders - Studies in the Sociology of Deviance*, New York.

Bohnsack., R. (1989), *Generation, Milieu und Geschlecht - Ergebnisse aus Gruppendiskussionen mit Jugendlichen*, Opladen.

Bohnsack, R. (1992), »Dokumentarische Interpretation von Orientierungsmustern, Verstehen - Interpretieren - Typenbildung in wissenssoziologischer Analyse«, in: Meuser, M. and R. Sackmann (eds.), *Analyse sozialer Deutungsmuster*, Pfaffenweiler.

Bohnsack, R. (1993), *Rekonstruktive Sozialforschung - Einführung in Methodologie und Praxis qualitativer Forschung*, Opladen (2. edition).

Bohnsack, R. (1995), »Auf der Suche nach habitueller Übereinstimmung - Peer-groups: Cliquen, Hooligans und Rockgruppen als

Gegenstand rekonstruktiver Sozialforschung«, in: Krüger/Marotzki (eds.): *Erziehungswissenschaftliche Biographieforschung*, Opladen.

Bohnsack, R. (1995), »Dokumentarische Methode«, in: R. Hitzler and A. Honer, (eds.), *Sozialwissenschaftliche Hermeneutik*, Opladen.

Bohnsack, R., P. Loos, B. Schäffer, K. Städtler and B. Wild (1995), *Die Suche nach Gemeinsamkeit und die Gewalt der Gruppe - Hooligans, Musikgruppen und andere Jugendcliquen*, Opladen.

Bohnsack, R. (1996), »Gruppendiskussionsverfahren und Milieuanalyse«, in: Friebertshäuser, B., A. Prenge (eds.), *Handbuch qualitativer Forschungsmethoden der Erziehungswissenschaft*, Weinheim/München.

Buford, B. (1991), *Among the thugs*, London.

Clark, J. et al. (1976), »Style«, in: Hall, St. and T.Jefferson, *Through Rituals - Youth subcultures in post-war Britain*, London.

Douglas, M. (1970), *Natural Symbols - Explorations in Cosmology*, London.

Giddens, A. (1984), *The Constitution of Society - Outline of the Theory of Structuration*, Cambridge.

Glaser, B.G. and A. Strauss (1969), *The Discovery of Grounded Theory*, Chicago.

Goffman, E. (1972), *Interaction Ritual - Essays on Face-to-Face Behaviour*, Harmondsworth, Middlessex.

Gurwitsch, A. (1977), *Die mitmenschlichen Begegnungen in der Milieuwelt*, Berlin/New York (Habilitationsschrift 1931).

Heitmeyer, W. (1992), »Soziale Desintegration und Gewalt - Lebenswelten und Perspektiven von Jugendlichen«, in: *DVJI-Journal*, 1-2, pp. 76-84.

Heitmeyer, W. et al. (1992), *Die Bielefelder Rechtsextremismusstudie*, Weinheim/München.

Lekschas, J. et al. (1983), *Kriminologie. Theoretische Grundlagen und Analysen*, Berlin.

Mannheim, K (1952a), »On the Interpretation of Weltanschauung«, in: Mannheim, K., *Essays on The Sociology of Knowledge*, London.

Mannheim, K. (1952b), »The Problem of Generations«, in: Mannheim, K., *Essays on the Sociology of Knowledge*, London.

Mannheim, K. (1982), *Structures of Thinking*, London.

Mannheim, K. (1991), »Sociology of Knowledge«, in: Mannheim, K., *Ideology and Utopia*, London.

Mariak, V., K.F. Schumann (1992), »Zur Episodenhaftigkeit von Kriminalität im Jugendalter«, in: Ewald/Woweries (eds.): *Entwicklungsperspektiven von Kriminalität und Strafrecht - Festschrift für John Lekschas*, Bonn.

Matthes, J. (1992), »The Operation Called ›Vergleichen‹«, in: Matthes, J. (ed.), *Zwischen den Kulturen? Die Sozialwissenschaften vor dem Problem des Kulturvergleichs*, Göttingen.

Matza, D. (1964), *Delinquency and Drift*, New York/London/Sydney.

Mead, G.H. (1934), *Mind, Self and Society*, Chicago.

Neidhardt, F. (1981), »Über Zufall, Eigendynamik und Institutionalisierbarkeit absurder Prozese«, in: v. Akmann u. Thurn (eds.), *Soziologie in weltbürgerlicher Absicht - Festschrift für René König*, Opladen.

Peters, H. (1985), »Jugendkriminalität«, in: *Gegenwartskunde*, no. 3.

Schumann, K.F. (1964), »Gewalttaten als Gefahr für die wissenschaftliche Integrität von Kriminologie«, in: *Kriminologisches Journal*, vol.26, no.4.

Willems, H. et al. (1993), *Fremdenfeindliche Gewalt*, Opladen.

Willis, P. (1977), *Learning to labour - How working class kids get working class jobs*, Saxon House.

Youniss, J. (1984), »Moral, kommunikative Beziehungen und die Entwicklung der Reziprozität«, in: Edelstein, W. and J. Habermas, (eds.), *Soziale Interaktion und soziales Verstehen*, Frankfurt.

Meredith W. Watts/Jürgen Zinnecker

Varieties of Violence-Proneness Among Male Youth

We hope, using a recently-conducted survey of German youth, to make a contribution to the contemporary discussion of politically motivated aggressiveness in the younger generation. Although the study was not designed to study right-wing extremism per se, it contains a variety of information on pre-ideological forms of violence-readiness among German youth (a significant portion of which is nourished by right-wing, conservatively-oriented protest). We will argue that an understanding of such aggression among youth cannot be understood by means of a simple transfer of adult-oriented theories of authoritarianism or party preference, but must additionally take into account the character of adolescent aggression.

In light of the political controversial and scientifically uncertain nature of the discussion of »youth and right-wing violence,« we believe it necessary before the presentation and interpretation of the research results, to describe as clearly as possible the theoretical background against which the investigation should be viewed. In this discussion, we do not focus on ideological or political goals, but rather on the general nature of youthful male aggression. This approach is not intended to diminish the political relevance of the violence, but simply, for the moment, to invert the nature of the question. We ask what types of aggression there are, and how »political« each seems to be.

Taking for the moment the perspective of the broader concerns of youth sociology, we point to the fact that at least a portion of recent manifestations of violence should be seen as an aspect of public street violence in general. This street violence has to do with a historically long-lived means of expression of male adolescence, though its actual form of expression is stimulated and given »political« content by specific social conditions and opportunity structures. But because youth has a history of violence qua violence, the possible political content of such behavior should not be assumed, but rather be made the object of the investigation.

Theory

Modern industrial societies of the western variety generally understand themselves as internally pacified societies. The nationstate possesses the monopoly of power and citizens are disarmed.[1] The most important internal conflicts are carried out in the judicial system where agencies of the nation-state possess a monopoly; »selfjustice« is for the most part specifically excluded from the citizens' options. However, the monopoly on force and on law is never complete. In everyday community life, as well in moments of historical crisis, both monopolies can be seriously challenged. The nation-state's management of public order, and the associated public discussion of that issue are, in that sense, continuously concerned - sometimes more, sometimes less - with the material and symbolic maintenance of these two monopolies (Elias 1989).

Male youth and young adult males have from the beginning been prominent among the social groups that threatened the legal monopoly of force and placed it in question. While youth may claim for itself a certain right to public, territorial street violence and selfjustice, the state seeks to contain and direct physical violence through pedagogical and police measures (see Gillis 1980; Shorter 1988). The conflict is by no means just a problem of contemporary society, or even of urban society in particular; the particular proclivity of young men for the direct use of physical force is multiply anchored in the social history of patriarchal, western industrial societies.[2]

Young men served - and continue to serve for a certain age-bounded period of their life-history - as a warrior caste, when the maintenance of individual national societies were threatened by warlike conflicts. In patriarchal societies adult males enjoyed certain private authority for the physical use of force over women and youth; young men could aspire to this form of sex-based domination, often through their comparatively privileged opportunities to display physical strength and aggression. For males that lacked other resources for the acquisition of social power and recognition, use of violence offered - at least potentially - an alternative source of power in social relationships. This social tactic can have a compensatory aspect - promoting a need for recognition, identity and power where it may be denied in the currently dominant social systems. In some historical epochs a closed class or economic system may have presented insurmountable barriers; in others (as in contemporary western industrial society), real, imagined or threatened failure in the educational and occupational systems may be the major threat to violence-prone young males. It might even be argued that most displays of such aggression in modern society serve compensatory needs not met by modern institutions of employment and achievement of recognition/status. The social »sublimation« of adolescent male aggression into productive channels is particularly problematic where conventional (»legitimate«) access to employment, housing and partner markets are blocked.

Of particular meaning for the intimate relationship between young men and direct physical force is masculine socialization. Under current conditions this still implies a widespread basic rule that young males can attain sex-related identity through their readiness to engage in physical confrontation. This assumes that such tactics will be more or less successful as a form of selfassertion (e.g., that it will be rewarded in some fashion). This is not universally true for all young males, but it exists as a potential in a variety of micro-environments (e.g., among peer groups and gangs) and may in some era enjoy a macro-legitimation (as in state-sponsored militant youth groups or, more diffusely, when political and social leaders tolerate or encourage aggression against internal minorities). In this way fighting and physical force find a firm place - first in the repertoire of male-specific play interests (see Maccoby and Jacklin 1974), and potentially on the »political« level if such tactics are generalized to broader social relations.

We assume that in socialization to »masculinity« a body-theme is developed that is oriented toward fighting and physical confrontation.[3] It is not necessary to argue that this process deterministically produces aggressiveness in every male; such an overgeneralization ignores obvious differences among individuals, socialization circumstances, and the diverse incentive/opportunity structures in which aggression might be displayed. The only theoretical assumption necessary is that there exists a gradient of aggressive potential in which some are more actively predisposed to physical assertion than others, and all (or most) have a latent repertoire of aggressive behavior that can be elicited under certain circumstances. The immediate »micro-« field of interactions and incentives, as well as the »macro-legitimation« provided by the political culture (e.g., widespread xenophobia and cognitive targeting of »outsiders«) both serve as immediate and diffuse »triggers« for the actual behavior.

However, we do not for the moment wish to focus on the historical specifics of German politics, nor on the more diffuse issue of gender-related socialization. At issue here is the relationship between adolescent male aggression and what was referred to above as the incomplete establishment of the state's monopoly on the use of force and the administration of law. The principle of nonviolent community coexistence has never been equally binding on all age groups in society. It is part of a set of differential age norms: the strongest taboos and sanctions are applied to the physical use of force by adult citizens. Children have greater freedom; adolescents are somewhere between the two norms. The older young people become, the more they acquire individual standing under the law and the stronger become the pressures to relinquish this »privilege« of childhood.[4]

When viewed from the point of view of age-specific norms for the renunciation of violence, confrontations between male youth and the adult society show an interesting social peculiarity: Young men - or specific subgroups of them - claim the right to be excluded for a relatively long period of time from the strict commandment of violence-renunciation that applies to adults. The state answers this demand with ambivalence. On the one hand it provides and encourages the violence of young males in specific, socially-prescribed roles (as members of internal or external uniformed forced for order or defense), and therefore cannot fully deny or suppress violence-proneness. On the other hand, governmental and private representatives of the adult society attempt to set narrow limits to the particular phase in the life course of young men during which direct physical force will be tolerated. It establishes, in other words, an age-related differentiation for the use of aggression; this differentiation is based on a societal ambivalence toward male violence. Not surprisingly, public policy and public opinion vary in their views of violence, seeing it at times as a social problem (e.g., as »criminal«) and at others as a rude, but understandable expression of sentiments found elsewhere in society (as when the Chinese Red Guards were eventually criticized for being too zealous, young Iranian males as too brutal in enforcing Islamic order, or when conservative German politicians find attacks on foreigners to be »understandable,« but extreme).

There is no simple relationship between adolescent male violence and the broader political order; it varies with historical period and with the sources of legitimation (and de-legitimation) in the broader political culture. The aggressive potential of young males can be a threat to social order, but it can also be a useful tool for carrying out »order-maintaining« activities that are outside the conventional limits of the adult-managed administration of the law. The legitimation and political content of violence therefore take place within the broader context of the society's political culture and, more specifically, the role it wishes its young males to play. Where the messages are ambivalent, or undecipherable, or where they point to goals that are virtually unattainable for many, regression to the »simpler« tactics of aggression may be the result. If the society also provides concrete models and forms of legitimation (in its identification of appropriate targets of aggression, e.g., particular social groups, such as indigenous minorities, foreigners, or refugees), the cognitive link between aggressive potential on the one hand, and specifically politically relevant targets on the other, can be established. This is not necessarily an ideological process requiring a high level of political sophistication; rather, it is a process of »cognitive targeting« that becomes political through its selection of targets for aggression. The actual perpetrators may have an elaborate ideology of inequality and violence, but as a bare minimum only a »temperamental« bias toward aggression, a set of plausible targets, an opportunity to attack without major risk, and some degree of justification (»legitimation,« whether provided by the immediate micro-sphere of interpersonal relations or by higher levels of political authority).

We do not mean to imply that adolescent male aggression is a constant, and that the choice of targets is arbitrary (and therefore of doubtful or minimal political content). On the contrary, some targets of aggression are more likely to be chosen than others. Contemporary right-wing extremism has a set of sometimes interchangeable, but nonetheless finite, victims. Specific contemporary conditions (e.g., urbanization, competitive employment and housing markets) combine with specific ideological currents in the society, to provide a greater »opportunity« for expression of particular forms of aggression. In the early 1990's, those conditions favor, in many western industrial societies, the expression violence against »outsiders.« The outsiders may, of course be social (foreigners and minorities, but also the sociallymarginal such as the homeless and the handicapped), or political/cultural antagonists (e.g., members of the »punk« youth style, or leftist youth gangs).

A related issue concerns the social location of masculine street violence, which can generally be localized in the urban underclass. In Europe, youth violence followed in the process of urbanization. Before it became a phenomenon of the large cities, it had expressed itself as traditional group violence in rural regions - for example as censure of undesired competitors in the local market for sexual partners and mates (Mitterauer 1986; Gillis 1980). In the urban context violence became more highly territorial, transforming itself into group struggles for control of the streets in urban neighborhoods.[5]

From the beginning one of the central goals of urban youth education in Germany was to contain the violence associated with male youth (which expressed itself above all in the formation of territorial groups), and to direct it into socially-acceptable paths. The German youth policy (»Jugendpflege«), which was formed around 1900, was particularly committed to this goal. The primary target group of this policy development were the fourteen-year old cohorts who fell into a care- and control-gap between graduation from primary education (»Volksschule«) and entry into military service.

Of course, it is also possible to trace back to the middle ages the struggle of the schools and the universities for the »disarmament« of their pupils and students.[6] In this process the educational system played a contradictory role. While the institutionalized education of male youth promoted a pedagogically controlled »pacification« of male youth, the very institutionalization of this group provided new opportunities for them to organize themselves into potentially violent groups beyond neighborhood territories. This had the effect of generalizing male aggression beyond physical territories (e.g., neighborhoods) into symbolic and cultural territories. In general, this social process represents the transition from local conflict to »political« conflict.

The process of pacification had differential effects by social class and educational level. With respect to the present, it is clear that the pacification of educationally privileged youth in high schools and universities has been fairly successful - at least in comparison to male street violence in metropolitan areas.[7] The relative pacification of the educationally privileged male youth in high schools and universities, however, contrasts with those male adolescents that are not integrated in either educational or occupational systems. These less-integrated individuals are more likely to express their potential aggressiveness through various subcultural forms (e.g., as in skinhead groups, or as soccer hooligans), everyday behavioral action (e.g., in neighborhood gangs, or in everyday aggression against peers or adults). In the former case the physical locations are likely to be »cultural spaces« such as youth centers, temporary action sites (such as a demonstration at a refugee hostel), or large sport centers (usually soccer stadiums); in the latter, locations are more likely to be territorially-defined neighborhoods, or the everyday ambient of young people such as the family, school, and ordinary public spaces where aggressive behavior occurs more or less spontaneously in response to an opportunity to test strength against peers or to provoke adults.

Each of the above forms of expression can have a »political« component depending on the targets of aggression and the response of governmental agencies. But a third form of aggressive expression is by its nature political in that its targets are quasi-ideologically defined and its goals, however inchoate they may sometimes appear, are aimed toward a change in the distribution of political power (»sending a message to the politicians«), an alteration in the distribution of public goods and services (e.g., jobs, housing, construction of nuclear power plants), or a change in the material and symbolic status of some groups (e.g., foreigners, asylum seekers). This class of political aggression assumed new meaning through the »participatory revolution« of recent decades (Barnes and Kaase 1979; Jennings and van Deth 1990; Watts 1992; Watts forthcoming).

A significant growth in the prevalence and legitimacy of »unconventional« (noninstitutional) political action forms has had a significant impact on the creation of actionistic opportunity structures for young males. The increase of expressive outlets for politically-oriented protest behavior in the streets and in the media gives adolescents new opportunities for forceful or even violent action. The social location of such activity is likely to be less restricted and clearly fixated as, for example, in the case of soccer-hooligans or of multiethnic street gangs. One thinks of the relatively widespread participation of young people in the left-wing »autonomic scene« or of potentially violent social protest movements. In this generally left-oriented scene, the participants tend to be educationally privileged high school and university students. Though their educational institutions were more or less »pacified« after the late 1960's and early 1970's (and therefore no longer provide as extensive an opportunity structure for actionism), the open, streetoriented nature of noninstitutional political action creates a »movable« opportunity structure in which escalation to violence can occur.

Since the public opportunities and occasions in which male violence can be expressed are so differentiated, the question presents itself whether there is a relationship between the »choice« of a public form and social location of violence on the one hand, and characteristics of youth on the other hand. Are there different paths to the emergence of violence on the part of skinheads or hooligan groups, in the emergence of aggressive relationships among peers to one another (and between youth and adults), and in the choice of specifically political forms of action?

To reiterate the general theoretical perspective that underlies our analysis: We believe it useful to discuss violence-proneness in the historical and structural context of male adolescence (we deal with gender differences in a separate analysis). By viewing this »masculine« action field we can reach a more meaningful judgment about the political character of violence-proneness articulated by this group. In the contemporary mass-media discourse there is characteristically a double misunderstanding: Politically-relevant action of young males is often prematurely declared to be specifically »political« in the sense of ideologically focused, policy-relevant behavior. This may or may not be a mistaken attribution - since actionistic groups (e.g., skinheads) may choose opportunistic targets, the likelihood of the behavior being labelled »political« is quite variable. If the target is a homeless urban dweller or member of a »punk« group, the behavior will be normally be interpreted as nonpolitical; if the target is a foreigner (particularly an asylum-seeker), the behavior will normally be labelled political. In these examples, the behavior and targets may be more or less interchangeable, though both result from adolescent aggressiveness and actionism. When cognitive targeting of ethnic or political groups takes place, then adolescent violence-proneness is combined with ideological content (however inchoate and superficial) and takes on a particular political character. But even here it does not lose its other face - that of adolescent male aggression.

Since both aspects are present - adolescent violence and political content - in varying degrees, a complex »recoding« and labelling takes place on the part of public officials and the media. For example, when the political protest of youth deviates from the officially legitimated framework of political action, it may be recoded as youth-delinquent behavior. That renders it less »dangerous« to the system, attributes it to social deficits on the part of youth, and »personalizes« it by assigning it as a pathology to individuals (who may or may not act in groups). This depoliticizes the behavior, and directs attention away from structural problems in the political, economic and cultural environment.

The opposite case presents itself as well. Often, youth »play« with political symbols as a means of expression, though their explicit ideological commitment may be minimal. If those symbolic elements recall the political past of Germany (e.g., the Third Reich), the behavior will generally be reinterpreted as having explicit political content. Some have even argued that this process of attribution and symbolic labelling is itself the cause for youthful groups becoming »ideo-logical« - the label provides what they wanted all along; namely, attention and recognition. This, however, causes the »political« to vanish theoretically and denigrates it to the level of »just another« mode of adolescent expression or, even more problematically, of »re-bellion.«

Though rebellion is an important element, youth-cultural styles do have a de facto ideological component. This is often shown most clearly in the language games of these styles which typically demon-strate a provocative recombination (»bricolage«) of elements from a the broader social and political culture. The symbolic elements are not unique, but exaggerated and recombined versions of the broader cultural symbol set. Right-wing extremist ideas have less »toxic« forms among conservative politicians who fret over »Überfremdung«, the »flood« of asylum-seekers, a tight employment market, and short-ages in housing. The expression of these broader forms of concern in the political culture provide a »macrolegitimation« for cognitive tar-geting. The right-wing form can become virulent when it is further intensified by incorporation of symbolic elements from the »brown« past, or from contemporary forms of political racism and neo-Nazism.

Within the context of a survey project we unfortunately cannot deal satisfactorily with the dynamic of this macro-legitimation, nor with the behavioral dynamics that link neo-Nazi organizations with broader circles of adolescent male aggression. However, within the framework of the available date base we do have the opportunity to view more closely the potential political content of youthful mascu-line violence-proneness on an individual basis. We ask whether the youth who show a certain type of violence-readiness also demon-strate certain characteristic social values, orientations and political preferences. Though this approach does not deal with the explicit political content of violence acceptance as much as we might wish, it does allow us to test whether male youth, who report (1) identifica-tion with aggressive youth styles, or (2) frequent use of physical force against others in their daily lives, or (3) show a high level of approval for violent political tactics, are more likely to show a pref-erence for particular values, particular political preferences and orientations toward (the self in) society. We not only expect that there will be different types of aggressiveness, but also that a specific youth variant will show a superficial »antiauthoritarianism« that is associated with a particular, youthspecific variety of hedonistic, rebellious self-assertion.

Variables

By the selection of politically-relevant variables, with whose help we wish to characterize various groups of violence-prone male youth, we draw upon a variety of measures that were employed in an interdisciplinary study of German youth. Among those measures are:
– Basic value orientations (e.g., so-called materialistic values)
– Orientation to the social future
– Evaluation of one's personal future
– Orientation toward the present (hedonism)
– Youth centrism (»ethnocentric« perception of youth as a socially-discriminated minority)
– Attitude of the individual toward social demands and expectations (willingness to adapt, self-assertion)
– Approval of particular political action forms (e.g., demonstrations, »harder« methods such as property damage and physical confrontation)
– Party preferences (e.g., Republikaner), and placement on a left-right party spectrum
– Attitudes toward social movements (»new social movements« = environment, peace, anti-nuclear power)
– Political Alienation.

Composition of the actual instruments is described in more detail in the Appendix.

A Subissue: Typology Construction
from Survey Data

There remains a technical/theoretical issue to be discussed before presenting the actual data - that of using broad sample surveys to study specialized phenomena that occur only in intensified form in a small portion of the population. Such features mays be »crystallized« in the target groups, but are likely to occur in the general population only in attenuated form. In the case of violence-acceptance and the willingness to use force, a sample of the general youth population will show relationships that are likely to be only weakened reflections of the actual relationships that exist in the active target groups. Since we know that age and gender have an association with violence acceptance, we can achieve some clarity by focusing on the most actionistic group - males in their late teens and early twenties.[8]

Within that general population, there is a further methodological problem of separating an appropriate »target« group of likely activists (or actionists) from the broader population. They may be operationally defined either by self-reported identification with, or membership in, the appropriate target group(s), or they can be defined by the construction of an empirical typology. Such a typology employs concepts that are theoretically central to the target group as we understand them conceptually (e.g., high »authoritarianism«).

The success of such a typology depends on the theory underlying it; we must take care that the operational definition of the typology does not already contain within it a tautological conclusion about who is violent. For example, if we identify »violence-acceptors« prima facie as skinheads (or neo-nazis, or leftist actionists, or convicted juvenile delinquents, etc.) we have implicitly located the violence in a specific group and may easily neglect other contributing groups or motivating factors. Furthermore, if we define violence-acceptors as those with a particular set of attitudes (e.g., rebellious, peer- group-oriented, prone to street violence), the target group may indeed by prone to socially problematic, aggressive behavior, but the objects of their aggression may or may not be »political« (and they may, or may not, be associated with right-extremist thinking). Lastly, identification of a target group according to political tactics is a possibility, but it does not distinguish between forms of motivation - acceptors of aggressive political behavior may come from anywhere in the political spectrum.

Obviously the problem of defining violence-acceptance, and of identifying potentially aggressive youth, is not simply a matter of empirical definition; it is closely related to our theoretical understanding of the sources and consequences of violence acceptance. Our approach to this problem follows from our theoretical position that there are multiple paths or basic models that can lead to right-extremist identification. These forms flow into each other, and they interact with right- extremist political groups and messages in a dynamic fashion. But we believe it is conceptually useful for youth to differentiate the types into (1) subcultural (group) identification with aggressive styles, (2) everyday aggressive behavior, and (3) approval of aggressive political tactics. The results of these definitions are discussed below; first, however the data base requires a brief description.

Data

A youth survey generally known under the title »Shell Youth Study« serves as our data foundation (Jugendwerk der Deutschen Shell 1992). The data provide a quota sample of sufficient quality to provide an appropriate portrayal of the German population between 13 and 29 years of age for West and East Germany. Some 4005 youth and young adults were questioned in standardized oral interviews lasting about one and one-half hours. The field research extended through summer months of 1991. For comparative purposes, the region of the former East Germany was oversampled compared to the total (West Germany : East Germany = 2:1). For the current analysis a subsample was selected that included all 15 to 20 year-old male respondents. This produced an analyses group of 704 respondents, 456 from West Germany and 248 from East Germany.

Results

Table 1 shows the results of the three operational definitions used to develop typologies of aggressive youth groups. The first typology forms a target group of those who identify with or generally approve of the skinheads and soccer-hooligans. This type numbers 25, and is contrasted with the 184 male youth who most strongly reject both subcultural groups.

Table 1: Alternative Definitions and Measurement of Violence-Acceptance German Males, 15-20

Operational Definition	Target Group	n	Contrast Group	n
Aggressive Subcultures	Skins (1,2) + Hooligans (1,2)	25	Skins (5) + Hooligans (5)	184
Everyday Youth Aggression	Provoke (2,3) + Fight (2,3)	67	Provoke (1) + Fight (1)	434
Political Aggression	Hard (5-7)	21	Hard (1)	490

Note: for Skins + Hooligans scores 1 = belong to/live like them, 2 = do not belong to them, but find them good; for political aggression, the contrast group consists of respondents scoring »1«, or rejection of both damage to property and violence against persons, scores 5-7 are combinations of strongly approve or approve of the two tactics; for »everyday youth aggression« scores 2 and 3 are »often« or »occasionally«, 1 = »never«.
Data Source: Jugend '92 (Fischer and Zinnecker, 1992)

The second typology is based on a set of questions about everyday expressive behavior and includes incidence of fighting with peers and deliberate provocation of older people. The typology identifies 21 male adolescents who »often« provoke older people, and who report engaging often in fights. A large contrast group (490) reported »never« engaging in either behavior.

The third typology is based on aggressive political tactics; the »target« group contains 67 respondents who express strong or moderate approval for aggressive political tactics (causing damage to property; and engaging in physical confrontation with other persons, including police). A large contrast group of 434 respondents strongly rejected both.

Before we examine the regression analysis, it is useful to look at the amount of overlap among the three typologies. The first technique for such a comparison is to look at the correlations among the measures from which the typologies were constructed; the second is to directly examine the overlap in the violence-prone identified in each way. Identification with aggressive subcultural styles correlated .11 with the behavioral and .16 with the political measures; the behavioral and political measures together correlated at .38. This suggests that »hard« political tactics are more appealing to those for whom everyday behavioral aggression is also a common occurrence. Political aggression is, on the other hand, less closely associated with aggressively-styled subcultures such as skinheads and soccer hooligans. The actual numerical overlap of the »target« groups from the three procedures shows the subcultural group sharing eight individuals with the behavioral and three with the political groups; the behavioral and political groups shared seventeen. Again, though it is difficult to say anything conclusive because of the small numbers involved, the evidence points to a closer relationship between the behavioral and political dimensions, than between any other pairing of types.

These results support in part the thesis (e.g., Heitmeyer 1987) that political »acting out« is essentially a generalization of violence experienced in everyday life. However, we find, as hypothesized, that all types of aggression are not identical. Not only is it noteworthy that the »behavioral« and »political« forms show a moderate level of intercorrelation, but also that the subcultural form is only marginally related to approval of political violence.

A last comment on the regional distribution of the types: If they are similarly distributed in East and West, we would expect them to exist in our sample in a 2:1 relationship; that is roughly the case with 65% and 62% for the behavioral and political types, respectively. The subcultural type shows signs of a higher East German identification with skinheads/hooligans (56% West versus 44% East), though the numbers are too small to draw any serious conclusions.

The next stage of the analysis utilizes logistic regression analysis (e.g., Norusis 1990) to differentiate between the pre-identified in our three typologies. The method is preferable to discriminant analysis in cases such as this one where the dependent variable is dichotomous and where it is inappropriate to assume that the underlying variable is normally distributed. This is, of course, the case with each of our three typologies.

As an orienting hypothesis, we expect that if there are different forms of aggression represented by the three typologies, the regression of a set of criterion variables on each of the typologies should produce somewhat different results. Table 2 presents an overview of the three logistic regression analyses that test this proposition. To test that the variables have different priorities for the three types of aggression, the statistical algorithm was a stepwise regression whereby only those variables contributing to the prediction were included in the equation (according to a maximum likelihood criterion).

As expected, the logistic regressions produced somewhat different results for each form of aggression. Identification with aggressive youth subcultures (skinheads and hooligans) was associated with two value orientations: the target group was more strongly inclined to value »order and national security« than the nonaggressive contrast group, but they were lower in their attachment to »power and authority.« This is the opposite of what classic authoritarianism theory might predict, and reflects what we argue above is the ambivalent relationship between youth and the authority of the state. This subcultural group, though perhaps »authoritarian« in its views of outgroups nevertheless sees itself as being in rebellion against established (adult) power and authority. While skinheads and football hooligans may be internally hierarchical or oriented toward a strong leader (see Farin and Seidel-Pielen 1993; Schumann 1990; Stock and Mühlberg 1990), they tend to reject outside authority that limits their range of action (see Willis 1981). This produces among some youth a special blend of authoritarianism and rebellion.

Table 2: Summary of Logistic Regression (Males 15-20)

Criterion	Group Definition		
	Subcultural Behavioral	Everyday Behavioral	Political Variables
Order/National Security	+		
Educational Achievement	-	-	
Power & Authority	-	+	
REPS	+	+	
Youth Centrism		+	
Demonstrations (DEMO)			+
Willingness to Adapt			-
New Social Movements			-

Note: »+« indicates a positive relationship with violence acceptance; »-« indicates the factor is negatively associated (coefficients based on logistic regression). The factors are order to illustrate differences among violence-acceptance dimensions. See Appendix for description of measures.

The subcultural form of violence-proneness is generally associated with lower educational attainment, as well as with identification with the right-wing Republikaner (REP) party. Though the skinheads may not necessarily display an integrated ideology, the xenophobic program of the REPS obviously provides some of the »macrolegitimation« for skinhead aggression against foreigners. The negative correlation with education confirms the general perception of the skinheads as underclass, xenophobic brawlers.

The second type of violence-acceptance (»everyday«/behavioral) is associated with lower educational attainment and with REP identification as well, but its antecedents have a different accent. Here the emphasis is on rebellion in the sense of an »ethnocentric« view of youth as a pseudo-social class that is in opposition to the »class« of adults. This self-other conceptualization sets youth apart, and denigrates the wisdom and nurturance of adults in general (see the composition of the scale in the Appendix). The target group - which reports engaging often in »provoking adults« and »fighting« - differs from the first group in its positive evaluation of the »power and authority.« This comes closer to the classic notion of authoritarianism, and is consistent with the thesis (Heitmeyer 1987) that acceptance of hierarchic thinking predisposes youth toward rightist ideology and behavior.

In this case, it seems likely that youthful aggression and ethnocentrism are associated, at least for rebellious male adolescents, with power and authority in the »micro-« sphere of social relations. Although we cannot directly demonstrate this proposition with the current data, we suspect that this micro-power (within groups) differs from the »macro-« power (official agencies) that is rejected by the subcultural groups in the first typology.[9] What in any case is clear is that there is not a single syndrome of everyday violence, values and sociopolitical orientations that is associated with rightist identification. Rather, there seem to be multiple paths, some more »authoritarian« than others.

The third typology differs still further. This target group is not strongly associated with Republikaner identification, but it does show, surprisingly, a negative relationship with New Social Movements. Through the »participatory revolution« of the 1970's we have come to expect approval of political aggression (damage to property, physical confrontation with persons) to be associated with the left-progressive activism. Here, of course, Hausbesetzer (urban squatters), masked anti-nuclear power demonstrators, and militant ecologists come to mind. This association may still hold for the broader population, and perhaps even with the youth population in general. But for our sample of adolescent males the association is moderately negative - indicating that for this age/sex group political aggression is increasingly associated with the right.

This shift of political aggression to the right is, to be sure, one that occurred during the 1980's in many nations; in the United States, for example, many of the most visibly violent demonstrations were conducted by conservative anti-abortion groups (often involving physical confrontation with the opposition and the police, property damage, and in at least one case the fatal shooting of a doctor). Thus, our data show concretely what has been increasingly the case in practical politics - that the participatory tactics of the left have been adopted by groups on the right, and that politically aggressive tactics which appealed to young leftists of the 1970's are appealing to male adolescents on the right in the 1990's.

Thus far our overview supports our basic contention that there are (among male adolescents at least) different paths to political aggression and right-extremism. Beyond this is the somewhat unexpected finding that the most expressly political form is not primarily associated with left progressivism for this population group. The logistic regression allowed a comparison of the empirical priority of a set of variables and a test of the central thesis that the three aggressive forms had different antecedents. A related and more extended question concerns a broader set of connections between our typologies and a variety of factors. For this, we display in Table 3 a set of t-tests that compare the mean scores of a set of variables according the three typologies. This no longer shows the specific priority of predictors, but simply presents a broad view of the associated factors.

The table is divided with by horizontal lines according to the factors that accent differences among the three typologies. The table includes the factors identified in the logistic regression, but additional variables have been added to enrich the picture somewhat. Horizontal lines separate groups of variables roughly according their ability to discriminate one form of aggression from another.

As before, educational achievement and »power and authority« discriminate well for the first two groups. It is clear here that the subcultural type is the least attracted to power and authority (mean = 6.0) while the aggressive youth group is the most attracted (mean = 7.8).

In the second group of comparisons, Youth Centrism is clearly the highest for the youth in favor of hard political tactics. As a further collateral test we examined a modified version of Zimbardo's scales (Kohr 1992; Zimbardo; Gonzalez and Zimbardo 1985) scale »hedonistic view of the present.« This scale, which measures the orientation toward excitement, risk, unpredictability, and immediate everyday experience (as opposed to future planning), shows the same pattern as Youth Centrism - the politically aggressive are the highest, followed by those identified as everyday youth aggression.

Table 3: Summary of T-Test Analysis (T = »target« group; C = »contrast« group). See Appendix for description of measures (»*« = statistical significance at the .05 level, »**« = beyond the .01 level).

	Group Definition								
	Subcultural Behavioral			Everyday Behavioral			Political Behavioral		
	T	C		T	C		T	C	
n=	25	184		67	434		21	507	
Educational Achievement	2.6	3.2	(**)	2.9	3.2	(**)	2.9	3.1	
Power & Authority	6.0	6.3	(**)	7.8	6.3	(**)	7.0	6.4	
Hedonistic Present	11.8	11.8		12.1	11.1	(**)	13.1	11.3	(**)
Youth Centrism	26.1	24.5		26.6	23.2	(**)	27.4	23.4	(**)
Order/National Security	11.4	10.0	(*)	10.3	10.5		8.0	10.1	(**)
Demonstrations	3.7	4.2		4.0	3.8		5.7	3.6	(**)
Willingness to Adept	13.4	13.4		13.0	13.6		11.1	13.8	(**)
Self Assertion	14.0	14.1		14.4	13.5	(**)	15.5	13.5	(**)
Political Party	1.9	3.9	(**)	2.7	3.7	(**)	2.6	3.5	
Republikaner	.32	.01	(**)	.16	.01	(**)	.14	.03	
New Social Movements	2.5	4.0	(**)	3.0	4.0	(**)	2.6	4.1	(**)
Future of Society	1.9	1.6	(**)	1.7	1.8		1.6	1.8	
Personal Future	2.4	2.5		2.4	2.5		2.1	2.6	(*)
Political Interest	1.4	1.7	(*)	1.5	1.6		1.6	1.6	
Politcal Alienation	15.2	15.4		14.9	14.5		15.1	14.7	

Figures in the third group of rows show that the aggressive sub-cultural youth are more oriented toward order and national security, the politically aggressive the least so. The politically aggressive are also more favorable toward »demonstrations« (both approved and non-approved); aggressive youth also displayed higher approval to-ward demonstrations than their contrast group, but the aggressive subcultural youth showed less approval.

Comparisons in the fourth group of rows confirm that the first two types are more associated with parties of the right, and more specifi-cally with the REPS. The last group shows some association with the REPS, but the association is not significant. This is because, we be-lieve, the politically aggressive groups contain some members of both right and left. Because of the particular composition of this group of adolescent males however, those on the right are more strongly repre-sented than would be the case for youth as a whole or for the adult population. All types are less oriented toward New Social Move-ments than their respective contrast groups, and all target (aggres-sive) groups place a higher value on personal self-assertion. The most assertive of all are those leaning toward political aggression.

Lastly, an interesting difference emerges in the respective views of the three types toward the future. The most significant difference is for those identifying with aggressive subcultures -they have the most positive view of the »future of society«. They are only average in their views of their personal futures, though. The most negative personal futures are expected by the politically aggressive.

Predicting Right-Wing Party Preference

In the previous section we used the Republikaner party as a factor to test the right-wing nature of the various aggressive types. The num-ber of REP identifiers in the sample was not large, but we found them nevertheless to be of some intrinsic interest. Therefore, we asked the reverse question - what variables best distinguish REPidentifiers from all others. To answer the question we used logistic regression once again to »predict« what young males were most likely to show an identification with the Republikaner Party.

The best predictors are the indexes »youth violence (subcultural)[+],« »youth aggression[+],« and »new social movements[-]« (we used the continuous forms of the indexes rather than the dichotomous forms that were used in the previous analysis to form the typologies). This means that, for the adolescent male youth in our data set, the most closely associated factors with REP identification are the first two measures of aggression (the more aggressive the youth, the more likely to identify with the REPS), and with rejection of New Social Movements (the greater the identification with the Peace, Anti-Nuclear and Ecological Movements, the less the identification with the REPS). The latter association is not surprising, but it is a significant factor that the REPS are favorably received by adolescent males who identify with subcultural and everyday aggressive styles.

Discussion

We have tried to approach the question of political content empirically without presupposing any specific relationship with the hypothesized »paths« to violence-proneness. This does not mean that we take less seriously the political content, and the political impact, of adolescent male violence. Rather, we wished to test whether there were alternative paths to aggression (and to right-wing identification). This means, at least for the moment, focusing on that aspect of aggression which has the distinct stamp of adolescent male aggression.

However, we do not wish to leave the impression that political aggression is »merely« another form in which adolescent violence-proneness can be expressed. On the other hand, when the perpetrators and sympathizers are in that age/sex group, it is worth remembering that such behavior is not just »political« in the cognitive and ideological sense. With this age group, violence-proneness has elements of both. We look at this research as at least a first attempt to approach the association between the »political« and the »adolescent« components.

How can the three masculine-adolescent forms of violence-proneness be characterized with respect to values and orientations? The first type, which signals violence-proneness in the context of publicly visible expressive subcultures - skinhead, hooligans - is anchored in a particular social location. These youth embody, with their emphasis on order and national security, traditional insecurity values. Correspondingly, their protest readiness is clearly located with the right-extremist »Republikaner« party. The traditional, milieu-connected orientation goes along with a decided disadvantage in the area of education - a sign of social immobility during adolescence.

We also found that male adolescents in this group place great value on nonconformity and resistance against conventional social hierarchy in a way that seems to differ from adult authoritarians (for whom clear power and authority relationships with the state may be more highly valued). This reflects the endemic conflict between adolescent male aggressiveness and the desire of the state to maintain its monopoly on force and the administration of law.

The second type of violence-prone adolescents shows the strongest trademark in the area of personal efficacy and selfassertion. Obviously this is a concentration of violence-prone male youth for whom physical force represents a means for gaining personal control over the immediate environment. Their need for control is oriented to the here and now (the hedonistic present), and is directed both toward peers and the older generation. In the political realm they are rather unremarkable and average in comparison to the contrast group. We are apparently dealing here with a behavioral option: (physical and verbal) violence-proneness suits them - for reasons that deserve closer investigation - for the satisfaction of their specific social, everyday needs for control.

The third type shows a more definite political framework than the first two. Here we find male adolescents whose readiness to use force against persons and property is expressed in the broader context of »politics of the street.« Their trademark is their low willingness to adapt to social demands and expectations. This includes a high degree of »youth centrism«, an ethnocentric demarcation from the adult world. That occurs in a strongly hedonistic orientation toward the present. Recognizable in this profile is its proximity to both the leftist scene of »autonomic violence«, but also with elements of attractive-ness to the right.

The negative association with New Social Movements may indi-cate not only the rejection of these groups by the right, but also a lack of interest in them among actionistic leftist youth (for whom these older movements may now be too tame). At the same time, these movements have consistently attracted a high proportion of females who have for more than a decade showed a »progressive bonus« compared to their male counterparts (this bonus increases with edu-cational level). This »feminization« points to an obvious counter-program to the masculine actionism to which young males pay hom-age. As a practical consequence, it is likely to be difficult to activate any »peace« potential among the violence-prone young men. The negative association of New Social Movements with the political form of violence-acceptance attests to this phenomenon.

Two political orientations that belong to all three types of vio-lence-proneness deserve particular attention - the relatively frequent sympathy for the right-wing Republikaner party (whereby there rests a strong affinity with the subcultural violence-type ›skinheads‹, and on the other side the relative distance from new social movements ›peace, environment, anti-nuclear power‹. Within the »legitimate« spectrum of the German party system, the Republikaner Party clearly has an appeal for violence-prone young males. This is quite consis-tent with electoral research which has repeated pointed to a dispro-portional appeal to males among voters for the right-wing Repub-likaner party (see Hoffmann-Güttig 1989; Roth 1989), it is different, however, in the link we believe to have established with various forms of adolescent aggressiveness.

We point lastly to several questions that have remained open in this paper and which require further investigation. We were con-cerned with testing for the existence of the three hypothetical forms of violence-proneness among young males. As demonstration of the need for such a differentiation, we found that, apart from their com-monalities, each type of violence-acceptance was associated with different social-political values and orientations. Neglected in this analysis were differences in socialization and life history. Here of course we would also expect to find commonalities, but an important area of qualitative research would be to examine differences in bio-graphical paths that lead to the various forms of violence-proneness.

An additional factor that has not been dealt with here is the diffi-cult and politically divisive question if, and in which respect we have to distinguish between a »left-progressive« and a »rightconservative« readiness to use violence. In order to make a contribution here the left-right scheme would have to be built into the typology construc-tion (see Hoffmann-Lange et al. 1993). Because of the complexity of that analysis, we hope to pursue that question further with the current data base and in the design of subsequent research.

Lastly, we point to an question that needs further clarification - whether the values and orientations that we found in the group of violent-prone young males also appear among other age and gender groups. We hope to turn our attention to this question in a future analysis.

Notes

1 This varies in practice, of course, with the Federal Republic of Germany more »disarmed,« while the citizens - and youth - of the United States have much broader access to firearms.
2 The conditions of this phenomenon are decidedly overdetermined. That allows us to leave undiscussed (for the moment), the extent to which this is an anthropologi-cal or biosocial constant. Though there is certainly evidence for such a position, it is remarkable how little youth-theoretical models have made use of this perspec-tive.
3 This is not to deny the extent to which combative body images are increasingly demonstrable among young girls (Zinnecker 1989).
4 Naturally these age norms are subject to historical change and are constantly in flux (It would be worthwhile to analyze the history of youth law within the frame-work of this confrontation.). Here we can see as regulative the pedagogical guide-lines that are formulated for the behavior of children together and for their rela-tionship with adults. It appears that the norms of family pedagogy are increasingly oriented toward an early acquisition of »peacefulness« on the part of children (at least for young males).
5 See Trasher as the classic case study for Chicago at the beginning of the 20th cen-tury (Trasher 1927).
6 See, for example, accounts of student and pupil unrest in Germany, England, and the United States by Dunning 1977; Kett 1977 and Gillis 1980.
7 This statement must in any event be revised with respect to the mandatory school system in childhood and early adolescence. These pedagogical institutions suffer

now as before - possibly increasingly - from a pupil violence that is difficult for instructors to control (see Grauer and Zinnecker 1978). However, unlike the United States where the question of violence in the schools is more closely related to questions of criminality, weapons and drugs, in Germany there is currently a closer link with the debate over xenophobic violence.

8 The figures for 1992 illustrate the situation. Of the roughly 2000 acts of violence counted in 1992, 70 percent of the perpetrators were males between sixteen and twenty-one years of age. (Bundesministerium des Innern 1991; Deutsche Jugend 1992, 503-4).

9 This difference between micro- and macro- authority is significant for measuring the alleged relationship between »authoritarianism« and radical-right political orientations. At least for youth, it seems important to distinguish whether the psychological referent »authority« is external to the adolescent's group (e.g., governmental, school, parental) or internal (oneself or a friend as a strong leader).

Appendix

Scales and Other Items Employed in the Analysis

Orientation toward a hedonistic present (Gonzalez and Zimbardo 1985; Zimbardo n.d.; Jugendwerk der Deutschen Shell 1992, p. 82) [alpha = .68]
It is often fun to be simply carried along/I like to take each day at a time/I do things impulsively, making decisions on the spur of the moment/I take risks to put excitement in my life (last two items from Gonzalez and Zimbardo,1985, 24-5) [Original: Manchmal macht es mir Spaß, mich einfach treiben zu lassen/Ich tue am liebsten spontan das, wozu ich gerade Lust habe/Ich lebe gern in den Tag hinein/Um etwas Aufregendes zu erleben, riskiere ich schon mal was].

Value Orientations [Power/Authority; Order/National Security] (Jugendwerk der Deutschen Shell 1992, vol 4, 89-94; Krebs 1992)

Willingness to Adapt (Jugendwerk der Deutschen Shell 1992, vol 4, 9798; Watts et al. 1989). [alpha = .69]

Self Assertion (Jugendwerk der Deutschen Shell 1992, vol 4, 99-100; Watts et al. 1989). [alpha = .59]

Youth Centrism (Jugendwerk der Deutschen Shell 1992, vol 4, 110-112; Watts et al 1989). [alpha = .67]

Political Measures:

Demonstrations. Summed index of preference (each on a 1 to four scale) for approved and non-approved demonstrations (Kaase 1990).

New Social Movements. Summed index of identification with »peace,« »ecology,« and »anti-nuclear power« movements (each on a scale from »1« representing »belong to the group/live like they do« to »5« (»they are enemies/I fight them«).

Political Alienation (Jugendwerk der Deutschen Shell 1992, vol 4, 101102; Fischer and Kohr 1980) [alpha = .80]

Political Interest. Single item: Are you interested in politics? (recoded 2 = »yes«, 1 = »no«)

Typologies of Violence Acceptance:

Subcultural [Aggressive Youth Groups]. Summed index of identification with »skinheads,« and »soccer hooligans« (each on a scale from »1« representing »belong to the group/live like they do« to »5«, »they are enemies/I fight them«. For typology construction see Note, Table 2.

Behavioral [Youth Aggression]. Summed index of items »provoke older people, frighten them,« and »get into a serious fight with another person« (on a three-point scale from »often,« to »never«). For typology construction, see Note, Table 2.

Political [Hard Political Tactics]. Summed index of preference (each on a 1 to four scale) for »causing property damage« and »use of violence against persons, including police« (Kaase 1990). For typology construction, see Note, Table 2.

Political Party. Six-point index created by ranking parties from right to left, each number corresponding to the following: Republikaner, Christian Democratic Union/Christian Social Union, Free Democratic Party, Social Democratic Party, Greens, Party of Democratic Socialism.

Republikaner. Simple dichotomous measure indicating preference for the Republikaner Party (REPS) or not.

View of the Future:

»Future of Society«. One can look at the future, at the way things will go in our society, more pessimistically or more optimistically. How is that with you? [Original: Man kann ja in die Zukunft, wie das Leben in unserer Gesellschaft weitergehen wird, eher düster oder eher zuversichtlich sehen. Wie ist das bei Dir?] (recoded to 1 = »more optimistic«, 2 = »more pessimistic«)

»Personal Future«. One can look at one's own future, the way things will go in one's own life, more pessimistically or more optimistically. How is that with you? [Man kann die eigene Zukunft, wie das eigene Leben weitergehen wird, eher düster oder eher zuversichtlich sehen. Wie ist das bei Dir?]» (recoded to 1 = »more optimistic«, 2 = »mixed ...«, 3 = »more pessimistic«).

References

Barnes, S.H. and M. Kaase (1979), *Political Action: Mass Participation in Five Western Democracies*, Beverly Hills.

Behnken, I., C. Günther, O. Kabat vel Job, S. Keiser, U. Karig, H.H. Krüger, B. Lindner, H.-J. von Wensierski and J. Zinnecker (1991), *Schülerstudie '90. Jugendliche im Prozeß der Vereinigung*, Weinheim/München.

Böhnisch, L. and R. Winter (1993), *Männliche Sozialisation. Bewältigungsprobleme männlicher Geschlechtsidentität in Lebenslauf*, Weinheim/München.

Bundesministerium des Innern (1992), *Verfassungsschutzbericht 1991*, Bonn.

Cavalli, A. (1988), »Zeiterfahrungen von Jugendlichen. Versuch einer Typologie«, in: *Zerstörung and Wiederaneignung von Zeit*, ed. R. Zoll, pp. 387-404, Frankfurt.

Deutsche Jugend (1992), *Dokumente* , 11/92, pp. 502-504.

Dunning, E. (1977), »Macht und Herrschaft in den public schools (1750 -1850)«, in: *Materialien zu Norbert Elias' Zivilisationstheorie*, ed. P. Gleichmann et al., Frankfurt.

Eckert, R. (1992), »Politische Beteiligung, Proteste und Gewalttätigkeit«, in: *Protestwähler und Wahlverweigerer. Krise der Demokratie?*, ed. K. Starzacher, K. Schacht, B. Friedrich and T. Lief, Köln.

Elias, N. (1989), »Zivilisation und Gewalt. Über das Staatsmonopol der körperlichen Gewalt und seine Durchbrechungen«, in: Elias, N., *Studien über die Deutschen*, Frankfurt.

Farin, K. and E. Seidel-Pielen (1993), *Skinheads*, München.

Fischer, A. (1992), »Politik und jugendliche Lebenswelt. Gruppen-porträts«, in: *Jugendwerk der Deutschen Shell, Jugend '92*, vol. 2, ed. J. Zinnecker, Opladen.

Fischer, A., W. Fuchs and J. Zinnecker (1985), *Jugendliche und Erwachsene '85. Ein Generationsvergleich*, Opladen.

Fischer, A. and J. Zinnecker (eds.) (1992), *Jugend '92*, 4 vols., Opladen.

Gillis, J.R. (1980), *Geschichte der Jugend. Tradition und Wandel im Verhältnis der Altersgruppen und Generationen in Europa von der zweiten Hälfte des 18. Jahrhunderts bis zur Gegenwart*, Weinheim/Basel.

Gonzalez, A. and P. Zimbardo (1985), »Time in Perspective«, in: *Psychology Today*, 19 (3), pp. 21-26.

Grauer, G. and J. Zinnecker (1978), »Schülergewalt. Über unter-schlagene und dramatisierte Seiten des Schülerlebens«, in: *Schüler im Schulbetrieb*, ed. G.-B. Reinert and J. Zinnecker, Reinbek bei Hamburg.

Heitmeyer, W. (1987), *Rechtsextremistische Orientierungen bei Jugendlichen*, 3d ed., Weinheim/München.

Heitmeyer, W., H. Buhse, J. Liebe-Freund, K. Müller, J. Müller, H. Ritz, G. Siller and J. Vossen (1992), *Die Bielefelder Rechtsex-tremismus- Studie. Erste Langzeituntersuchung zur politischen Sozialisation männlicher Jugendlicher*, Weinheim/München.

Hoffmann-Güttig (1989), »Die neue Rechte: Die Männerparteien«, in: *Aus Politik und Zeitgeschichte*, B41-42/89.

Hoffmann-Lange, U., H. Schneider and M. Gille (1993), »Politische Gewaltbereitschaft Jugendlicher«, in: Deutsches Jugendinstitut, *Gewalt gegen Fremde*, München/Weinheim.

Hopf, W. (1991), »Familiale und schulische Bedingungen rechtsex-treme Orientierungen von Jugendlichen«, in: *Zeitschrift für Sozializationsforschung und Erziehungssoziologie*, 1/91, pp. 43-59.

Jaschke, H.-G., (1992), »Nicht-demokratische politische Partizipation in der sozial polarisierten Stadt. Zur Entwicklung rechtsradikaler und fremdenfeindlicher Protestpotentiale in Frankfurt am Main«, in: K. Starzacher, K. Schacht, B. Friedrich and T. Lief (eds.),

Protestwähler und Wahlverweigerer. Krise der Demokratie?, Köln.

Jennings, M.K. and J.W. van Deth (1990), *Continuities in Political Action*, Berlin/New York.

Jugendwerk der Deutschen Shell (1992), *Jugend '92*, ed. A. Fischer and J. Zinnecker, 4 vols., Opladen.

Kaase, M. (1990), »The Cumulativeness and Dimensionality of Participation Scales«, in: *Continuities in Political Action*, ed. M.K.Jennings and J.W.van Deth, pp. 393-395, Berlin/New York.

Kett, J.F. (1977), *Rites of Passage. Adolescence in America: 1790 to the Present*, New York.

Kohr, H.-U. (1992), »Zeit-, Lebens- und Zukunftsorientierungen«, in: *Jugendwerk der Deutschen Shell, Jugend '92*, vol. 2, ed. J. Zinnecker, pp. 145-168, Opladen.

Krebs, D. (1992), »Werte in den alten und neuen Bundesländern«, in: *Jugendwerk der Deutschen Shell, Jugend '92*, vol. 2, ed. J. Zinnecker, pp. 35-48, Opladen.

Maccoby, E.E. and C.N. Jacklin (1974), *The Psychology of Sex Differences*, Stanford.

Mitterauer, M. (1986), *Sozialgeschichte der Jugend*, Frankfurt.

Norusis, M.J. (1990), *SPSS/PC+ Advanced Statistics*, Chicago.

Schwartz, S.H. (1992), »Cultural Dimensions of Values: Toward an Understanding of National Differences«, in: *Individualism and Collectivism*, ed. U. Kim and H. Triandis.

Schwartz, S.H. and W. Bilsky (1990), »Toward a Theory of the Universal Content and Structure of Values: Extensions and Cross-Cultural Replications«, in: *Journal of Personality and Social Psychology*, 59, pp. 878-891.

Schwartz, S.H., S. Roccas and L. Sagiv (1992), »Universals in the Content and Structure of Values: Theoretical Advances and Empirical Tests in 20 Countries«, in: *Advances in Experimental Social Psychology*, 25.

Schubarth, W and U. Hoffmann-Lange (1992), »Nationalistische und rechtsextremistische Orientierungen«, in: Deutsches Jugendinstitut, *Schüler an der Schwelle zur Deutschen Einheit*, pp. 114-127, Opladen.

Schumann, F. (1990), *Glatzen am Alex. Rechtsextremismus in der DDR*, Berlin.

Stock, M. and P. Mühlberg (1990), *Die Szene von innen. Skinheads, Grufties, Heavy Metals, Punks*, Berlin.

Shorter, E. (1988), »Jugend, Gewalt und soziale Kontrolle in drei Jahrhunderten«, in: *Jugend im internationalen Vergleich*, ed. W. Ferchhoff and T. Olk, pp. 45-51, Weinheim/München.

Thrasher, F.M. (1927), *The Gang: A Study of 1313 Gangs in Chicago*, Chicago.

Watts, M.W. (1990), »Orientations Toward Conventional and Unconventional Political Participation Among German Youth«, in: *Comparative Political Studies*, 23, pp. 283-313.

Watts, M.W. (1992), »Legitimität unkonventioneller politischer Beteiligung: Unterschiedliche Spuren der ›partizipatorischen Revolutionen‹ in West und Ost«, in: Jugendwerk der Deutschen Shell, *Jugend '92*, vol. 2, ed.J. Zinnecker, pp. 73-89, Opladen.

Watts, M.W. (forthcoming), »A ›Participatory Revolution‹ Among the German ›Unification Generation‹? Youth Attitudes Toward Noninstitutional Participation after the East German Revolution«, in: *European Journal of Political Science*.

Watts, M.W., A. Fischer, W. Fuchs and J. Zinnecker (1989), *Contemporary German Youth and Their Elders*, New York.

Willis, P. (1981), *›Profane Culture‹. Rocker, Hippies: Subversive Stile der Jugendkultur*, Frankfurt/Main.

Zimbardo, P., *Stanford Time Perspective Inventory*, Department of Psychology. Stanford University.

Zinnecker, J. (1989), »Körper und Sport im Zivilisationsprozeß«, in: *Bewegungswelt von Kindern und Jugendlichen*, ed. W.-D. Brettschneider, pp. 296-310, Schoendorf.

Metin Alkan

Racism and Schooling Experiences of Turkish Students in Secondary Education in the Netherlands

Since the Dutch government formulated for the first time in 1980 integrated policies directed towards migrants and the improvement of their social position, there has been a great deal of both academic and popular interest concerning the performance of children from a variety of ethnic minority groups within the educational system. In many studies and reports, the trend has been to suggest that ethnic minorities have been underachieving in education. Attempts to identify and explain factors contributing to underachievement have often been set within a social pathology research model. The focus has been on a set of real or supposed individual characteristics, searching for deficiencies and shortcomings of ethnic minority children and their backgrounds. In essence, a large majority of research has been centered around questions relating to the educability of minority children within the context of the demands and expectations of the Dutch school programs. Among the most popular models of explanation of underachievement have been the social disadvantage, limited proficiency in Dutch language, and ethnic-cultural backgrounds and characteristics of various groups under consideration. The social disadvantage view is based on the assumtion that children from ethnic minority groups and those of indigenious working-class families are to a high degree comparable with respect to their educational chances.

According to this view, the underachievement of ethnic minority children in education has nothing to do with their ethnicity; it is a logical consequence of the fact that their parents belong to the lowest socio-economic class (De Jong 1987; Kerkhoff 1988, 1989; Van Langen and Jungbluth 1990). This assumed similarity between ethnic minority and lower-class Dutch children has been the main reason for developing an educational policy for all underpriviliged children in 1980's (Eldering 1989). Language problems and linguistic deprivation have also received attention. In this context, the underachievement of minority children in education has been related to their limited proficiency in the Dutch language in meeting the requirements of the abstract and cognitively demanding school language. Since the late 1980's, the educational policy has concentrated primarily on the teaching of Dutch as a second language (Appel 1984, 1994; Extra and Vallen 1989; Driessen 1992). Within the framework of ethnic-cultural backgrounds and characteristics, the focus of research studies has been on the problems of adjustment to Dutch school practices, differences between home and school, parents' educational background, pupils' early childhood development, family structure and pedagogy, and identity problems (Driessen 1992; Ledoux et.al. 1992; Verkuyten 1988; for a review of educational research on underachievement of ethnic minority children, see Eldering 1989; Teunissen 1990; Alkan and Kabdan 1995). Structural factors such as the distribution and selection mechanisms, and other organizational and conceptual strategies within the school system have been largely neglegted in these explanations of differential outcomes for ethnic minority and white majority children.

The focus on the characteristics of learners from ethnic minority groups in the majority of studies is connected with a particular application of the concept of ethnicity in the formulation of research questions and methodological approaches. Similar to such factors as the parents' educational background or the length of stay in the Netherlands, the so-called ›ethnic-factor‹ is often treated in these studies as isolable and as functioning independently, rather than in an interactive way. Or, it is viewed as subjective, ascriptive descriptions, shaping the specific personal characteristics of pupils from ethnic minority communities. Matthijssen (1993) suggested, for example, that a combination of the following »ethnic-specific« characteristics of minority children in schools makes them a group at risk: an extreme importance attached to receiving a diploma (»eagerness and tenacity in processing learning tasks as if their lives depend on it«), an undisputed authority of the teacher (»an intense obedience and servility, a limiteless submission to the authority of the teacher«), social isolation experienced with teachers and students (»feelings of being excluded, lack of self-confidence and social skills, and fear of making mistakes«), an isolation to a certain extent from parents (»as a result of parents' lack of understanding of school tasks and problems«), specific sorts of language problems (»they miss lots of information, because the teacher speaks too fast«), and »light and unconscious forms of discrimination, with which the most students do not seem to be having trouble« (pp. 51-52).

While the main thrust of the majority of research studies has been concerned with the ethnic minority children as the problem within the education system, there has been a small number of studies, concerned specifically with the analysis of the process of schooling itself and the practices which place these children at a disadvantage. In these studies, the problem is posed with respect to the question of how the structures and processes of the educational system and of individual schools might be failing to facilitate the full academic development of minority pupils. Coenen and Vallen (1991), for instance, revealed that national tests administered in the last year of the primary school tend to be culturally and linguistically biased to the disadvantage of ethnic minority children with respect to the school advice that they receive for their further schooling at the secondary level. According to a study conducted by De Lange (1987), expectations of teachers are clearly low for Surinamese, and especially for Turkish and Maroccan children in the first cycle of secondary education. The low expectation of teachers is reflected negatively in their interactions with students within the context of classroom instructional processes (see also Bervoets, 1992; Van Erp et al., 1992). Studies by Van den Berg and Reinsch (1983), Van Dijk (1987) and Mok (1990) demonstrate the existence of subtle forms of racism in school textbooks. Hofman (1993) concluded that school process variables like parental involvement, degree of attention for student counselling, and the extent of integration of minority languages and cultures in the school curriculum substantially determine the career efficiency and study perspectives of ethnic minority children. Indeed, as Meijnen and Riemersma (1992) revealed, there are schools in the Netherlands that succeed in providing ethnic minority children with an academic achievement at the level of or even higher than the average of the total school population. Similarly, Matthijssen (1993) and Van der Werf, Mitert and Reezigt (1994) pointed to various aspects of institutional realities and processes in schools to account for the underachievement of ethnic minority children in education. Among the proposals that emerge from these studies for the improvement of school success of these children are the creation of a positive school climate, a well-structured school curriculum, order and regularity in classroom activities, and a friendly, positive and personal approach by teachers to minority children.

Findings of these research studies into various aspects of school structures and processes indicate the need to move away from the rather narrow and one-sided focus on factors relating to minority pupil characteristics in explaining patterns of achievement and underachievement. Inequalities and disadvantages involved in the education of ethnic groups need to be considered from the viewpoint of the structure and functioning of the school system. Inevitably within such a relatively new research area of the structure and workings of the educational system itself, much work remains to be done. One such area is in relation to the experience of schooling, which this article is concerned with. Here, the research problem is conceptualized in terms of describing and analyzing the ways in which racism and inequality are produced and reproduced by/in schools and how students experience these processes (see Gillborn 1990; Mac and Ghaill 1989; Wright 1992). The central focus here is on the actual patterns of interaction within the context of the school and classroom, with a particular attention given to the ways in which ethnicity informs the educational experiences and outcomes of ethnic minority students. Ethnicity, a dynamic and complex concept, refers to how members of a group perceive themselves and how, in turn, they are perceived by others. Ethnic relations in education relate to the nature, intensity and scope of a continuing interaction that take place between students and various dimensions of the school.

The forces which shape this interaction need to be taken into account. This requires an insight into the characteristics and perspectives of students as well as the structure and functioning of the school system, and it requires a clarity about the kinds of changes which are seen as desirable and possible. The focus on interaction provides a more holistic, comprehensive, and dynamic view than do other explanations of differential achievement. The school attempts to shape and regulate this interaction through decisions, measures and teaching-learning activities that are designed and implemented in response to the perceived needs and characteristics of the students. This is reflected in the nature of teacher-student relations, decisions concerning the school careers of students, assessment and evaluation of student progress, and in the interactional, social, management, and organizational aspects of classroom and school environment. Obviously, the school occupies a powerful, but not an independent position in this process of structuring ethnic relations in education. The nature of demands, reactions and expectations of ethnic minority groups needs to be considered. Similarly, students develop perspectives, interpretations, coping and survival strategies, and specific forms of resistence and responses with respect to their school experiences.

The data reproduced below originate from a recently completed study with a group of Turkish students in various types of secondary schools in Amsterdam (Alkan and Kabdan 1995). The initial question of the study was: How do Turkish students evaluate the factors that determine their chances of success or failure in secondary education? In-depth interviews were conducted with 47 Turkish students from four different types of schools. The students were from 27 schools out of the 59 secondary schools that exist in the city of Amsterdam. Informal interviewing method (McCracken 1988) was thought to be best suited to the purpose of the study. In this type of interviewing, the researcher starts with an agenda, or a list of general topics to cover, as well as an opening statement and open-ended questions designed to elicit the participants' perspectives without sensitizing the participants to any hypotheses of the researchers. In this study, the focus was on specific domains of interest, and the interview agenda was developed after a basic review of literature. The specific domains included: primary school period school advice received at the end of the primary school, racism and discrimination in schools and society, school-based friendship patterns, relations with teachers, counselling, parental support, and motivational factors. During the interviews, students were able to provide their views on a wide range of issues relating to these domains within the context of their own experiences and personal observations. In the following part of the paper, the schooling experiences of Turkish students will be reported in relation to three areas: school advice, relations with teachers, and racism in schools and society.

School Advice for Secondary Education

The type of secondary school students can follow depends on how well they have done atprimary school in general, and their test scores in the last year of the primary school. Parents have the right to choose a secondary school, but the school decides whether or not to admit the child, through a consideration of the advice given by the primary school. Findings of mainstream research concerning the performance of children from ethnic minority groups in primary education suggest that the Dutch language proficiency is the most important cause of underachievement of these children, which, in turn, plays a decisive role in the unequal participation in secondary education. Minority children tend to score poorly on tests of language proficiency, mathematics, social competence, and intelligence (De Jong 1987; Eldering 1989; Mulder and Tesser 1992; Kloprogge et.al. 1994). Consequently, compared with the Dutch students, the representation of Turkish students in the various types of secondary schools displays enormous inequalities. The school placement advice given at the end of the primary school period determines this unequal representation to a large extent. According to a study conducted by Mulder and Tesser (1992), while close to 50 % of Turkish students received an advice for IVBO (individualized pre-vocational education) and VBO (pre-vocational education), 23 % of Dutch students received the same advice. The percentage of Turkish students with an advice for HAVO (senior general secondary education) and VWO (pre-university education) was 7,9, and for the Dutch students 32,9.

Against the background of such findings, we posed the Turkish students in the interview group questions relating to their experiences during the primary school period. Among the areas covered were the educational opportunities provided for their learning needs, attitudes towards the school, learning problems that they experienced, difficult years or periods, and the type and duration of any specific help which they received. The students appeared quite positive about their experiences during the primary school period. They indicated that they liked their teachers, got along well with their classmates, and had little or no difficulty with their lessons. Except some initial difficulties mentioned by some students, involved primarily in learning of or functioning with the Dutch language, there was no indication of any important problem relating to their education at that level. They were not confronted by their teachers with a learning problem that they would be experiencing. And there was no special provision for helping them. What surprised some of these students was the fact that they came to realize only in the last year of the primary school that they had not learned enough to succeed in tests at a level which they had expected of themselves.

»The last year was the most difficult period. We took many tests. No one helped us. I thought, ›why can't I do well in these tests, why is it so difficult, have I not learned anything so far?‹

Especially the last year was difficult. I couldn't succeed at a level I wanted. I felt like I was stupid. I thought also that the school advice was very low. I would have wanted to study at a higher level, but it didn't work out that way.«

In the interview group, almost half of the students said that they were not happy with the advice they had received from their primary schools. As the most important reason for this, they indicated the low expectation of teachers regarding students' abilities. In the following account, a fifth year HAVO student, who intends to transfer to VWO in order to be able to go to university, illustrates this point:

»For the last four years, I have been the most successful student in my class. When they gave me a MAVO advice in the last year of the primary school, I couldn't believe it. ... If I had known then what I know now, I would have chosen for VWO. I would have said, ›My grades are just as good as the other students, why do they get a HAVO/VWO advice and I get a MAVO advice?‹ ... I think that the teacher had no confidence in me. A year later when I passed to the second class, I went to see that teacher to show my report. He said he knew I would be successful. I asked him why he had given me a MAVO advice. He said he didn't know. Probably, he didn't trust me then.«

In the interview group there were other students with a comparable position to the above student. Despite the low advice of the primary school, they succeeded to transfer to a secondary school of their level and choice.

»I should have gone directly to HAVO. But they sent me to MAVO. I am now in the forth year of HAVO. This way, I lost one year.«

The school advice appears especially problematic from the viewpoint of those students who were placed in a VBO-school. These students experienced this as an injustice and they were of opinion that they were discriminated against by their primary school teachers. One student described his experience as follows:

»Until the last year of the primary school, there was no discrimination. In the last year, the teacher gave me VBO advice. But I wanted to go to a higher level. Nevertheless, what the teacher wanted happened. We couldn't do anything about it. We went to the community centre to ask for help. They said, ›if your teacher thinks so, we can't do anything about it.‹ ... The teacher had said to me, ›you can't even make it in the VBO‹. This made me so angry and ambitious at the sametime. When I transfered from VBO to MAVO, I went to the school to show my report. But the teacher was sick. He was not at the school.«

Some students problematized their school advice from the viewpoint of their ethnic identity. They compared their situation with that of Dutch students, and believed that teachers tended to give a lower advice to students of ethnic minority origin. They perceived this as an act of discrimination, and in some cases, as a source of motivation to succeed and prove themselves. In the following account, it is possible to see the elements of low teacher expectation, comparison with Dutch students, the role of prejudice against the ethnic group, and the problematization of student's language proficiency. It should be noted that this student, similar to the cases mentioned above, found it important to go back to the primary school a year later in order to confront the teacher with what she thought as an injustice done to herself.

»I wanted a school with not many minority children in it. I wanted to become a lawyer. I thought that a MAVO/HAVO school was suitable to my level. I could do HAVO. I had confidence in myself. But the teacher wanted to send me to VBO. I resisted to it. I insisted that I go to MAVO. I did this with a determined attitude of ›despite this teacher, and for my own future‹. Sometimes they say things about Turks. Like, we can not do it. But somebody has got to try. My brother supported me too. They gave me a VBO advice, because they thought of me as inferior. My test result were not bad at all. There was a Dutch girl who had the same scores. She got a MAVO advice, and I got VBO. I said, ›How can this be?‹ They said, ›Her Dutch is better than yours‹. I said, ›You do this only because she is Dutch, don't you?‹ But they denied it. Against their wish, I went to a MAVO school. In my second year I made it to the MAVO/HAVO. I took my report to the school to show it to that teacher. He said to me, »well done«.

Among the students interviewed, the feeling was shared that primary schools generally discriminate against students of ethnic minority origin by giving them a lower advice. Thus, they tended to perceive their own school advice also within the context of the experiences of other Turkish students in their environment.

»After the primary school they wanted to send me to MAVO. My older sister had gonethrough the same experience. Therefore, she made it sure that I could go to VWO. They said in the school that I could not make it in the VWO. They said, ›It is for your own good. You can't do it‹. But they knew very well that I didn't have bad grades. Although my sister had also very good grades, they sent her to VBO. That is very bad.«

Several students in the interview group found it important, therefore, that the coming generations of Turkish students their families should be suspicious of the correctness of the advice which they will receive. They pointed out that the given school advice was influenced by the stereotyped attitudes of teachers against ethnic minority groups in general, and the Turkish minority in particular.

»I didn't do any test in the last year of the primary school. They adviced me to go to VBO. My mother was against it. ... They thought that, because I am Turkish, I was going to getmarried and drop out of school anyway. ... I am now in the second class of MBO. When I am finished I'll go on to higher education. ... If we hadn't objected it, I wouldn't have been here at this level now. I would still continue with my education. But, to get to the level where I am now, it would have taken me a longer time. Much longer. You have to make all kinds of turns.«

As can be expected, the majority of the students follows their school advice, even though they may think that they could have studied at a higher level. Within the interview group, the students that fall into this category pointed out that they were unhappy and regretful, and they lacked a feeling of personal attachment to the school, and found the lessons rather easy.

As mentioned earlier, the school advice given at the end of the primary school plays a critical role with respect to the position and the level of success of the Turkish students at the secondary school level. Despite the research evidence indicating problems of underachievement at the primary school level, there seems to be institutional factors at work influencing these processes in a negative way. Taking the student experiences as a basis, the biased assessment and testing procedures and the stereotyped attitudes and low expectations of ethnic minorities among the teachers should be considered among these factors. As the above data suggest, there exists a discrepancy between the given school advice and the actual position and achievement level of the students. Similarly, a discrepancy exists between student expectations and the given school advice (for similar findings, see Nelissen and Bilgin 1995).

Student-Teacher Relations

A particular problem of ethnic relations in education is the ways in which ethno-cultural differences are perceived and acted upon by teachers in their interactions with students. Several studies substantiate the influence of teacher bias and expectancy on student performance. These biases or preconceived judgments may lead to specific teacher behaviors, which create interpersonal barriers for the involvement of these students in learning. Exclusion, stereotyping, fragmentation, imbalance and linguistic bias are processes, indicative of biased teacher behavior that adversely affects the potential success of students. It may be safe to assume, therefore, as Cummins (1988) emphasized, that the most direct determinant of minority student outcomes is the type of interaction students experience with teachers. Minority students are empowered or disabled as a direct result of their interactions with teachers. These interactions are mediated by the role definitions of teachers which are moulded by a variety of influences.

With respect to their interaction with teachers, all the students in the interview group spoke of the importance of having a positive and close relation with their teachers. They expected that teachers show respect, understanding, support en encouragement, and equal treatment. In general, the students appeared highly sensitive and extremely perceptive of teacher behavior and attitudes.

»It is very important for me to have a warm relationship with the teachers. When my teachers don't help me, I feel very lonesome. ... I don't want that teachers give me a special sort of attention. I don't want that. They should treat us in an equal way. ... To me, a teacher should understand the special circumstances of a student. He should be considerate.

I like my teachers very much. Some of them teach very well, and some are very helpful. When you have a problem with your lessons or another problem, they help you.

I can speak about everything with my teachers. I have good relations with them. This has a positive influence on my success. They give me confidence, they say I can do it. Then I work harder and do better.«

Besides a friendly and close personal relationship, a certain amount of stress in the form of high expectations serves to improve performance. The students mentioned positive experiences with teachers who related their high expectations to them directly and in an encouraging way.

»Some of my teachers say, if I don't do something well, ›Is this really you? First you had a nine, and now two. How is this possible?‹ I am pleased with this type of interest.

In this school, the interest that teachers have in us is very good. For instance, the math teacher has been very supportive of me. When I think sometimes that I won't be able to do well, he says, ›You can do it, come on, we'll work together‹.

The teacher says, ›You didn't do well in your exam, how could this happen?‹ Such an interest from a teacher gives me confidence. I feel stronger and try to improve my performance.«

The students want to be treated equally by their teachers, and they find it unacceptable that some teachers appear to make a distinction between minority and Dutch students. In the mean time, they expect that teachers display certain attitudes and sensitivities towards ethnic minority students.

»Teachers should be considerate of the background of a minority student. They should respecthis culture. They should know their way with him and speak with him.

Teachers should behave friendly to minority students. They should help them. Dutch students feel generally at ease. That is not always the case with minority students.«

The students talked also about their experiences with prejudiced and discriminatory teachers. As they did so, they referred essentially to a particular teacher and in some cases they used the term »some teachers«. They also made statements referring to teachers in general. The remarks of the students about the problematic aspects of their interactions with teachers were concerned with open discriminatory acts, prejudice over ethnic groups, differential treatment of minority and majority students, and discriminatory assessment of learning outcomes. Below, a selection of specific accounts of these interactions is described and analyzed.

In the experiences of some student, it is possible to detect teacher attitudes which take the form of an explicitly prejudiced interaction with students and discriminatory practices. Among the negative responses to Turkish students expressed by teachers, within or outside the classroom context, were also an open disapproval of the customs and traditions. Such teacher behavior added to the negative experiences of school of some of these students. In some cases, the students mentioned experiences in which some teachers were even involved in the use of direct forms of racist and ethnicist verbal abuse. As the following accounts make it clear, these attacks include accusation of theft, cursing of religious and cultural practices, and degrading remarks over the ethnic identity of the students.

»There is a teacher who gives English and sale practice. I don't trust him. He hates minorities. If a Turkish or Moroccan boy comes into the class with something new, he asks always where he lifted it. ... There is no problem among the students in this school. If there is racism, it comes from the teachers.«

»One of the teachers says things in the form of a joke. He calls Turks, for example, because they fast during the Ramadan, ›hungery apes‹ and Moroccans ›camels‹.

They [teachers] say that Turks should be ashamed of themselves.

There is this teacher who often says in a degrading tone, ›you Turks, you Moroccans‹, when we make a mistake. He makes me so angry.

A teacher in this school said to a student that he stank, and that he had to wash himself first and then come back. He would never say something like that to a Dutch student.«

The above accounts relate to the observable, clear-cut instances of racist discriminatory acts by some teacher. The students mentioned also experiences in which stereotypical views of some teachers over the ethnic group are revealed.

»Teachers have certain ideas over us, because we are Turkish or Moroccan. In the first place, they should get rid of these ideas. ... Some teachers have reacted to me in a very strange manner. Like, ›Are you really so free, can you do this all, do you really think so, are you not going to get married?‹. When I hear such things from them, I feel like saying, ›Who do you think you are‹. There exists so much ignorance, so many stereotypes. When they get to know you better, it disappears. But that doesn't mean that they will not do the same thing again with others.«

In their talks with the students, teachers relate their prejudice and low expectations of the ethnic group in a variety of ways. Even when a teacher praises a student for his success, this could be perceived by the student as an act of humiliation towards his own ethnic group.

»One of the teachers said to me that I was exceptional. He said that there were not many others like me. Among the Turks, of course. Only I was so. ... The fact that I am successful amazes them.«

In relation to teacher prejudice and discrimination, the students mentioned also that they could see a difference in the way in which teachers behave towards Dutch students and students of ethnic minority origin.

»The teachers show more interest in the Dutch students and they discriminate against us. We are all their students. They shouldn't do something like that.

There are some teachers that act cool and distant to minority students, simply because they are foreigners.

Some teachers are nicer to the Dutch students. I see that. I just feel it.«

According to some students, teachers' differential treatment of minority and majority students results in discriminatory assessment practices.

»In the assessment of our homeworks and exams, teachers discriminate sometimes between us and the Dutch students. This is very bad.

For example, there is a Dutch girl and a Turkish girl. For the same work, she gets an eight and the Turkish girl a five. To me, this is discrimination.

There are teachers in this school that discriminate. ... For example, we make a presentation in the class. You see that a Dutch student doesn't do well. But you prepare yourself at home very well before you come to school. The Dutch student says that he did not prepare at all. He gets a nine and you get a six. Perhaps the Dutch student speaks a bit clearer, but the teacher doesn't want to see that you have worked much harder. Teachers are nicer to Dutch students.«

Asked about how they react to teacher prejudice and discrimination, some students said that they confronted the teacher with it. Those students who said that they had not had a direct experience with discrimination by teachers indicated that, in case it would happen, they would relate the matter to the school director. The students thought in general that there was little that could be done about the subtle and indirect forms of teacher discrimination. In taking a stance against teacher discrimination, some students seemed to calculate the formal power the teachers have over themselves.

Racism in Schools and Society

During the interviews, the students reflected their views on the nature of ethnic relations within their schools and in their environment. As institutions, schools operate within a larger society, which has powerful and dynamic forces that affect teachers and students directly and indirectly. Recent attitudinal surveys indicate a widespread racist sentiment among the different layers of the Dutch society. According to a study conducted by the Dutch Interdisciplinary Institute for Demographic Research, more than 50 % of the sample surveyed expressed the wish that migrants, who are unemployed for more than a year, should return to their countries of origin. Also the majority of the respondents found that the government should stimulate migrants to return back to their countries with some financial help. Compared with the results of a similar survey in 1990, the attitudes of the Dutch people towards migrants became more negative (Van Leusten and Moors 1995). According to another study, the majority of the Dutch population still would like to consider the Netherlands a white man's country (Van Leusden and Moors 1988). In a survey of youth attitudes, two-third of the sample expressed the opinion that there should be no more foreigners permitted into the Netherlands and almost 20 % of the sample defined ethnic minority groups as a »threat«. There is a growing group among the youngsters, holding »biological racist ideas«; 7.8 % of the sample found that migrants were less intelligent than the Dutch and expressed the opinion that they must be sent back to their homelands (Kleinpenning 1993).

In the interviews, the students spoke of their concern about the deteriorating racial climate in the Dutch society.

»I don't like it here anymore like I used to. In the past, I didn't want to be anywhere else. But now, I feel less so. They look down at Turkish people in the Netherlands. I never used to think about discrimination or so. The other day I read in the newspaper that one third of the Dutch people don't want any foreigners here. That surprised me. One third or two third, I don't remember. I try to be careful now.

When you say racism, I think of things like ›Get out of our city, what are you doing here‹.Then I feel like a tourist. I mean, an illegal person. I become very angry. I want to hit that person.

I am really angry about racism. When they say, ›Go back to your country‹, I say, ›What would have happened in this country if we hadn't come. We did the dirty work while you were sitting at home. You say to us now that we live on your tax money. ... In order to prevent racism, they must talk about it in schools. We did not come here with bad intentions‹.

They throw bombs to mosques. In Germany, they attact Turkish people. I see such things on television. It is really absurd.«

Problems involved in ethnic relations in the larger society affect the schools system in a variety of ways. In the large cities where minority populations are concentrated, school segregation has become a serious problem not only at the primary but also at the secondary level. As a result of the combination of discriminatory housing policies and White-flight, the majority of children from ethnic groups receive their education in the so-called black schools. During the interviews, the students indicated the negative consequences of this development with respect to the quality of education, school climate, the quality of physical environment of the schools, the discipline in the classroom and contacts with Dutch students.

»The first three years, I was happy with my school. But, not any more. Everything is changed. There are other teachers and students. The climate in the school is changed. They used to treat us better.

There are big differences between this school and other schools: outside, canteen, the way in which teachers deal with the homework. In this school they don't look at our homeworks.

This school used to be good. But, as the number of minority students increased, the discipline faded away. ... I would like a school in which there is discipline and there are more Dutch students. Speaking with them would help us learn Dutch better.«

Especially, the lack of discipline was problematized by the students in schools with a large minority student representation. They spoke of their preference for a school in which the composition of student population is multi-ethnic, the administration and teachers have authority over the students, classroom activities take place in an harmonious and orderly manner, the teachers take their jobs seriously, control homework, and follow student progress.

Many of the students who attended schools with a high concentration of ethnic minority students pointed out that they did not experience racism within the school. Those students who mentioned some specific incidents of racism expressed their disappointment in the lack of attention from their their teachers and school administration in confronting such acts. In other words, teachers, although aware of the racial harrassment experienced by Turkish students, seem reluctant to formally address to this issue.

»There is no racism in the school. We are all foreigners anyway. Sometimes, teachers discriminate. But, it is not really obvious.

In my second year here, I met racism. The Dutch students said to me things like ›Stupid Turk, go back to your country.‹ I went to talk with the school director about it. He told me not to pay attention to such things. The school administration doesn't take such things seriously.

If someone says something racist to me, I tell my teacher about it. But he doesn't bring us together to talk it out.«

Independent of the fact whether they have had a direct experience with racist discrimination, the students appeared highly concerned with racism in schools and in the society. They emphasized that schools should take an active role in dealing with these processes. Among the points which they mentioned were a clear school policy on anti-racism, disciplinary measures against racist acts, teaching about racism and discrimination, and clearly stated guidelines for the selection and appointment of teachers.

Another issue here is the actual patterns of interaction between students and their relationship to ethnicity, that is, how far ethnicity informs the formation and structure of school-based frienship groupings. There was not a single student in the interview group who had a close Dutch friend in his/her friendship group. For some students, the reason for this was the absence of Dutch students in the school or in the environment. Yet, in schools with a multi-ethnic student population, the friendship relations between the Dutch and Turkish students leave much to be desired. The Turkish students prefer as friends students from their own group or from other ethnic minority groups. Among the reasons given for this preference were the lack of solidarity, stereotypical attitudes and discriminatory acts which they experienced with the Dutch students.

Conclusion

The interview material reported above illuminates the point that characteristics of ethnic minority student populations are not sufficient to explain or predict academic achievement. School variables must be taken into account. An important factor which contributes potentially to underachievement and unequal representation of the Turkish students is stereotyped attitudes of teachers which take the form of an explicitly prejudiced interaction with students and low expectations of students' abilities and achievement. Students are extremely perceptive and are capable of understanding the meaning of these attitudes. The students' ethnicity influence their interaction with teachers and their experience of teacher expectations. Stereotyping of minority students appears to play an important part in misassessment and misplacement, as well as other aspects of school experiences of these students. A systematic monitoring and evaluation of school advice given at the end of the primary school period is a necessity.

Dealing with differential achievement patterns requires the elimination of racist discriminations, exclusion and prejudice and a greater appreciation of cultural diversity, both in society and in the schools. Improvement in educational outcomes for ethnic minority students depends significantly on changes in teacher attitudes toward minority students, adaptations in curriculum and instruction, and the use of culturally and linguistically unbiased testing and assessment procedures. Changing the basic attitudinal orientation and knowledge base of teachers is necessary. Teachers should be provided with opportunities to examine their expectations and perceptions of ethnic minor-

ity students. Finally, there is an urgent need for more research information on overt and covered racism in schools and in the education
system, and how this relates to performance of ethnic minority pupils
and wider educational issues.

References

Alkan, M. and R. Kabdan (1995), *Goed onderwijs, een goede baan
en een gelukkig leven*, Amsterdam.
Appel, R. (1984), *Immigrant children learning Dutch,*. Doordrecht.
Appel, R. and A. Vermeer (1994), *Tweede-taalverwerving en tweede
taalonderwijs*, Bussum.
Berg, H. van den and P. Reinsch (1983), *Racisme in schoolboeken,*
Amsterdam.
Bervoets, M. (1992), *Aandacht voor slimme sakina*, Amsterdam.
Coenen, M. and T. Vallen (1991), »Itembias in de eindtoets basison-
derwijs«, in: *Pedagogische Studien*, no. 1, pp. 15-27.
Cummins, J. (1988), »From multicultural to anti-racist education: An
analysis of programmes and policies in Ontario«, in: Cummins, J.
and T. Skutnabb-Kangas (eds.), *Minority education: From Shame
to struggle*, Clevedon, Philadelphia.
Dijk, T.A. van (1987), *Schoolvoorbeelden van racisme*, Amsterdam.
Driessen (1992), *De onderwijspositie van allochtone leerlingen. De
rol van sociaaleconomische en etnische-culturele factoren, met
speciaale aandacht voor het onderwijs in eigen taal en cultuur*,
Nijmegen.
Eldering, L. (1989), »Ethnic minority children in Dutch schools: Un-
derachievement and its explanations«, in: L. Eldering en J. Klo-
progge (eds.), *Different Cultures Same School*, Amsterdam/Lisse,
pp. 107-136.
Erp, M. van e.a. (1992), *Overeenkomst en verschil*, Amsterdam.
Extra, G. and T. Vallen (1989), »Meertaligheid en samenleving«, in:
Entzinger, H.B. and P.J.J. Stijnen (red.), *Etnische minderheden in
Nederland*, Baarn.
Gillborn, D. (1990), *»Race«, Ethnicity and Education: Teaching and
Learning in Multi-Ethnic Schools*, London.

Hofman, W.H.A. (1993), *Effectief onderwijs aan allochtone leerlingen*, Delft.

Jong, M.J. de (1987), *Herkomst, kennis en kansen*, Lisse.

Kerkhoff, A. (1988), *Taalvaardigheid en schoolsucces. De relatie tussen taalvaardigheid Nederlands en Schoolsucces van allochtone en autochtone leerlingen aan het eind vande basis-school*, Amsterdam/Lisse.

Kerkhoff, A. (1989), »De geschiedenis herhaalt zich: onderwijskansen van allochtone kinderen«, in: *Migrantenstudies*, 5, 2, 1989, pp. 32-48.

Kleinpenning (1993), *Reported in De Volkskrant*, 11 september 1993.

Kloprogge, Jo, L. Mulder, G. Walraven and G.van der Verf (1994), *Verwachtingen en realiteit kruipen naar elkaar toe*, Den Haag.

Lange, R. de (1987), »Houden leraren wel genoeg van hun allochtone leerlingen?«, in: *Didaktief*, 17, 4, pp. 6-9.

Langen, A. van and P. Jungbluth (1990), *Onderwijskansen van Migranten. De rol van sociaal-economische en culturele factoren*, Amsterdam /Lisse.

Ledoux, G., P. Deckers, E. de Bruijn and E. Voncken (1992), *Met het oog op de toekomst. Ideeën over onderwijs en arbeid van ouders en kinderen uit de doelgroepen van het onderwijsvoorrangsbeleid*, Amsterdam.

Leusden, H and H. Moors (1988), »Mede-landers?«, in: *Demos*. vol. 4, no. 5, pp. 33-36.

Leusden, H and H. Moors (1995), »Leeftijd en opleiding sterk bepalend voor meningen over allochtonen«, in: *Demos*, vol. 11, no. 6, pp. 44-46.

Mac an Ghaill, M. (1989), »Coming of age in 1980's in England: reconceptualizing black students' schooling experience«, in: *British Journal of Sociology of Education*, 10.

Matthijssen, M.A.J.M. (1993), *Lessen in orde voor migranten. Leerlingperspectieven van allochtonen in het voortgezet onderwijs*, Amersfoort.

McKracken, G. (1988), *The long interview*, Newbury Park.

Meijnen, G.W. and F.S.J. Riemersma (1992), *Schoolcarrières: een klassekwestie?*, Amsterdam.

Mok, I. (1990), *Anti-racisme en schoolboeken*, Amsterdam.

Mulder, L. and P. Tesser (1992), *De schoolkeuze van allochtone leerlingen*, Nijmegen.

Nelissen, Carien and Sibel Bilgin (1995), *De school thuis*, Rijswijk.

Teunissen, F. (1990), »Onderwijs«, in: H.B. Entzinger and P.J.J. Stijnen (red.), *Etnische minderheden in Nederland*, Amsterdam, pp. 141-167.

Verkuyten, M. (1988), *Zelfbeleving en identiteit van jongeren uit etnische minderheden*, Gouda.

Wright, C. (1992), »Multiracial primary school classrooms«, in: Gill, D., B. Mayor and M. Blair (eds.), *Racism and Education: Structures and Strategies*, London.

Anton Trant/Elizabeth McSkeane

Wider Horizons for Young People: A Case Study in Reconciliation in Ireland, North and South

Background of Conflict in Ireland

This paper is entitled a case-study in reconciliation. The word reconciliation implies estrangement, alienation and enmity between people who should be friends. In other words it implies a state of conflict between rivals. It is important therefore to try to understand the underlying causes of this conflict, else how can we attempt to reconcile the rival parties? If people are to seek forgiveness from one another they must first know what sin they have committed.

Ireland is a small island of about 100.000 square kilometres in area. Its people for the most part speak the same language and practise one form or other of the Christian faith. We have a common history of being colonised by our neighbouring island, Britain, for several hundred years, and have benefited or suffered from this process - depending on which point of view you take. We share the same material culture and to an outsider we look alike, wear the same kind of clothes, eat the same kind of food, drive the same kind of cars and look at the same kind of television programmes - more or less.

Yet for all that Ireland is a divided country. A political border winds its tortuous way over 400 kilometres, dividing fields and farms rivers and lakes, roads and railways, - and even in one case - so it is said - somebody's house. If you walk, along this border, in some places you are in danger of losing your way and may find yourself wandering from one part of the country into the other and back again without being aware that you have changed jurisdictions. This border, however, is but a symbol of a deeper division - a division of minds and hearts among the people who live together on the island. We cannot live at peace with each other, neither can we agree on the way the island as a whole should be governed. We are a divided country and a divided people.

The reasons for these divisions have been explored at great length by all manner of people - politicians, church leaders, historians, sociologists, economists, psychologists, anthropologists, journalists, novelists, dramatists, poets and even film makers. The volume of research and scholarly publications on what is sometimes called the Irish question is enormous. There has been a huge outflow of scholarly work since 1969, the beginning of the current phase of »the Troubles«, so much so that one researcher, Professor John Whyte, was able to examine no fewer than 540 serious titles which had appeared mostly between 1969 and 1990, all purporting to explain the reasons for the conflict (White 1990). What we can we say then in a short paper like this without risking a distortion of the truth by an oversimplification of the facts? We must try nonetheless to give some kind of explanation, otherwise, as we said at the beginning, of the paper we cannot seriously talk of reconciliation.

It is possible to distinguish three broad categories among the various theories on the reasons for the present troubles in Ireland. The first would put the blame on Britain, arguing that the problem is chiefly caused by the British occupation of the six north-eastern counties of Ireland, the entity officially known as Northern Ireland. This view sees the solution essentially dependent on Britain withdrawing its forces from Northern Ireland, thereby paving the way for the unification of both parts of Ireland, North and South. The view in its extreme form is that of the IRA, a paramilitary organisation which up to very recently has pursued its aims through physical force.

The second view would put the blame on the South, the Irish Republic, which comprises the greater part of the island. This view, which is held by a large number of Unionists in Northern Ireland (people who owe their allegiance to Britain and who want Northern Ireland to remain an integral part of the United Kingdom), sees the main problem to be the fact that the Irish Republic lays claim to the whole island of Ireland, a claim which is supported by a large minority in Northern Ireland, as well as by many people in the South. The view in its extreme form is held by the Unionist paramilitary organisations, which like the IRA have up to recently promoted their aims through violence.

The third view sees the problem as being chiefly within Northern Ireland itself because within that small entity there are two sharply divided communities, unionist and nationalist, the first largely Protestant, the second Catholic, the one calling itself British, the other Irish, with the former traditionally in a position of dominance and power and the latter increasingly rejecting a position of subservience and lack of status.

The first two explanations are variations of nationalism; the third can be described as a theory of inter-community conflict. All three lead us to conclude that there are three strands to the problem and therefore three related dimensions to any solution which will emerge. We may express it like this: the situation is a complex amalgam of three sets of relationships:

– within Northern Ireland, between two antagonistic communities, who live side by side in the same jurisdiction;
– within Ireland as a whole, between the people both North and South, who have to share the same small island;
– between Ireland and Britain, who have to agree on the best way the island is governed.

A last point about the conflict before we turn to possible ways of reconciliation, is that it would appear safe to assume from what we have said above that the core of the problem is essentially linked with the issue of identity; in other words there are different ways in which people in Ireland express their identity and these ways are sometimes in conflict with each other. Hence, the views and perceptions that people hold about each other are often expressed in hostile terms. These perceptions may or may not be grounded in reality; the important thing is that people hold to these views firmly, often passionately, and sometimes are prepared to kill because of them.

Anton Trant / Elizabeth McSkeane

The Way of Reconciliation

In Ireland today, you will sometimes hear people speak in despairing tones of the conflict which has now persisted for a quarter of a century in Northern Ireland, and which has sometimes overflowed into the South and into Britain. The legacy of bitterness and enmity created by the Troubles now seems so deep that no solution seems possible and no matter what remedy is suggested you will always find one group or other which will remain intransigent. The old slogans »no surrender« and »not an inch« are still very powerful catch-cries.

Yet it has to be said that the conflict has also generated a wide variety of peace and reconciliation initiatives at all levels of society. It is fair to say that there is a groundswell of good will and yearning for peace, a readiness to come together to see if any basis can be found for mutual understanding and co-operation. There are many individuals and organisations devoted to these ideals and, in recent years there has been a great ferment in thinking about causes and possible solutions. In this paper I shall very briefly describe one particular reconciliation initiative - not untypical of much of what is going on in Ireland today.

In 1986 an organisation called the International Fund for Ireland was established by both the British and Irish Governments with the aim »to promote economic and social advance and to encourage contact, dialogue and reconciliation between nationalists and unionists throughout Ireland« (Annual Report 1987/88). This organisation is an international fund in the sense that it has attracted financial support from abroad - largely from the US and the European Union, and also from Canada and New Zealand. To date the International Fund for Ireland has received UK£240 million in such donations. The Fund comprises a series of programmes in North/South co-operation in areas like tourism, urban development, business enterprise, rural development and community regeneration. All these programmes regulate the giving of grants to foster initiatives as varied as building hotels and industrial complexes to reopening a disused canal as a means of communication and leisure pursuits between North and South.

One of the Fund's programmes is different from the others in that it is centred on people and on promoting their training and employment opportunities. It does this by sending groups abroad for periods of about two months - mainly to the US, Canada and the countries of the European Union - to places where they can obtain relevant training and work experience. Every group, which comprises about 15 to 20 people, has to contain two dimensions - it must have both Catholics and Protestants from Northern Ireland, and also there must be participants from the South as well as the North. To ensure that each project group functions as a unit requires considerable preparation and leadership well in advance of the actual overseas experience, and when you consider the different backgrounds of the people who make up the group - Catholic and Protestant, and North as well as South - this is a considerable achievement.

The Programme covers a wide spectrum of people, from managers of businesses to young people with poor qualifications and poor prospects of employment. The Programme is called - appropriately enough - »Wider Horizons« and it is oriented largely towards people in the age range 16-28 years. It seeks to make an impact on people's lives by sending them into a situation very different from the one they are used to, and so hopefully enhance their employability and deepen their understanding of each other. Thus the Programme can be said to have a two-fold aim: to promote mutual understanding and reconciliation through vocational preparation and professional development.

The Practice of Reconciliation within Wider Horizons

One of the most noticeable effects of the Wider Horizons experience is the opportunity it gives to the participants to re-evaluate their own situations back home. Coping with the demands of living in a strange environment creates a separation which for some people is as much psychological as physical, a space which allows them to see familiar situations from new points of view. One project group report describes how the participants who travelled to the US in 1991 as part of a younger managers' development programme learned much about their own culture as a result of their time in the US:

»Trainee managers reported on what they felt had been a real widening of horizons in their approach both to Northern Ireland and to the Republic. For some, the project had enabled them to visit the other side of the Irish Border for the first time. They felt that their time abroad had enabled them to see their own communities in perspective, and while they seldom talked amongst themselves about national and denominational differences, the experience of explaining such differences to Americans had proved valuable in clarifying their own minds. Some were now interested in working in the hospitality industry on the other side of the Border from their own home.« (Trant and McSkeane 1994, 45-46)

Contact with people from other cultures, for whom Ireland and its troubles are distant and even inexplicable, can challenge Wider Horizons participants to explain their own tradition not only to their overseas hosts but to themselves. This is turn can lay the ground for sympathy and understanding between neighbours, who in Ireland consider each other as strangers. For the twenty young marketing students who trained and worked in San Francisco in 1989, the experience revealed as much about Ireland as it did about the US:

»The most important exploration of differences and sensitivities appears to have taken place across the Border as opposed to across the already in some senses well-explored Northern cross-community boundary. Many Southerners found that they had learned greatly about the North in the company of the Northern students. The majority had never visited the North, and confessed themselves previously ill-informed on the area; all were now intending to visit. One Southern girl felt that finding out about the North was an ›eye-opener... an interesting analogy‹.

Another Southern girl who had worked in the Soviet Union thought that in its depth of interest and novelty talking to Northerners was ›like finding out about Russia‹. Northerners also felt that they had learned about the other part of Ireland. To some, the trip to Galway was as novel an experience as the trip to San Francisco.« (Trant and McSkeane 1994, 47-48)

It seems, therefore, that ignorance and preconceptions exist not only between the communities on both sides of the Northern divide, but on both sides of the Border. It is revealing to know that to some young people on this island, Galway or Belfast may seem as exotic, or as alien, as San Francisco or Moscow. Conversely, young Northerners sometimes discover how much they have in common with each other as compared with their Southern counterparts. »We have more to argue about«, one young Northern Protestant observed, and sounded pleasantly surprised (ibid.).

A significant feature of the project reports to date is the infrequency with which sectarian conflict is reported within the groups. Considering that Wider Horizons has brought together four and a half thousand people from the different traditions in Ireland, this is quite remarkable. It may be that the novelty and exhilaration of enjoying new experiences and facing unfamiliar challenges makes the participants more inclined to put their differences aside than they would at home. It is possible also that there is a self-selecting process at work, whereby people who agree to take part in a project which promotes contact with an alien tradition are already less prejudiced and therefore less likely to engage in sectarian conflict than those who do not participate in such projects. Or it may be that those who write the project reports are, understandably, less than eager to publicise unpleasant behaviour. Whatever the reasons, the fact remains that in over a hundred reports surveyed, only a very small number document conflict of any kind, and this arises more often as a result of personality clashes or professional differences between the organisers than among the people in their care. This suggests that the very fact of being together may be a significant factor in helping to dissolve the sectarian and political barriers which divide people.

This surmise is supported by the theory known as the »contact hypothesis«, which was formulated in the US in the wake of World War II and sought to combat hostile perceptions of Japanese and other ethnic groups perceived by white Americans as »the enemy«. The theory implies that bringing together individual members of conflict groups automatically results in a modification of attitudes and behaviour which are based on ignorance and prejudice. This is the reasoning underlying several contact programmes in Northern Ireland among them the Holiday Schemes Project which brought Protestant and Catholic children together for community holidays. The Department of Education, Northern Ireland, which funded the Holiday Schemes Project, described it as a »practical means of facilitating the coming together of children and young people in circumstances that will contribute to increased understanding between the two traditions« (ibid.).

The contact theory supports the view that in order to promote harmony and mutual understanding among conflict groups, it is sufficient to bring about contact between them. Reconciliation »just happens« of its own accord and therefore inputs which make specific mention of religion, politics or prejudice reduction are neither necessary or desirable. Many Wider Horizons projects come into this category in that they do not include explicitly structured guidance on reconciliation issues.

Is Contact Enough?

The question however remains - is contact alone enough? To date, the vast majority of Wider Horizons projects have operated from the premise that it is, and some of the anecdotal evidence summarised above seems to support this. However, it must be pointed out that in the absence of more extensive documentation or supportive field research, this is a conclusion which cannot be drawn with certainty. Contact by itself may not be sufficient to ensure reconciliation. Some researchers now argue it is unlikely when two groups are brought together that harmony will necessarily ensue, unless contact is augmented by additional factors. In other words, if integration and mutual understanding are left to happen as a natural and inevitable consequence of people simply being together, reconciliation very possibly may not happen at all. And even if it does, the breaking down of barriers between individuals need make no difference to their perception of the alien group to which their new friends belong (Ruddle and O'Connor 1992, 21-25). This is not to say that contact is not important but rather points to the conclusion that contact without the support of specially designed activities, which encourage growth in mutual understanding, cannot be depended upon to produce the ambitious effects embodied in a programme like Wider Horizons.

It is also important to remember that conflict within any particular group can be exacerbated by factors which are not political or religious in origin. This is illustrated in the case of a Wider Horizons group which met for the first time at a pre-departure residential seminar. By the end of the seminar all the participants were on excellent terms with each other. Political and religious boundaries appeared to have dissolved and cross-Border and cross-community friendships had emerged. It was nevertheless a very divided group and the most obvious division was that of age. While some of the participants were still in their teens, most were in their mid-twenties and at least two were approaching thirty. A divergence of attitudes and aspirations, which one would expect from people with such different life experiences, had begun to emerge and it was obvious that some of the younger people were irritated by the well-meaning advice proffered by their elders and would-be-mentors.

Educational attainment and aspirations divided this group still further. While a few participants had completed post-primary schooling and hoped to continue to further education or a professional career, most were interested in manual skills and had few qualifications, with at least one young man having difficulties with reading. Another division was gender; the young women in the group were seriously out-numbered and openly admitted to feeling disregarded or even occasionally threatened by the overwhelming male presence. Add to this the natural variations in personality and temperament, which make some people dominate a group and others wish to hide in it, and we get some idea of the potential tensions and conflicts which made up the project. In fact the group was probably little more divided than many other Wider Horizons groups but the point to be emphasised here is that when conflicts do arise in such a group they may be sparked by differences in age, personality, education and gender as much as by religious and political allegiances.

For this reason the theoretical framework offered by Taijfel's Social Identity Theory (SIT) may be useful in unravelling the effects of programmes like Wider Horizons which aim to promote reconciliation among divided people. SIT locates the study of conflict and its resolution in the question of identity, and specifically focuses on the link between group membership and the development of a positive self-concept. People, according to the SIT model, tend to simplify the complexities of their environment by creating social categories such as »us« and »them« - the in-group to which one »belongs« and the alien or out-group. The in-group is homogenised and differences between members mitigated so that everyone who belongs feels more or less the same in important and pre-defined ways - for example in religious persuasion or in the football team supported. On the other hand differences between the in-group and the out-group are exaggerated, and this is but a short step to identifying »them« as »the enemy«. An important spin-off from such an over-simplification is the positive sense of self which derives from the belief that one's own group is somehow »better« than the despised out-group. As Tajfel himself put it:

»In order for large numbers of individuals to be able to hate or dislike or discriminate against other individuals seen as belonging to a common social category, they must first have acquired a sense of belonging to groups (or social categories) which are clearly distinct from and stand in certain relation to those they hate, dislike or discriminate against.« (Taijfel 1978, 50)

It is not difficult to imagine how this model can illuminate the Catholic/Nationalist - Protestant/Unionist polarisation in the Northern conflict. Ed Cairns, a social psychologist at the University of Ulster, has assembled evidence from a number of research studies which indicated that the SIT theory fits the Northern Ireland situation in several respects (Cairns 1987). The theory can also help to explain the preoccupation with identity that many observers have noted in Northern Ireland (Whyte 1990, 97).

Necessary Conditions for Reconciliation

A study of the research literature on reconciliation seems to indicate that there are five broad conditions necessary for successful work in this field: (1) maintaining an intergroup as well as an interpersonal focus in the contact situation; (2) ensuring that there is equality of status among all the participants; (3) recognising differences as well as similarities; (4) co-operating together in the pursuit of superordinate goals; and (5) creating a safe and suitable environment (see Ruddle and O'Connor 1992; Falconer 1988; Hurley 1994). In describing these five conditions we shall look at the performance of Wider Horizons under each heading, and in doing so we shall attempt an assessment of the Programme's contribution toward prejudice reduction and mutual understanding.

Intergroup Focus: The intergroup approach is based on the premise that if attitudes are to change then contact must take place in a situation where the interaction that occurs is between individuals as representing the different conflicting groups rather than individuals as individuals. Brown and Turner argue that where intergroup contact leads to positive changes in attitude, this is because of basic changes in the attitudes of the groups towards each other rather than the outcome of new friendships between various individuals (Brown and Turner 1981). According to this view changes in interpersonal relations are an effect rather than a cause of a more general change in intergroup relations.

An intergroup as well as an interpersonal focus is a basic tenet in Wider Horizons and is possibly the most significant contribution the Programme is making in the field of reconciliation. In an overview of reconciliation projects in Northern Ireland, one researcher has pointed out that the intergroup approach is the exception rather than the rule and that the bulk of projects could be regarded as encouraging superficial contact only (McCartney 1985, 25). The intergroup approach in Wider Horizons entails lengthy periods of negotiation between sponsors, agreement on procedures, joint planning, organising various preparatory, overseas and follow-up activities, and generally ensuring that the project group develops into a cohesive and harmonious unit. This is no mean undertaking when one takes into account the several different sub-groups which can take part in a project.

Equality of Status: Allport, one of the earliest researchers in the area of prejudice and tolerance, argued that participants in a successful reconciliation project must be of equal status, pursue equal goals, and be given social and institutional support (Allport 1954, 22). The

301

most obvious application of this to Wider Horizons is to ensure that in all its projects the proportions of cross-community and cross-Border participation are equitable. The Programme's official policy on this is unambiguous: participation should be one third Northern Protestant, one third Northern Catholic and one third from the South.

Recognition of Differences as well as Similarities: This is sometimes described as avoiding the »culture of politeness«, which Ruddle and O'Connor, describe in the following terms:

»When groups first meet in the contact situation, their behaviour initially is likely to be polite and superficial. Each side strives to establish safe patterns of interaction and, to do so, seeks out similarities or common needs. This pattern is reinforced by the prevailing social value to be polite at all costs. While this approach of smoothing over differences may mean that an atmosphere of bonhomie prevails, however, if the contact continues in this mode it means that no controversial information is shared and unchallenged myths may be perpetuated.« (Allport 1954, 24)

In order to overcome the culture of politeness and to create genuine intergroup contact, it is necessary that people acknowledge that differences do divide them and that these differences be discussed and explored in a positive manner. This implies confronting what Ed Cairns called the »denial syndrome« - the frequently observed convention that politics and religion are to be avoided as topics of conversation in »mixed company« (Cairns 1987, 161). It should be emphasised that the exploration of differences and mutual suspicions in Wider Horizons is always carried out with great care and in a non-threatening manner and it is generally felt that the way forward in this regard is the careful preparation of leaders to handle reconciliation issues.

Co-operating in the Pursuit of Superordinate Goals: For a reconciliation project to be successful, it is important that the group learn to co-operate together in the pursuit of goals which the members could not have achieved on their own. This is especially the situation in Wider Horizons, where the superordinate goal in question is for the entire group to have a successful training and work experience overseas. This is the Programme's central attraction, the factor that induces people of different backgrounds and traditions to overcome their mutual suspicions and antipathies and allow themselves to be bonded into a new unity. Within this unity, however, it is important to recognise the distinctive contribution that each of the constituent subgroups makes to the common endeavour. Otherwise, there is a risk of hostility reasserting itself, as the subgroups feel their own identity to be threatened.

Creating a Safe and Suitable Environment: Taking part in the process of reconciliation can be a risky exercise, where people feel vulnerable and exposed. It is imperative, therefore, that reconciliation happens within a context of safety and trust where the participants know they will be respected and treated in a responsible and non-judgemental fashion. Creating a safe and suitable environment for its participants is the long-standing practice of Wider Horizons. At a practical level it means that procedures and ground-rules are thoroughly worked out and clearly understood by all, and that a common code of acceptable conduct is agreed.

Is there Hope for the Future?

What are we learning from the entire experience? First of all, there is an immense need for people and institutions North and South to get to know each other better and try to dispel some of the mistrust born of a centuries-old antagonism. We have learnt that one of the best ways of doing this is to identify issues and concerns that are common to all sides of the divide - issues such as unemployment, the need for community regeneration, ways of co-operating in developing marketing and trading opportunities, exploring areas like tourism, agriculture, education and training that affect everybody on the island - the list can be a very long one.

The second point is to take the necessary steps, once a common issue has been identified,to do something co-operative about it - in other words to put together a common project with agreed objectives and procedures. This has been the preoccupation of Wider Horizons - working out the dynamics of forming and maintaining co-operative groups in pursuit of common goals that have been mutually identified and agreed.

How successful have we been? Our evaluation studies so far tell us a number of things. In some projects, particularly those composed of managers, the focus has been on economic targets such as increased sales and marketing opportunities, increased turnover, greater awareness of the need for strategic business planning, and expansion of the businesses involved with a consequent rise in numbers employed. These of course are general statements and it is not always possible to say precisely how far Wider Horizons has contributed. On the whole, however, the evidence is positive and encouraging.

An encouraging picture also emerges from projects devoted to the needs of unemployed and poorly qualified young people (who incidentally are in the majority). Here the emphasis seems to be more on the enhancement of general skills and attitudes - such as increased self-confidence and growth in personal and social attributes - what are sometimes termed 'soft skills'. It can be argued of course that these so called soft skills are no less important for enhancing employability than the hard economic targets emphasised in the managers' projects.

When we turn to the reconciliation aspect of Wider Horizons we find plenty of scope for debate. The targets here are much harder to measure because possibly there is a greater difficulty in defining them in the first place. At a general level however it can be said that bringing people together from different sides of the divide in a meaningful and non-threatening way is a very beneficial experience. There is plenty of evidence to show that participants on Wider Horizons projects do genuinely learn to look beyond the stereotypes they hold of each other, and in many cases actually form close friendships. How long these friendships can persist after the project is over is of course another matter and this is something which the Programme is currently addressing - the problem of follow-up.

In the eight years of its existence so far Wider Horizons has demonstrated that it can work successfully in a variety of situations. The Programme has built up a considerable body of expertise on how projects should be planned and carried out. Many valuable lessons have been learnt, especially with regard to the need for a thorough preparation of the participants and the development of leadership qualities in the supervisors. On the whole we have reasonable grounds to be happy with Wider Horizons: it is an idea which has proved itself with widely differing groups in a great variety of contexts. The next stage for the Programme will be to widen its practice and increase the level of its activities.

A little over a year ago, after twenty-five years of violence, peace has at last come to Ireland. Some people speak in hushed tones about it, as if afraid for its fragile nature. Others are more confident and agree with President Clinton's message to the White House Conference for Trade and Investment in Ireland, in May 1995 - »a return to the violence of the past quarter century would be unacceptable« (Irish Times, 24 May 1995). Whatever one's views on the peace process, one thing, however, seems sure: people have to work hard to bring about peace and perhaps harder still to maintain it. The task in front of us is becoming clear: we must exert ourselves as never before to build up the peace and pass it on to future generations. This is the challenge now facing Wider Horizons: helping to consolidate the peace process in Ireland.

Wider Horizons has no motto but a suitable one could well be this: »better to light one candle than curse the darkness«. In the eight years of its existence the Programme has lit many candles: six thousand people in over 300 different projects have benefited from the experience of living, training and working overseas in structured and meaningful situations. It is important to recognise, however, that countless other candles have also been lit by various organisations and individuals who have laboured in the field of reconciliation, sometimes in isolation from each other. Perhaps the time has now come to make common cause in bringing all these lights together to ensure that the darkness of violence never again falls on our land. This would indeed give some hope for the future.

References

Allport, G. (1954), *The Nature of Prejudice* (quoted in Ruddle, H. and J. O'Connor (1992), *A Model of Managed Co-operation*, Dublin).

Annual Report (1987/88), International Fund for Ireland.

Brown, R. and J. Turner (1981), »Interpersonal and Intergroup Behaviour«, in: Turner, J. and H. Giles (eds.), *Intergroup Behaviour*, Oxford.

Cairns, E. (1987), *Caught in Crossfire: Children and the Northern Ireland Conflict*, Belfast.

Falconer, A. (1988), *Reconciling Memories*, Dublin.

Hurley, M. (1994), *Reconciliation in Religion and Society*, Belfast.

McCartney, C. (1985), »An Overview of Reconciliation Projects« (quoted in Ruddle, H. and J. O'Connor (1992), *A Model of Managed Co-operation*, Dublin).

Ruddle, H. and J. O'Connor (1992), *A Model of Managed Co-operation: An Evaluation of Co-Operation North's School and Youth Links Scheme*, Dublin.

Taijfel, H. (1978), *Differentiation between Social Groups: Studies in the Social Psychology of Intergroup Relations*, London.

Trant, A. and E. McSkeane (1994), *An Evaluation of Wider Horizons*, Dublin.

Whyte, J. (1990), *Interpreting Northern Ireland*, Oxford.

Monika Reinfelder

The Misogynist Violence
of Fortress Europe

The last few years have seen a tightening of control by member states of the European Union that has served to fortify the walls of a fortress intent to keep at bay non-Europeans, in particular if they are Black or of so-called ethnic groups undesired by »indigenous« Europeans. Those already living in the fortress have experienced the state's legal, political and economic aggression as well as the violence of an angry mob anxious to preserve its tribal territory. It will be argued here, however, that Fortress Europe is not only racist, but that it is also extremely misogynist. This means that racist, nationalist and xenophobic violence affects Black and »ethnic« women differently, and often worse, than men. It will be argued that gender oppression compounds the danger of racist violence, that women are doubly at risk when their communities are under threat. Far from constituting a diversion, an understanding of violence against women, in particular against Black, refugee and migrant women, will contribute to the analysis of racist, nationalist and xenophobic violence. It will also inform policy, be it legal, economic, educational or otherwise, required for provisions for those affected.

In the UK a Black person is 50 times more likely to be racially attacked than a white person. But in all ethnic (including white) groups women stand a 66% chance of being physically attacked not because of their ethnicity, but because they are women. In addition, femicide, the most extreme form of violence against women, knows no respect for ethnicity, nationality or race: half of all women murdered are not killed by racist thugs, but by their male partner. This gender specific violence is taken less seriously than racist violence, although it is much more widespread. For example, Germany in 1992 showed 12 racist murders - rightly generating outrage. The hundreds of femicides were met with silence (Emma 1993). The reason for this is that racist and xenophobic murders are seen as a political issue, while femicide or misogynist murder, alongside other forms of violence against women, is still dismissed as a private issue. The politicisation of gender specific violence is long overdue.

While violence against women is depoliticised or even denied, most analyses of racist violence are gender neutral. The perpetrators are mostly referred to as »youth«, again a gender neutral term. Yet in 96.3% of racist offences the perpetrators are male. Few women are involved in the perpetration of racist violence; of the 3.7% cases where women are engaged in racist offences, most relate to propaganda rather than violence. In Germany's local elections half as many women than men voted for the Republicans. Women have noted the relationship between the racism and the misogyny so clearly expressed by right wing politics.

There have indeed always been women who participated in violence. Female politicians have initiated wars. During slavery white women colluded with, or were actively involved in, violent actions against slaves. Vron Ware has shown more recent involvement on the part of white women in the perpetuation of racism in a variety of forms (Ware 1992). Women have also been involved in so-called »terrorist« activities, although Robin Morgan argues that usually they were the »brides« of male terrorists and became involved because of their attachment to a male (Morgan 1989). (This does not protect them from femicide as in the case of Nicole Bargenda who was raped and murdered by her neo-Nazi mates.)

However, the above examples should not detract from the fact that violence is practiced predominantly by white men in the form of racial attacks and men of all ethnic groups in the home. In the UK, 1 in 4 women is battered by her male partner, and 1 million women report domestic violence to the police annually. According to the Metropolitan Police these figures are just the tip of the iceberg as 8 out of 10 women do not report domestic violence to the police (Justice 1993). An American study showed that violence will occur at least once in two-thirds of all marriages (Red 1992). It is now common knowledge that 1 in 3 women is subjected to rape, and 1 in 2 girls will have experienced sexual abuse by the age of eighteen. The majority of these crimes are committed by men known to the women and girls. In many countries, including Germany, rape in marriage is still not a crime. It is also now commonplace that rape is an act of power, not the result of some uncontrolled sexual urge or temporary loss of control. Rape is usually premeditated by the perpetrator and has at its aim the intimidation, control and humiliation of women and girls. This is clearly demonstrated, yet again, by the rapes of women in Bosnia. These rapes are often committed by neighbours or former school mates whose intention is to humiliate women of a different ethnic group. This example demonstrates how race and gender oppression intersect for women. The violence they are experiencing is a dual attack on their ethnicity and their sex.

Even the United Nations is now pushed into an acknowledgement of violence against women as a human rights abuse. At the United Nations World Conference on Human Rights in Vienna an International Tribunal heard women from all over the world testifying to their experiences of male violence. They spoke of rape, sexual abuse of children, sexual harassment, genital mutilation, forced sterilisation, dowry burning and many other forms of violent abuse inflicted on women and girls all over the world. The perpetrators are husbands or other male relatives, state officials, soldiers or other men in a position of authority over women. Amnesty International, too, testifies to the use of rape and sexual abuse in the torture of women in detention, as well as women being raped by security forces in several countries. In Peru, for example, army officers refused investigations into allegations of rape by soldiers on the basis that »rape is to be expected when troops are conducting counterinsurgency operations«.

Public space, in any country, is not save for women, Pubs, streets, public transport, parks, in particular at night, carry a high risk. Women are under a permanent curfew, albeit one that is very ineffective as a »protective« device given that women, as we have seen above, are even more at risk if they stay in their homes, the most dangerous of all places for women whose homes are accessible to men. The curfew is however effective in providing exclusive territorial rights for men. Men learn to take for granted a »natural« right to territory. This is now to be defended against »aliens«. A fortress of sameness is built where those who are different or do not belong are objectified as the Other and kept out through immigration controls, legislation, and violence.

This fortress affects men and women differently. Exposure to domestic violence is compounded by racist legislation and immigration controls. Women who join migrant husbands are legally defined as dependants and do not posses an automatic right of entry into the labour market. This situation puts them in an even more precarious position as it ties them to a man they may not necessarily be safe to stay with. Domestic violence against women amongst the migrant population occurs no more or less than in the »host« population, but migrant women have the additional disadvantage of no longer being able to stay in a country when they are not linked to the legal status of their husbands. The choice is between staying with a violent man and keeping the right of residence or escaping from their violent situation and facing deportation. It is not unknown for survivors of domestic violence to have sought help from social services and as a result to have been deported.

For others, as a recent study in the UK has shown, being subjected to more threats of violence from a racist police force will prevent Black women from seeking police protection (Kelkar 1985). If, as in some cases, women are given protection and are rehoused, the new housing may well be available as a result of another family having had to leave because of racial attacks. Therefore, the move would merely constitute an exchange of individual male violence for racist group violence. In addition, Black women in the UK are only too aware of the criminalisation of Black men and the false identification of domestic violence as a »black crime«, and therefore choose to abstain from feeding into the stereotyping of the Black community or from subjecting their community to further police harassment.

Turkish women in Germany experience a similar fate. A German man's violence is either denied or explained away as a psychological disturbance, while a Turkish man is seen to be violent on the basis of being Turkish. Thus, male violence against Turkish women is interpreted as »cultural«, as their ethnic characteristic, rather than as a patriarchal practice upheld by Turkish and German men, for that matter, men irrespective of any nationality. Violence in the Turkish family is readily acknowledged, while its existence is denied in German heterosexual households. Given this identification of domestic violence as a Turkish (accepted) cultural practice and the denial of racism against the Turkish community, no refuges for Turkish women are provided, subjecting them to possible racism if admitted to a mixed refuge.

Even less protection is available to women who arrive in Europe as sexual slaves. According to the United Nations, trafficking in women is more profitable than arms or drug smuggling. In Europe women are either forced to participate in the multi-billion pornography industry or are used as prostitutes. Some are sold into sexual slavery by traders in their own country, others are lured to Europe under the pretence of an offer for a »good« job. Others arrive as mail-order brides. The women, who are mostly from South-East Asia, have no residence rights. A »bride« who is subjected to physical violence and raped by her »husband« will not be able to report her attacker to the police as separation or divorce will lead to her deportation. If she does escape her assailant little other than prostitution is open to her as she will not be in possession of a work permit, thereby subjecting herself to repeated daily rape by punters and violence by a pimp. A Kenyan speaker at an event organised by the Campaign Against Pornography in the UK reported an encounter she had with a woman from her country at the hairdressers. The woman broke down crying while her male partner quickly nipped out to get a packet of cigarettes, telling a saga of constant beatings, rapes and total isolation after she had been brought to London. In Germany, where mail order brides were predominantly from South-East Asia attempts are made to target other ethnic groups. With recent developments in Eastern Europe Polish women are brought into the Fortress as marketable commodities and expelled when the »goods« don't meet the buyers' requirements:

»Poles are cheaper than Asians both in terms of capital investment and in maintenance: what is a cheap train ticket in comparison to a 5.000DM air ticket from Bangkok or Manila? And, whereas a Thai is unprepared for cold German winters - one has to buy her clothes - a Pole brings her own boots and a fur coat. And she is as good in bed and industrious in the kitchen«. (Bild, 9.1.1991)

The above examples constitute some of the reasons why a number of Non-Governmental Organisations are demanding that »persecution on the basis of sex« is included into the definition of a refugee. At present the definition exclusively refers to persecution on the grounds of race, religion, nationality, membership of a particular social group or holding a political opinion. The 1984 resolution by the European Parliament calling upon states to consider women who have been persecuted on the basis of sex as a »particular social group« has not been given consideration by member states. The judges' recommendation at the Women's Tribunal in Vienna identified rape and abuse of women as a form of torture, irrespective if it occurs at a police station or in a bedroom. Women subjected to such torture are not offered asylum, be it in the country were the offence is committed or elsewhere. This leads to further abuse and often culminates in femicide. Fortress Europe, having tightened its frontiers, will continue to refuse to provide a sanctuary for those persecuted simply because they are women.

There is however a difference in misogynist violence and racist violence, in the hatred of women and the hatred of »foreigners«. »Race« is, of course, a social construct and the presence of any racially constructed group deemed inferior is only tolerated in situations where its physical presence is perceived to bring benefits to the group constructing the Other. The most obvious example is slavery. Temporary cheap labour or domestic service are others. Otherwise any group designated inferior is not tolerated in close proximity. Women, in contrast, live in such proximity with perpetrators of violence. They are the daughters, sisters, mothers, wives, lovers of those who subject women to violence. Women's immediate presence is needed for the domestic, sexual, emotional and intellectual servicing of men. This exposes women to far greater a danger than those who are ghettoised by the violence of the oppressing group. Ironically it often also subjects them to a greater danger of racist violence, as the killing of the Turkish women in Solingen demonstrated: the women fell victim to racist murder as well as a moral code and the genderised division of labour that keeps women in the home.

The famous Montreal killings, like »honour killings«, show that women who challenge male conventions are particularly at risk. Defiance of imposed rules, or the venturing into male territory, in particular the showing of independence and autonomy, and the withdrawal of support, approval and the domestic, sexual, emotional and intellectual servicing of men is the worst sin a woman can commit. This provides also an explanation of the worldwide oppression of lesbians whose independence from men constitutes the ultimate affront to the male ego.

Lesbians all over the world are facing incarceration in psychiatric hospitals, violence, even death, or are receiving death threats. The International Lesbian and Gay Association received an inquiry about a Russian lesbian seeking asylum in Germany. The local authority processing the application wanted to know if there was documentation of lesbians being incarcerated into Russian psychiatric hospitals as the asylum seeker had claimed. Although it is well known that this is the fate of Lesbians not only in Russia, but also in Rumania, Mexico and probably other countries, no documentation exists. This makes it very difficult for lesbians to seek asylum, or to press for sexual orientation to be included in the definition of a refugee. Germany can pride itself on having granted asylum to an Iranian lesbian in 1992 who, if deported, would have faced the death sentence. The execution methods in Iran are particularly cruelling, ranging from being hurled of a cliff or mountain to public stoning or beheading.

To reiterate the above: far from being an irrelevant diversion, a discussion about violence against women does move towards an explanation of racist violence. If men are capable of physically abusing those who live with them in close proximity and know they can get away with it they are also likely to physically abuse others whom they want to exercise control over or, at least, condone such abuse. Without wanting to conflate misogynist and racist violence I would, however, suggest that there is a relationship between the two. I am in no doubt that those who commit racist violence also abuse women and children and have inflicted, and are continuing to inflict, violence on women. Further study and acknowledgement of gender violence will contribute to an understanding of racist, nationalist and xenophobic violence and hopefully induce resistance to both.

References

Emma (1993), no.1 and no.5.

Justice for Women (1993), *London Justice for Women Collective*, London.

Kelkar, G. (1985), »Woman and Structural Violence in India«, in: *Women's Studies Quaterly*, 13, nos.3/4.

Mama, A. (1989), *The Hidden Struggle: Statutory and Voluntary Sector Responses to Violence Against Black Women in The Home*, London.

Morgan, R. (1989), *The Demon Lover: On the Sexuality of Terrorism*, London.

Red, M. (ed.) (1982), *The Abusive Partner*, New York.

Ware, V. (1992), *Beyond the Pale: White Women, Racism and History*, London.

Diane L. Brook

Racism, Violence, and the Liberation Struggle: The Impact on South African Education

Introduction

Demands for equality in education in South Africa have been central to the liberation struggle. In this paper, the relationship between education and liberation/reform is considered in terms of the tensions between demands for educational equality and the self-destructive forces of mass action centered on the schools. Observations offered here are from ongoing case study research in South African schools.

Sweeping reforms to reshape South African education along non-racial lines aim to eradicate a legacy of entrenched racism and white privilege. The Education Renewal Strategy (1991) includes initiatives for streamlining the four racially segregated education systems into a single nonracial system, with initiatives for decentralization, comprehensive curriculum reform, community participation, equalization of educational opportunity, nine years of universal compulsory schooling, and a dual emphasis on general and vocational/technical education to meet national development needs. Undergirding the educational reform strategy is a commitment to developing a new multiracial, democratic society and a new formulation of nationalism as a product of political, social, and economic transformation.

The multisector reforms currently in early-stage implementation under the DeKlerk administration are accompanied by, and a function of, the ongoing liberation struggle in South Africa that has gathered momentum since 1976 and particularly from 1986 onwards when riots in Soweto township against educational inequality spread to become a series of national crises to which the government responded with policy shifts. The intersection of education and liberation-struggle has spawned violence and wreaked havoc on African education; yet it has also been protest against racism and oppression in aspects of schooling that has led to many of the significant changes underway in all sectors.

Education is not the only arena impacted by violence in the liberation struggle. For instance, campaigns in the »people's war« of the African National Congress (ANC) targeted African schooling, the police force, and black local authorities because they were viewed as instruments of white domination. During the 1980s the ANC embarked on a strategy to make the country ungovernable with persistent attacks on these »soft targets,« aimed at forcing the government to address the injustices founded on racism and white privilege that permeated all sectors. African youth were mobilized in the campaign. They were described by Oliver Tambo, then president of the ANC, as »young lions« who would assist in bringing African education to a standstill during the 1980s (Kane-Berman 1993). Protests and riots targeted education in particular and apartheid in general. A decade later, the mobilized youth have become a major headache, frequently referred to as the »delinquent youth culture« in the townships, and beyond the control of the leadership of organizations such as the ANC. Violence, attack and counterattack, and intimidation have taken on a life of their own that has created a basis for mutual concern on the part of opposition groups (ANC, Inkatha, and others) and the government, given the risk the violence poses to a workable new system. The use of coercion in consumer boycotts, work stayaways, and education-related protests has become a fact of life in South Africa (Pereira 1992).

The Current Situation in Education

South Africa has four racially segregated, and grossly inequitably funded public education systems: for whites, Africans, »coloreds« (people of mixed race), and Indians. Prior to the 1990s efforts to desegregate schooling were largely confined to a small number of progressive private schools that admitted nonwhite students during the

1976 township riots, and accelerated their »open« admissions policies during and after the crisis years of 1984-86 and the Soweto riots.

Rioting in the townships was sparked by the Department of Education and Training (DET) policy that forced use of Afrikaans as the
instructional medium in social studies and mathematics, a decree
widely perceived as a blatant act of oppression and white domination
through schooling. The rioting was fueled by already decades-old
resentment of white privilege and African disadvantage, and by the
expanding liberation movement. As the government lost control of
the situation in black schools, responding to repeated outbreaks of
violence and crises centered on the plight of black students, deregu-
lation of all schooling began first in practice and then in legislation
(McGurk 1993, 7).

In the 1990s the government's commitment to non-racial education was announced as the Education Renewal Strategy (SADNE
1991), an agenda for restructuring all schooling. Initial implementation has focused on structural and administrative adjustments with
curricular and certification reforms to follow. Under the Clase Models implemented in 1990, formerly all-white government schools
were allowed to change their admissions and financing policies,
which resulted in a modest amount of change: roughly 10% of formerly all-white schools opted to become »open« or nonracial schools
and integration was a small-scale one-way process in which black
student enrollments at these schools constituted only 0.6%. The decision to permit restructuring, refinancing, desegregation of white
government schools was less an altruistic step than a result of budg-
etary shortfalls in the House of Assembly (McGurk 1993, 8).

In private schools the degree of racial integration was higher, with
black enrollments as high as 24% and total non-white enrollments
sometimes exceeding 50%. Movements of white students into non-
white schools were almost non-existent (SAIRR 1992). In 1992 the
government introduced a policy of »rationalisation« of education in
an attempt to cope with the increasing diversity in school classifica-
tions and management types. All public schools become semi-private
schools and technically non-racial, with government financing only
of teacher salaries and with heavy emphasis on local level financing.

By August of 1992, 2,044 of the country's 2,082 white public schools were operating thus as »nonracial semi-private schools«, but with very limited non-white enrollments. In 1992, only 7,923 black pupils had been admitted to white government schools; by late 1993 the number had increased to 60,000 (SAIRR 1994, 5). However, nationally there were 3.5-5 million school-age children without places in school, and over 150,000 places were needed for African children alone, there were 47,286 elementary and 82,046 secondary vacant places in white schools. Under the policy of »rationalisation« many white suburban schools were closed (more than 20 in 1992 alone), and more than 4,000 teachers were laid off due to declining white enrollments. Rather than allow use of these schools by the DET, or by other agencies, to address the overwhelming shortages of places for black students, underused white schools were simply closed. Only a small number were turned over to the DET and then this gesture met with violent opposition from white conservatives who wanted the status quo preserved. The issue of underutilized and closed white schools has sparked outbreaks of violence on several occasions. Opposition groups seeking to focus public attention on the inequitable use of and access to educational resources staged occupations of some of these schools, using schoolchildren as pawns in the process.

Gradually, continued escalating violence and pressure for change, coupled with progress made in the ANC/government negotiations, resulted in the abandonment of several educational bastions of apartheid. For instance, the long standing policy of »Christian National Education«, dating to the 1948 »Beleid« era of white domination and Afrikaner nationalism, was abandoned (McGurk 1993, 2). In a major reversal, beginning in 1994 Afrikaans will no longer be compulsory in schools. Its forced use in township schools that sparked the 1976 Soweto riots ushered in the contemporary era of protest and reform (Carr 1990, 135-138).

Currently, the situation is as follows. The white education system remains the best funded, but it is undergoing sweeping changes in the form of reduced government support, and in restructuring and decentralization that allow racial integration and more local control. The degree of racial integration (and progressive reform of in-school curricula and policies) varies widely from school to school, largely dependent on the nature of the school's leadership. Indian and colored schools have undergone very little change in enrollments and financing, but more so than the complete absence of change in African schools. As a group, the private schools remain the most progressive, traditional leaders in pressing for democratic schooling opportunities. However, there are isolated formerly all-white government schools that have also taken the lead in establishing radically different (liberal, nonracial) programs. Urban and suburban schools have generally experienced more change than their rural counterparts. While the impact of the beginning reforms has been most keenly observed in formerly white government schools, largely as significantly altered enrollments-by-race and as financing/administrative arrangements, real (curricular and programmatic) efforts to eradicate the harmful effects of racism and prejudice have occurred in only a few pioneer schools. The township schools remain unchanged in enrollments, curricula, policies, and opportunities (or a lack thereof). In fact, in the township schools the politicization of schooling and the impact of the »liberation before education« battle cry have actually kept the schools from exposure to the changes underway, as a result of the continued violence and mass action in the townships.

African Education: The Crux of the Issue

Of the four systems, African education remains the least funded and most disadvantaged, administered by the Department of Education and Training rather than the Department of Education and Culture that oversees education for whites, Indians, and coloreds through the Houses of Assembly, Delegates, and Representatives, respectively. In fact, aside from the Department of National Education that oversees general policy, there are 18 separate education departments including 6 departments for the self-governing territories of Gazankulu, Katigwane, Kwazulu, Kwandebele, Quaqua, and Labowa, and 4 for the TBVC »states« of Transkei, Bophuthatswana, Venda, and Ciskei (SADNE 1992, 6). A key demand of the ANC is to have all education administered under a single agency. The term »own affairs«, a provision of the 1984 Tricameral Constitution, came into usage indicating these racially and territorially separate administrations of education, with white education disproportionately financed from the government's central treasury. Until the new single »dispensation« (one non-racial agency for education) announced in early 1993 is actually implemented, the splintering and segregation of education persists. The notion of »own affairs« is still invoked by conservatives who want white schools kept white at any cost.

The African education system exhibits several indicators of impoverishment. Its disadvantage in funding is perhaps the most clear-cut indicator, most often juxtaposed with the differences in funding of white education. The ratio of funding for white education to African education did narrow from 18:1 to 4:1 in the period 1969-1989 (SAIRR 1992, lXXXV), and some reversal occurred in the share of expenditures allotted to white versus African education. In 1969-70 white education received 70% of the education budget and African education 16%; in 1991-92 white education received 33% and African education 48%, with an additional R0.5 billion allotted to address African educational backlogs. However, given the size of the historical deficits in black educational allocations, expenditure reversals have been modest (McGurk 1993, 7). In 1991-92, the persistent gap was evident in per capita pupil expenditures of R1,248 for Africans, R2,701 for coloreds, and R4,448 for whites (SAIRR 1993b, 5). Figures for 1993-94 were R1,659 for Africans, R2,902 for coloreds, R3,702 for Indians, and R4,372 for whites, indicating persistent inequities despite reform measures (SAIRR 1994, 5).

Aside from historical deficits in funding, there are other indicators of so-called backlogs in African education. In 1991, pass rates in the matriculation examinations were 41% for Africans, 83% for coloreds, 95% for Indians, and 96% for whites (SAIRR 1993b, 5). Africans, constituting 74% of the population, accounted for only 25% of enrollments at technical colleges in 1992, despite a 230% increase in 1986-92 (SAIRR 1993a, 575) and only 19% in 1993; Africans were only 34% of university students in 1993 (SAIRR 1994, 5). Pupil/teacher ratios in DET (African) classrooms were 55:1 (primary schools) and 43:1 (secondary schools) in 1988, and 41:1 and 36:1 respectively in 1991, compared with ratios of 16:1 to 25:1 in the other three systems (SAIRR 1993a, 575,607). DET schools are drastically short of instructional materials; some have no functioning sanitary facilities or telephones. Teachers in DET schools are underpaid and underqualified compared to teachers in the other three systems, a major issue in the DET teachers strike in 1993, the first nationwide teachers' strike.

The tradition of unequal funding, inadequate provision of places for black students, forced use of instruments of control (such as Afrikaans), inadequate resources and teacher expertise, and resulting poor performance and opportunities for black students have combined in a volatile mix of township protests. Unfortunately, protests with just cause in education issues have been accompanied by a general escalation of violence and protest over a broader range of issues. Schools, students, teachers, and parents are often caught in the crossfire. African educational backlogs have been aggravated by unrest in the townships that accelerated in the 1984-86 protests under the battle cry of »liberation before education«. In essence, African students have become twice-victimized. The education to which they have access is grossly inadequate, and intermittent depending on the prevailing climate of attack and protest in the townships. Secondly, students have become targets for intimidation and coercion by groups engaging in violence and »mass action.« The impact on students in these and other schools will now be discussed.

The Impact of Racism and Violence, and Reform, on Schools

The impact of the liberation movement, official reforms, and the climate of violence and opposition can be considered differentially for township schools, urban and suburban schools, and rural schools. Costs for education have been steep. Some writers have characterised the education crisis (particularly in the townships) as nothing more than a political contest between a recalcitrant regime and undaunted black youths for control of education (see for instance, Mathiane 1990).

Township schools: Township schools and their students have been the most adversely impacted by the violence and actions undertaken

321

in the name of liberation, on top of the legacy of discrimination and oppression that was imposed officially. Schooling in many townships has degenerated into a state of anarchy. Students have been coerced into observing stayaways from school, staged as protests for a variety of reasons. With imposition of the Value Added Tax in 1991, students were supposedly »exempted« from the »voluntary« stayaways protesting the VAT (Kane-Berman 1993, 35). Some students were victims of necklacing, for writing their examinations in defiance of boycotts of black schools in 1986, organized as part of the »people's war« (Kane-Berman 1993, 43). Between 1984 and 1991 the DET reported damage to or destruction of 6,017 classrooms during rioting (Van Der Merwe 1991). Many secondary schools have been vandalized, some have been completely demolished. In Soweto township secondary schools that are still operational, 50% of school time in 1992 was lost and only 20% of the syllabus had been taught by August, a result of teacher and pupil stayaways and mass action over teacher salaries, school fees, and sympathetic strikes on issues in other sectors. The lost time in school hurt black students' performance on the matriculation examinations in which African students already have the poorest pass rates. Capricious actions by the DET aggravated the situation, such as in sudden raising of examination fees in 1992 that sparked rioting and refusals to pay. Physical assaults occurred on unpopular principals and teachers in schools. In Kathorus College of Education a lecturer was set alight by disgruntled students in February 1992. The government announced a »National Emergency Programme« in 1992 to address the deepening crisis in township education, particularly with reference to resources and financing (SAIRR 1993, 55-57). However, official measures proved weak against a growing force of youths taking control of school admissions and pupil promotions, and general administration of facilities. In June 1992 alone 16 schools were shut down as a result of the situation.

Visits by this researcher to several high schools in Soweto in 1993 revealed that many principals have been banished from their schools--they spend their days at the DET central offices in the city. Some facilities are occupied by gangs of armed youths. Others are open, but attempting to function without running water, electricity, doors and windows removed or damaged by rioting and vandalism. The isolated secondary schools that are functioning have principals who have actively resisted pressure and intimidation from gangs of armed youths seeking to close down all schools in the township. It is interesting to note that primary schools are little impacted by these forces, they are open and running as normal. The impact of adverse political socialization is quite tangible in secondary schools, where any instrumental value of education has been obliterated by anger focused on the DET, despair over the rewards of schooling, and by the higher cause of liberation.

The so-called »delinquent youth culture« in the townships has become a major problem for the authorities as well as the ANC and other opposition groups who are unable to control the cycle of violence and random attack that regularly sweeps parts of the country, particularly in the townships. Tambo's »young lions« have become unmanageable, in the process rendering the current generation of students further deprived of educational opportunity. The township schools are being held hostage by activists, teacher morale has been crippled, parents have been marginalised, and students have been victimised. Better off children have been removed from this setting, attending schools in the cities or abroad - with the result that the township pupil population is becoming progressively disadvantaged, losing hope not only for education but also for liberation (Pereira 1992, 21).

Urban and Suburban Schools: Several progressive schools have forged ahead of the reform process, initiating grass-roots programs such as multicultural, contextually based curricula in Integrated Studies, and social interaction and tolerance programs designed to mitigate the harmful effects of racism and violence on students who attend a progressive, nonracial school but who live in a still largely segregated society. While these pioneer schools are few in number, their impact is significant in that their programs are highly publicized and keenly observed by other schools as well as by the media and education officials who are endeavouring to shape new non-racial, decentralized policies for the future system. While the examples shown in this presentation are the most »non-racial« or multiracial schools in the country, their administrations and faculty daily battle

323

with the spillover of sustained racism and violence in the society outside. For instance, their African students have been targets of attacks by township youths who resent their attending a nonracial school. These students have been afraid to wear their uniforms to school for fear of attack. Outbreaks of violence have occasioned sleepovers at school because the administrators feared for the students' return to the townships. These schools recognize ongoing needs for counseling and values clarification to deal with students' conflicting notions of home and school sociocultural environments. The progressive schools have been the target of bombings and other acts of intimidation by conservatives disapproving of their liberal policies.

In contrast, many of the formerly-white government schools report little impact of events outside, but some of their principals also admit to having little real understanding of their black students' perceptions and needs. However, all sampled by this researcher did report knowing of acts of intimidation against their black students for attending a non-township school. Some of these schools have more than 90% black enrollments, yet they are still run essentially as white schools and without overt attention to issues of racism and the impact of violence on their students. There is much variation across schools in the degree to which administrators and faculties acknowledge that issues of racism and prejudice must be addressed in the reform process. This phenomenon has also been reported by other researchers (see Penny et al. 1993).

Rural Schools: Prior to 1993, rural schools were relatively untouched by the violence that was focused primarily on the township schools, and that secondarily spilled over into city schools. However, several incidents have occurred in rural schools in the northern Transvaal and Natal that indicate a spread to these more remote schools of the patterns of violence and intimidation previously seen mostly in townships. In some mission schools in the northern Transvaal, teachers and principals have been attacked; students have been intimidated and pressured to participate in mass actions of protest organized in the name of liberation (Thiernan, B., January 21 1994, personal communication). The development is cause for concern: rural schools too are being faced with the damaging intersection between demands for educational equality and tactics to further the »cause« of liberation on the part of one or another group or faction.

Conclusion

There exists widespread concern over the escalation in violence in South Africa in the last two years, accompanying the advancement of negotiations for a new Constitution and for elections to be held in April 1994. In the period September 1984 to November 1993 18,379 people were killed in political violence in South Africa (SAIRR 1994, 3). The Goldstone Commission Report (1992) underscored the difficulty in addressing the problems associated with persistent racism and opposition to change from the right, planned and random incidents of protest and violence on the left, the questions of possible government implication on either side, and the distortion of information fed the public. The country is besieged by an epidemic of blame and counteraccusation with the government security forces, ANC, Inkatha Freedom Party, and several conservative groups each being implicated in particular episodes of violence. Sorting out who is to blame is a major issue, one that still fails to address the toll taken on vulnerable populations such as schoolchildren. The overwhelming climate of uncertainty over the upcoming elections has aggravated concerns over violence and the potential for further violence. Frustrated expectations of students so long denied a fair and equal chance at education are a major potential source for still more unrest. With such massive backlogs to address in African education, it is a fragile hope that all students will indeed enjoy the fruits of a future nonracial, democratic education system.

As an outgrowth of the concern over the escalating levels of violence in all corners of society, the recent embracing of a National Peace Accord is significant. National Peace Day was observed in September 1993, and schools across the country participated with their own programs and pledges. Although such gestures may be little more than symbolic, they are testimony to a growing awareness on many levels of South African society that the agendas of various parties and groups will have to be subordinated to a new conception of nationalism and unity, devoid of the self-destructive effects of attack and retribution, if there is to be any hope for building a new multiracial and democratic society in South Africa. Furthermore, the relationship between liberation and education needs realignment in a »culture of learning« that will replace the »delinquent youth culture« that is subverting schooling for Africans in particular and for the nation in general.

References

Carr, W.J.P. (1990), *Soweto: Its creation, life, and decline*, South African Institute of Race Relations (SAIRR), Johannesburg.

Goldstone, R.J. (1992), *Second interim report to the State President*, Commission of inquiry regarding the prevention of public violence and intimidation, Cape Town, 29 April 1992.

Kane-Berman, J. (1993), *Political violence in South Africa*, SAIRR, Johannesburg.

Mathiane, N. (1990), *Beyond the headlines: Truths of Soweto life*, Johannesburg.

McGurk, N.J. (1993), *Politics and education: A realistic approach to the future for South Africa*, Consultation of the South African Association of Independent Schools, 11-15 July, 1993, Cape Town, Unpublished document.

Penny, A., S. Appel, J. Gultig, K. Hurley and R. Muir (1993), »The advent of racial integration in South African schools«, in: *Comparative Education Review*, 37(4), pp. 412-433.

Pereira, P. (1992), *Coercion, boycotts, and stayaways*, Spotlight 3/92, SAIRR, Johannesburg.

SADNE (South African Department of National Education) (1991), *Education Renewal Strategy: Discussion Document*, National Education Policy Branch, Pretoria.

SADNE (South African Department of National Education) (1992), *Education Realities in South Africa, 1991*, Report, National Education Policy Branch, Pretoria.

SAIRR (South African Institute of Race Relations) (1992), »Synopsis and Update: Education«, in: *Race Relations Survey 1991/92*, Johannesburg.

SAIRR (1993a), »Synopsis and Update: Education; Political Violence«, in: *Race Relations Survey 1992/93*, Johannesburg.

SAIRR (1993b), *State of the Nation Report*, Fast Facts 1/93, Johannesburg.

SAIRR (1994), *State of the Nation Report*, Fast Facts 1/94, Johannesburg.

Van Der Merwe, S. (1991), *Statement* by Dr. S. Van Der Merwe, Minister of Education and Training, 13 May, 1991.

List of Contributors

Prof. Dr. Ulrich Albrecht, Institut für Internationale Politik und Regionalstudien der Freien Universität Berlin (Germany)

Dr. Metin Alkan, Vakgroep Onderwijskunde, Faculteit der Pegagogische en Onderwijskundige Wetenschappen, Universiteit van Amsterdam (The Netherlands)

Dr. Floya Anthias, Department of Sociology, University of Greenwich (Great Britain)

Prof. Dr. Ralf Bohnsack, Institut für Schulpädagogik und Bildungssoziologie der Freien Universität Berlin (Germany)

Prof. Dr. Diane L. Brook, Department of Social Science Education, College of Education, University of Georgia (USA)

Dr. Christiane Buhmann, Institut für Sozial- und Kleinkindpädagogik der Freien Universität Berlin (Germany)

Dr. Bernhard Dieckmann, Institut für Allgemeine Pädagogik der Freien Universität Berlin (Germany)

Prof. Dr. Katherine C. Donahue, Department of Social Science, Plymouth State College, University System of New Hampshire (USA)

Prof. Dr. Hinderk M. Emrich, Abteilung Klinische Psychiatrie der Medizinischen Hochschule Hannover (Germany)

Dr. Robert Ferguson, Department of English, Media and Drama, Institut of Education, University of London (Great Britain)

Dr. Jagdish Gundara, Centre for Multicultural Education, Institut of Education, University of London (Great Britain)

Prof. Dr. Ulrich Herrmann, Seminar für Pädagogik der Universität Ulm (Germany)

Dr. Roger Hewitt, Culture, Communication and Societies, Institut of Education, University of London (Great Britain)

Dr. Crispin Jones, Department of International and Comparative Education, Institut of Education, University of London (Great Britain)

Prof. Dr. Uli Linke, Department of Anthropology, The State University of New Jersey (USA)

Dr. Elizabeth McSkeane, Curriculum Development Unit, Dublin (Ireland)

Prof. Dr. Yves Michaud, École Nationale Supérieure des Beaux-Arts de Paris, (France)

Prof. Dr. Edgar Morin, Centre d'Etudes Transdisciplinaires, École des Hautes Etudes en Sciences Sociales, Paris (France)

Prof. Dr. Panikos Panayi, School of Arts and Humanities, De Montfort University of Leicester (Great Britain)

Dr. Monika Reinfelder, Department of Policy Studies, Sociology of Education, Institut of Education, University of London (Great Britain)

Prof. Dr. Anton Trant, Curriculum Development Unit, Dublin (Ireland)

Prof. Dr. Meredith Watts, Department of Political Science, University of Wisconsin-Milwaukee (USA)

Dr. Michael Wimmer, Institut für Pädagogik, Fachbereich Erziehungswissenschaften der Martin-Luther-Universität Halle-Wittenberg (Germany)

Prof. Dr. Christoph Wulf, Interdisziplinäres Zentrum für Historische Anthropologie der Freien Universität Berlin (Germany)

Prof. Dr. Jürgen Zinnecker, Fachbereich Erziehungswissenschaften und Soziologie der Universität - Gesamthochschule Siegen (Germany)

Acknowledgements

The fact that the Congress »Violence« could take place in Berlin 1994 and its results could be published was due to particular efforts of many institutions and people who are expressly thanked here once again.

We would like to thank the directors of the *Marc-Bloch-Institut* in Berlin, Etienne François and Emmanuel Terray, the *Institut Français de Berlin* and its director, Bernard Genton, Ewald Brass and the *Deutsch-Französisches Jugendwerk,* the coordinator of the *Network Educational Science Amsterdam,* Gustavo Reparaz, and also the *Interdisciplinary Centre for Historical Anthropology* of the *Freie Universität Berlin.*

We owe particular thanks also to Andrew Boreham, Marlow F. Shute and John Lambert, which took over the translation of some German and French contributions.

Finally the colleagues of the Department of Education of the *Freie Universität Berlin* should be thanked for their enormous work connected with this publication.